MYTH AND POETICS

A series edited by

GREGORY NAGY

PHRASIKLEIA

An Anthropology of Reading in Ancient Greece

JESPER SVENBRO

Translated by Janet Lloyd

CORNELL UNIVERSITY PRESS

ITHACA AND LONDON

International Standard Book Number 0-8014-2519-0 (cloth)
International Standard Book Number 0-8014-9752-3 (paper)
Library of Congress Catalog Card Number 92-52773
Printed in the United States of America
Librarians: Library of Congress cataloging information
appears on the last page of the book.

♾ The paper in this book meets the minimum requirements
of the American National Standard for Information Sciences—
Permanence of Paper for Printed Library Materials, ANSI Z39.48-1984.

To the memory of
Eric A. Havelock

Contents

Foreword by Gregory Nagy		ix
Translations Consulted		xiii
Introduction		1
1	Phrasikleia: From Silence to Sound	8
2	I Write, Therefore I Efface Myself: The Speech-Act in the Earliest Greek Inscriptions	26
3	The Reader and the Reading Voice: The Instrumental Status of Reading Aloud	44
4	The Child as Signifier: The "Inscription" of the Proper Name	64
5	The Writer's Daughter: Kallirhoe and the Thirty Suitors	80
6	*Nómos*, "Exegesis," Reading: The Reading Voice and the Law	109
7	True Metempsychosis: Lycurgus, Numa, and the Tattooed Corpse of Epimenides	123
8	Death by Writing: Sappho, the Poem, and the Reader	145
9	The Inner Voice: On the Invention of Silent Reading	160
10	The Reader and the *erómenos*: The Pederastic Paradigm of Writing	187
	Index	217

Foreword

GREGORY NAGY

Phrasikleia: The Anthropology of Reading in Ancient Greece, by Jesper Svenbro, addresses a question of central importance and interest—the beginnings of literacy in Greece. This question, as the author argues, requires an anthropological understanding of reading as well as writing, viewed in the specific historical context of ancient Greek culture. For the Greeks, the concept of reading is to be grasped not just in intellectual or psychological terms, which Svenbro reconstructs by analyzing such distinct words as *anagignōskein, nemein,* or *epilegesthai,* all of which we translate simply as "read"; it also finds expression in myth and poetics. In fact, as Svenbro shows, a dazzling variety of traditional metaphors articulate the relationship between reader and writer. Some of these metaphors are built into the oldest myths that tell about the "discovery" of writing, while others come to life in the most sophisticated newer creations of the Greek poetic tradition.

The author finds a particularly striking poetic metaphor in his reinterpretation of Sappho's celebrated *Fragment* 31, which captures the synaesthesia of passion evoked by what seems on the surface a love triangle in the making. For Svenbro, the triangular relationship that links the passionately jealous first-person female speaker in the poem with the languidly distracted second-person female beloved and with the attractively attentive third-person male lover of the second person is tantamount to a relationship that links the

writer with the poem that she has written and with the reader who
reads that poem.

Svenbro shows many other kinds of erotic models as well, most
notably in the complex metaphorical world of Plato's *Phaedrus*.
Besides the sublime homoerotic model constructed by Socrates
himself in this dialogue, another such model is that of sexuality
without love, as problematized in the *Phaedrus* and as actually realized in some of the most notorious surviving ancient Greek graffiti.
A key to this negativized kind of homosexual relationship, a foil to
"Platonic love," is the power-play of sexual domination as exerted
by the older *erastēs* over the younger *erōmenos*.

Given that this relationship of *erastēs* and *erōmenos* serves as a
prime metaphor for the relationship of writer and reader in ancient
Greece, Svenbro's book refers to the reader consistently with the
pronoun "he," excluding explicit reference to any potential reader
who happens to be "she." As we contemplate the games of domination that come into play with the eroticized metaphors of reading,
this particular instance of gender omission may actually seem wel-
come. Although I personally find the ancient Greek mentality of ex-
clusion unwelcome in a hoped-for contemporary world of gender-
inclusiveness, where the reader can become interchangeably "he"
or "she," the default translation of the reader as an accessory "he" in
Phrasikleia is historically faithful to the metaphorical world of reading in ancient Greece. If Svenbro's interpretation is right, even
Sappho's projected reader defaults to a "he."

The feminine gender does indeed find its authority—but not so
much in the reading or decoding of ancient Greek writing as in its
encoding. It could even be said that the feminine gender *is* the code
of reading, as brought to life, for example, in the mythical figure of
Phoinike, who becomes in Svenbro's argument the very embodi-
ment of Greek letters or *phoinikēïa grammata*. So also with the
historical figure of Phrasikleia, the young woman who becomes
memorialized for all time in a poem inscribed on her statue—and
whose identity or even essence takes pride of place in Svenbro's
book. In the language of Phrasikleia's poetic inscription, her statue
speaks with her own authority as she proudly identifies herself in
the first person, equating her identity with what is called by the
poem a *sēma* or sign that presents to the world her three-

dimensional essence. Her words equate her own self with the *sēma* or sign that bears the inscribed words announcing that self. And her very name, *Phrasikleia,* proclaims that she both "draws attention" and "pays attention" (*phrazein,* as in *phrasi-*) to her own poetic "glory" (*kleos,* as in *-kleia*). In the world of the Phrasikleia inscription, the speech-act of poetry has *already* taken place in the fact of writing. The reader's voice, as reading out loud, is but an accessory to the fact.

Svenbro's elaborations on the ideas of Foucault and Derrida, and also his new insights into the distinctively Greek uses of "silent reading" as a means to achieve power, make his book a timely one for students of comparative literature and literary theory, not only Classics.[1] More than that, his reading of Phrasikleia's *sēma* in all the senses of that Greek word—sign, signal, symbol, and tomb— promises to become a classic in the history of semiotics.

1. Svenbro's findings are pertinent to such recent works as G. R. F. Ferrari, *Listening to the Cicadas: A Study of Plato's Phaedrus* (Cambridge, 1987), and William V. Harris, *Ancient Literacy* (Cambridge, Mass., 1989).

Translations Consulted

Loeb Classical Library (London and Cambridge, Mass.)

Apollonius of Rhodes, *Argonautica,* trans. R. C. Seaton, 1967.
Aristotle, *Parva Naturalia* (On Sense and Sensible Objects), trans. W. S. Hett, 1964.
    Politics, trans. H. Rackham, 1972.
Athenaeus, *The Deipnosophists,* trans. Charles Burton Gulick, 1959.
Clement of Alexandria, *The Exhortation to the Greeks,* trans. G. W. Butterworth, 1960.
Demosthenes, *De Falsa Legatione,* trans. J. H. Vince, 1963.
    Private Orations, trans. A. T. Murray, 1964.
Diogenes Laertius, trans. R. D. Hicks, 1980.
Herodotus, trans. A. D. Godley, 1956.
Hesiod, *The Homeric Hymns and Homerica,* trans. Hugh G. Evelyn-White, 1967.
Homer, *The Iliad,* trans. A. T. Murray, 1978.
    The Odyssey, trans. A. T. Murray, 1966.
Lysias, trans. W. R. M. Lamb, 1943.
Minor Attic Orators: Antiphon, Andocides, trans. K. J. Maidment, 1968.
Pausanias, *Description of Greece,* trans. W. H. S. Jones, 1967.
Pindar, *Olympian Odes,* trans. Sir John Sandys, 1946.
Plato, *Apology,* trans. Harold North Fowler, 1966.
    Charmides, trans. W. R. M. Lamb, 1964.
    Cratylus, trans. Harold North Fowler, 1970.
    Crito, trans. Harold North Fowler, 1966.
    Epistles, trans. R. G. Bury, 1981.

Laws, trans. R. G. Bury, 1967.
Minos, trans. W. R. M. Lamb, 1964.
Phaedo, trans. Harold North Fowler, 1966.
Phaedrus, trans. Harold North Fowler, 1966.
Statesman, trans. Harold North Fowler, 1962.
Symposium, trans. W. R. M. Lamb, 1927.
Pliny, *Natural History,* trans. W. H. S. Jones, 1969.
Plutarch, *Lives,* trans. Bernadotte Perrin, 1967.
Moralia: The Banquet of the Seven Sages, trans. Frank Cole Babbitt, 1962.
Moralia: Love Stories, trans. Harold North Fowler, 1969.
Strabo, *Geography,* trans. Horace Leonard Jones, 1969.

The University of Chicago Press (Chicago and London)

Aeschylus, *Eumenides,* trans. Richmond Lattimore, 1953.
Euripides, *Iphigenia in Tauris,* trans. Witter Bynner, 1952.
Medea, trans. Rex Warner, 1955.
Sophocles, *Antigone,* trans. Elizabeth Wyckoff, 1954.

PHRASIKLEIA

Introduction

Over the past decades, scholars of ancient Greek have become extremely interested in the alphabetic writing of the ancient Greeks, in all its many aspects. During the first half of the first millennium B.C. the Greeks borrowed the alphabet from the Semites, modifying it considerably for their own purposes. Alphabetic writing burst on a Greece accustomed to an oral tradition; and ever since 1963, when Eric Havelock's *Preface to Plato* appeared,[1] a whole stream of research has been devoted to determining how, when, and to what degree writing became established in Greek culture. Did Greece remain essentially "oral" up until the time of Plato? Or had writing sounded the knell for traditional culture long before? Considerable progress has unquestionably been made by research in this field, in particular, perhaps, by making the questions to be asked more specific and by identifying the unresolved problems.

Upon consulting the available bibliographical information, however, a scholar specializing in written communication in ancient Greece may well be surprised at how little attention has been devoted to *reading,* that is to say, to the receiving side that after all would seem to represent one-half, if not more, of the phenomenon. From a sociological point of view at least, it seems perverse to concentrate on the emission side, the act of writing, to such a degree that the number of books and articles devoted to various aspects of

1. E. A. Havelock, *Preface to Plato* (Cambridge, Mass., 1963).

I

writing in ancient Greece runs into hundreds, whereas studies on reading are extremely few and far between. Two to be noted in particular, however, are Pierre Chantraine's article on Greek verbs meaning 'to read' (1950) and Bernard Knox's study of silent reading (1968).[2] The situation is all the more curious in that, seen from a perspective in which an opposition is set up between orality and writing, reading would appear to represent a zone of interference which is of the greatest interest since it is known that the ancient Greeks normally tended to read aloud. Writing itself could thus logically claim to be "oral." For, as we shall see, Greek writing was first and foremost a machine for producing sounds.

In concentrating chiefly upon the emission side, scholars have in a way remained faithful to the Greeks' own way of looking at things. Those Greeks who did not quite simply reject writing, as Pythagoras and Socrates did, tended to prefer the activity of writing to the "passivity" of the reader (who is passive in that he is "subjected" to the writing). As soon as we recognize the *instrumental* nature that one who reads aloud assumes in relation to the writer, we are struck by the analogy between the categories of written communication and those of another Greek social practice, recently analyzed by Michel Foucault: I refer to pederasty.[3] The relationship between the *erastés* 'lover', who is active and dominant, and the *erómenos* 'beloved', who is passive and dominated, raises questions similar to those inherent in the relationship that binds the writer to the reader and tends to make reading the devalued underside of writing. The inscription on a kylix vessel found in Sicily and dating from 500 B.C. (to which we shall be returning) in its own crude way makes use of the terms of that analogy: "The writer of the inscription will 'bugger' [*pugíxei*] the reader." By making available his vocal apparatus, an inner (one might almost say "intimate") organ, to what is written, the reader puts himself into a passive role similar

2. P. Chantraine, "Les Verbes signifiant 'lire,'" in *Mélanges Grégoire*, 2 (Brussels, 1950), pp. 115–126; B. M. W. Knox, "Silent Reading in Antiquity," *Greek, Roman, and Byzantine Studies,* 9 (1968), pp. 421–435. For a recent bibliography on writing—and on reading—in the Greek world, see G. Camassa and S. Georgoudi, "Tracés bibliographiques," in *Les Savoirs de l'écriture en Grèce ancienne,* ed. M. Detienne (Lille, 1988), pp. 525–538.

3. M. Foucault, *The Use of Pleasure* (New York, 1985), pp. 185–215.

to that in a pederastic relationship. By reading it, he is subjected to the inscription.

One consequence of the Greeks' reading aloud is that the reader is thus presented as an *erómenos*. But there are others. The writer necessarily depends on the voice of the reader. At the moment of reading, the reader relinquishes his voice to what is written and to the absent writer. That means that his voice is not his own as he reads. While it is employed to bring the dead letters to life, it belongs to what is written. The reader is a vocal instrument used by the written word (or by the one who wrote it) in order to give the text a body, a sonorous reality. So when the reader of a funerary stele reads out the inscription "I am the tomb of Glaukos," logically there is no contradiction, for the voice that makes that "I" ring out belongs not to the reader, but to the stele bearing the inscription. No contradiction is involved, but a kind of violence undoubtedly is.

This opens up a whole field of inquiry for what one might call the microsociology of written communication. The fact that the written word (or the writer) makes use of the reader as he would make use of an instrument (that is to say, an object) constitutes the starting point. This starting point prompted me to study the relation between the writer and the reader not only as a pederastic relationship, but also as a "genealogical" one, for I was very soon led to formulate the hypothesis of a relationship of affiliation which, through the medium of the writing, linked the writer with the *lógos* 'speech' eventually read out loud. In contrast to the Platonic model, where the written *lógos* is the son of the writer,[4] this affiliation gives the writing a role of its own: it is the daughter of the writer and the mother of the *lógos* that is read aloud by the reader. The tension here is different from that which obtains in a pederastic relationship, for here the tension develops between a father and a suitor for his daughter's hand, the father who is loath to let his daughter go but needs a son-in-law, and a suitor who seeks to tear the daughter from her father and from the paternal home.

By choosing how the Greeks read rather than how they write as my subject of research, I thus arrive at a perspective that, at a stroke,

---

4. Plato, *Phaedrus* 275e. See the analysis of J. Derrida, *Dissemination* (London, 1981), pp. 75 f.

clarifies a number of hitherto perplexing factors. Let me take an example with implications that seem to me particularly important. Clearly, one of the first tasks in a study of reading in ancient Greece is that of drawing up an inventory of verbs meaning 'to read'. Four are listed in the above-mentioned article by Chantraine. But among the omissions of that great French scholar is the verb *némein*, which without the slightest doubt did possess the sense of 'to read'. Now, the Greek word for 'law' is *nómos*, for which no "truly satisfactory" etymology has yet been produced.[5] Formally speaking, however, *nómos* is a noun derived from *némein* and, accordingly, might be open to the sense of "reading." In a culture that set such a very high value on the spoken word, that the law should be something to be read aloud rather than written down is, no doubt, significant. In Greece, *nómos* is accounted king, and reading rules. The legislator can rely on this king (whose imperious voice will end up as the inner voice of conscience). And the "oral" prehistory of *némein* 'to cite, recite' allows us to glimpse how it was that an "oral distribution"—another possible translation of *nómos*—based on writing came to replace one based on memory.

Like the legislator, every writer counted on a reader so that his words at one remove could sound forth. It was essential that they should do so, to the Greeks, a people as it were obsessed with the idea of "resounding renown" or *kléos*. Writing could not do without a voice. In truth, letters were meaningless for the average Greek reader until they were spoken. Letters had to be pronounced aloud if the text was to become intelligible. Sound and sense coincided in the *lógos*, which was both *réson* and *raison*—'resonance' and 'reason'—to borrow the felicitous pun made by Francis Ponge.[6] By listening to the resonant sequence of sounds produced by the reader from the string of written words, the same reader could recognize the meaning of those words committed to writing. Not surprisingly, then, the Greeks chose as a technical term for 'to read' a verb meaning 'to recognize' (*anagignóskein*). And we immediately realize that, for those Greeks, whose reading was always done aloud, the letters themselves did not *represent* a voice. They did not picture a

5. E. Laroche, *Histoire de la racine* ★ *nem- en grec ancien* (Paris, 1949), p. 163.
6. F. Ponge, *Pour un Malherbe* (Paris, 1965), p. 97 and passim.

voice. Only a voice—the reader's—*prompted* by those letters could be produced, a voice that, for its part, could claim to represent the voice transcribed, even if that voice was a fictitious one.

Not until silent reading was conceptualized—possibly as early as the late sixth century B.C.—could writing be regarded as representing a voice. Now the letters could themselves "speak" directly to the eye, needing no voice to mediate. In his article on silent reading, Bernard Knox cites a few striking examples of this remarkable and, it must be admitted, marginal, or even parenthetical, phenomenon in Greek culture. For if the purpose of writing was to produce sound, silent reading inevitably has the air of an anomaly. Although Knox does not succeed in establishing a distinction between silent reading ("in one's head") and reading that is just inaudible to others (but which is, in principle, still "vocal"), it is possible to corroborate the findings of his inquiry by a study of the mental structure of silent reading. In short, the internalization of the voice in silent reading corresponds to the metaphor of "letters that speak," which became current at the point where silent reading began to be more or less commonly practiced. For anyone reading in silence, as Theseus does in Euripides' *Hippolytos,* the letters "speak," they "cry out" or even "sing." The eye *sees* the sound.

A written page can now become a scene. A scene? Certainly, a scene, as is attested by the Athenian poet Callias' *ABC Show* (second half of the fifth century B.C.). Surviving fragments allow us to form a general idea of this astounding play. In it the Ionian alphabet is literally set on stage and its twenty-four letters address the spectator in the same way as they were by then accustomed to address, in perfect silence, the metaphorical spectator whom the reader had become.

What motivated me to undertake the line of inquiry I have just summarized? I would say that, in a sense, it was the unease provoked by the contradictory figure of the reader or, to be more precise, by the two conflicting models of the reader with which we are familiar today. On the one hand is the reader despised by the writer, that is to say the ancient model which I have described above, consolidated by a certain romanticism that set up an opposition between the sublime poet and his vulgar readers. On the other is the reverse, more recent model, namely that of the "superreader" for whom the poem is simply a pretext for a reading that considers itself to be infinitely superior to its object.

Confronted by those two models of the reader, it is legitimate to wonder whether it would not be possible to postulate a more evenly balanced relationship between writer and reader without minimizing the specific features of each, as formulas such as "to read is to write" tend to do. At any rate, it was with just such a "more evenly balanced relationship" in mind that I began the present inquiry into Greek reading. I did not do so under the illusion that I would discover it ready-made among the ancient Greeks, but rather in the hope of coming up with a few ideas that might serve in its elaboration. In other words, I conceived this inquiry as a preliminary study on reading, to be carried out under the "laboratory conditions" provided by Greek culture.[7]

When I was reaching what then seemed the conclusion of my inquiry, I discovered something like—yet distinct from—that more evenly balanced relationship that I was seeking. And, to my astonishment, it was in Plato's *Phaedrus* that I found it, at the point where Socrates redefines not only the relationship between lovers in a pederastic union (as Michel Foucault has shown[8]), but also, through that very redefinition, the relationship between writer and reader, both of whom, as subjects, take part in one and the same search for truth.

In more or less elaborated forms, all the chapters in this book have been presented as lectures or seminar papers. I mention them all in order to give credit where credit is due, to all those from whose observations I have profited. I offer them my warmest thanks.

Chapter 1 was presented in February 1984 at the seminar organized by Jean-Pierre Darmon, Jean-Louis Durand, and François Lissarrague at the Ecole pratique des hautes études (fifth section) in Paris, and again three months later at the colloquium "Literacy and Society" organized by the Center for Sammenlignende Kultur-

7. See J.-P. Vernant, *Myth and Thought among the Greeks* (London, 1983), p. x. For an updated edition, with significant changes, see J.-P. Vernant, *Mythe et pensée chez les Grecs* (Paris, 1985).

8. M. Foucault, *The Use of Pleasure,* pp. 229–246.

forskning (and more particularly by Michael Harbsmeier, Minna Skafte Jensen, Mogens Trolle Larsen, and Karen Schousboe) at the University of Copenhagen. Chapter 2 is the paper I delivered at the colloquium "L'Ecriture, son autonomie et ses nouveaux objets intellectuels en Grèce ancienne," directed by Marcel Detienne of the Centre de recherches comparées sur les sociétés anciennes, in Paris in September 1984. Five months later I delivered it again as part of Florence Dupont's course at the Université de Paris IV. I had the chance to discuss Chapter 3 at the seminar run by Jean-Pierre Vernant in the Collège de France in March 1985. In Marcel Detienne's seminar at the EPHE (fifth section), I was able to read a preliminary text of what later became Chapters 2, 4, and 5. A draft of what became Chapters 6, 7, and 8 was discussed at a meeting of the "Corps du citoyen" group organized by Nicole Loraux and Yan Thomas in April 1985 (Ecole des hautes études en sciences sociales, Paris). I presented Chapter 9 at a second colloquium organized by the Center for Sammenlignende Kulturforskning—"*From Orality to Literacy and Back*"—in November 1985. The text of the final chapter of this book was delivered at a meeting of the "Corps du citoyen" group in January 1986.

I also thank Gregory Nagy of Harvard University, who read a preliminary version of Chapter 1 and commented on it, and Øivind Andersen, of the University of Trondheim in Norway, who helpfully read the first nonannotated version of the whole work. My gratitude also goes to Ann-Marie Habbe (who in 1977 first drew my attention to Phrasikleia), Luc Brisson, François Hartog, Carl Nylander, Göran Printz-Påhlson, Agnès and Alain Rouveret, Joseph Russo, Lars Rydbeck, Evelyne and John Scheid, Annie and Alain Schnapp, Sandro Veronesi, and Froma Zeitlin. Finally, I express my thanks to the director of the Centre de recherches comparées sur les societés anciennes, Pierre Vidal-Naquet, who kindly agreed to publish the French version of this book in the series for which he is editor-in-chief at the La Découverte publishing house, and who, after a meticulous reading of the manuscript, made many useful comments that I was happy to include in my notes.

J.S.

Phrasikleia:
From Silence to Sound

Among the myths dealing with the origin of the Greek alphabet, one seems to be quoted less frequently than the others, probably because of its overtly ethnocentric character.[1] In one stroke, it wipes out the Phoenician origin of writing, so important for those who wish to consider myth an allegorical staging of history. The myth I am thinking of is found in the fragments of the historian Skamon of Mytilene, author of a work in several volumes, titled *On Inventions*. According to Skamon—who lived in the fourth century B.C. and was the son of the historian Hellanikos[2]—the letters of the alphabet were called "Phoenician" after Phoinike, the daughter of the Attic king Aktaion, the inventor of writing. To quote Skamon, Aktaion "is said to have been without male offspring, but to have had three daughters, Aglauros, Herse and Pandrosos: [a fourth] Phoinike is said to have died when still a young girl [*parthénos*]. For this reason, Aktaion called the letters 'Phoenician' [*Phoinikḗïa tà*

---

1. The scholia to Dionysius Thrax list a dozen inventors of the alphabet, in particular Kadmos and Palamedes (*Anecdota Graeca* 2.774, 781–786 Bekker). See also L. H. Jeffery, "'Αρχαῖα γράμματα: Some Ancient Greek Views," in *Festschrift Grumach,* ed. W. C. Brice (Berlin, 1967), pp. 152–166. For Kadmos see R. Edwards, *Kadmos the Phoenician* (Amsterdam, 1979), pp. 22–23; for Palamedes see M. Detienne, "L'Écriture inventive," *Critique,* no. 475 (1986), pp. 1225–1234.

2. For the dates of Skamon, see F. Jacoby, "Skamon," *Pauly-Wissowa* 2, 3:1 (Stuttgart, 1927), col. 437, who cites the *Suda* (s.v. *Hellánikos*) where Skamon is given as the son of Hellanikos of Mytilene.

grámmata], wanting to bestow some kind of honor [*timế*] on his daughter."[3]

If this myth at first sight seems a mediocre mishmash of elements known from the traditions on Athenian autochthony, where Aglauros, Pandrosos, and Herse are the daughters of Kekrops, not Aktaion, it largely compensates for this "mediocrity" by connecting alphabetic writing with the commemoration of the dead.[4] The earliest Greek alphabetic documents that have come down to us do not, as one might have expected, concern economic activities in the strict sense (inventories, bookkeeping, and the like). Our earliest alphabetic documents are of a different kind: inscriptions on various objects dedicated to the gods or belonging to human beings, be it a statue, a drinking vessel, or a tombstone.[5] In fact, alphabetic writing found one of its first applications in the commemoration of the dead.

From the archaic period we have a great number of sepulchral inscriptions. But it very rarely happens that we are able to study an inscription together with the sepulchral monument to which it belongs, as the inscribed base is often all that remains of a monument, the statue being lost. For this reason, the 1972 discovery of Phrasikleia's *sêma* 'memorial' at present-day Merenda, in the ancient Attic deme of Myrrhinous (south of Marathon) becomes singularly important.[6] "For the first time in the history of archaic Greek sepulchral sculpture, we are in possession of a statue and an epi-

3. *FGrH* 476 F 3 = Photius and *Suda*, s.v. *Phoinikếia grámmata*. We will return to this legend at greater length in Chapter 5. "Letters" are *Phoinikếia grámmata* (Herodotus 5.58) or simply *phoinikếia* (*Sylloge*³, no. 38, 37–38 Dittenberger).

4. According to Tacitus, Kekrops is also believed to have invented the alphabet (*Annals* 11.14). A tradition reported by Cicero gives him as the originator of Attic funeral customs (*Laws* 2.63).

5. See L. H. Jeffery, *The Local Scripts of Archaic Greece* (Oxford, 1961); M. Guarducci, *Epigrafia greca*, 1–2 (Rome, 1967–1970); G. Pfohl, *Greek Poems on Stones*, vol. 1, *Epitaphs: From the Seventh to the Fifth Centuries B.C.*, Textus Minores, no. 36 (Leiden, 1967) (hereafter, "Pfohl"); M. Lazzarini, *Le formule delle dediche votive nella Grecia arcaica*, Atti della Accademia nazionale dei Lincei. Memorie. Classe di scienze morali, storiche e filologiche, 8th ser., 19:2 (Rome, 1976) (hereafter "Lazzarini"). For an overview, see G. Pfohl, "Die ältesten Inschriften der Griechen," *Quaderni Urbinati di Cultura Classica*, no. 7 (1969), pp. 7–25.

6. E. I. Mastrokostas, "Myrrhinous: La koré Phrasikleia, Oeuvre d'Aristion de Paros et un kouros de marbre," *Athens Annals of Archaeology*, 5 (1972), pp. 298–324.

gram, assuredly belonging together, which are both almost intact."[7] In fact, the base of the statue had already been found separately in the eighteenth century and was published more than a century ago from the manuscript of Michel Fourmont, who visited Greece between 1729 and 1730 and saw the inscribed base in the wall of the Panaghia church, some two hundred meters from the spot where the statue was found in 1972.[8] Nevertheless, the conditions of its interpretation have changed radically since the discovery of the statue to which it belongs. Some have mistakenly clung to interpretations produced before the new discovery, as if the statue itself had nothing to contribute.[9] But it is equally mistaken to treat the statue's epigram as a "simple text with no hidden meanings," while nevertheless considering the statue to be a masterpiece of sculpture.[10] What is a "simple text"?

Georges Daux describes the statue this way: "It is a life-size representation of a young woman; her right arm is held alongside the body, her hand pinching and slightly parting the folds of her khiton; her left forearm is placed horizontally across her chest, her left hand holding a flower, vertically, between her breasts. Thick sandals; a long khiton cinched at the waist by a belt, bestrewn with rosettes and bordered by a band decorated with meanders (as is the middle vertical ribbon) or with tongue-and-groove patterns; all these motifs are incised and painted. The young woman wears a necklace and earrings and a bracelet on each wrist. Her head is adorned by a diadem (crown [*stephánē*]) decorated with a string of pearls and, above, with a row of lotus flowers alternating with flower cups similar to the one that she holds in her left hand.[11] On either side of her head, three plaits of hair fall to her bosom. The

7. G. Daux, "Les Ambiguïtés du grec κόρη," *Comptes rendus de l'Académie des inscriptions et des belles-lettres* (1973), p. 383.

8. A. Boeckh, *Corpus Inscriptionum Graecarum*, 1, no. 28 (Berlin, 1828), pp. 46–47. See Mastrokostas, "Myrrhinous," pp. 318–319.

9. As N. M. Kontoleon does in an article published in 1975, "Περὶ τὸ σῆμα τῆς Φρασικλείας ('Απολογία μιᾶς ἑρμηνείας)," 'Αρχαιολογικὴ 'Εφημερίς" (1974), pp. 1–12, in which he defends the interpretation that he proposed in his lectures delivered at the Collège de France in 1967 (*Aspects de la Grèce pré-classique* [Paris, 1970], p. 53).

10. Daux, "Les Ambiguïtés du grec κόρη," p. 388.

11. Lotus calixes, according to Mastrokostas, "Myrrhinous," p. 317.

PHRASIKLEIA (detail). In this photograph taken before the restoration of the statue (whose left hand was broken off at the wrist), the hand holding the flower is simply placed across the chest. Photo courtesy Euthymios I. Mastrokostas ("Myrrhinous: La Koré Phrasikleia, ouevre d'Aristion de Paros et un kouros de marbre," *Athens Annals of Archaeology,* 5 [1972], p. 313).

statue is exceptionally well-preserved and still bears many traces of its original painted surface. It is the work of the Parian sculptor Aristion, whose name and origin are inscribed on the base. This sculptor, already known from other dedications (one complete, two restored), was active during the third quarter of the sixth century."[12]

The almost perfect state of preservation of this statue, which has been dated to around 540 B.C., is worth commenting on.[13] It was probably buried shortly after being completed; the absence of any traces of mutilation indicates that it was buried by people who were bent on protecting it from destruction.[14] Destruction by whom? In this case, not by the Persian invaders, since the fragments of pottery found around the statue preclude such a late date.[15] But the year 540 was probably the year when the tyrant Peisistratos returned to Athens, expelling the Alcmaeonid family.[16] According to Isocrates, the followers of Peisistratos "not only demolished the houses of the Alcmaeonids but they even opened their graves."[17] These circumstances suggest that the statue of Phrasikleia may have been buried by the Alcmaeonids on the return of Peisistratos. The artistic quality of the statue further confirms this hypothesis, as it conforms with what we know of the Alcmaeonids' interest in art.[18] But there is another fact worth taking into account: the name of the young girl. She is called Phrasikleia. The last element of her name is derived from the word *kléos* 'fame', a word of central importance not only to archaic Greek culture in general but to the Alcmaeonid family in particular.[19] Among the names given to its members,

12. Daux, "Les Ambiguïtés du grec κόρη," pp. 383–384.

13. L. H. Jeffery, "The Inscribed Gravestones of Archaic Attica," *Annals of the British School at Athens* 57 (1962), p. 139.

14. I am indebted to Carl Nylander for this observation.

15. Mastrokostas, "Myrrhinous," p. 324.

16. F. Schachermeyr, "Peisistratos," *Pauly-Wissowa*, 19:1 (Stuttgart, 1937), col. 171–172.

17. Isocrates *The Team of Horses* 26.

18. On the Athenian sculptor Antenor see P. Lévêque and P. Vidal-Naquet, *Clisthène l'Athénien*, Annales littéraires de l'université de Besançon, 65 (Paris, 1964), pp. 83–89.

19. See M. Detienne, *Les Maîtres de vérité dans la Grèce archaïque* (Paris, 1967), p. 20; G. Nagy, *Comparative Studies in Greek and Indic Meter* (Cambridge, Mass., 1974), pp. 231–255; and Nagy, *The Best of the Achaeans* (Baltimore, 1979), pp. 15–18.

Megaklês (approximately) "great fame" is repeated in almost obses-
sional fashion from generation to generation; and *Kleisthénēs* 'fame-
strong' and *Periklês* "wide fame" (despite the fact that Perikles was
only related to the Alcmaeonids on his mother's side) are other
examples that show how gripped the Alcmaeonids were by the idea
of *kléos*.[20] Consequently, it would not be unreasonable to assume
that the young girl called Phrasikleia belonged to the Alcmaeonid
family.

If Phrasikleia's memorial may thus have a value as a *document* for
the history of sixth-century Athens, it is also a *monument* in its own
right, to use Michel Foucault's distinction.[21] And precisely as a
monument, obeying rules of its own, is the Phrasikleia ensemble—
statue and epigram—the subject of this book.

We may infer from Pierre Chantraine's *Dictionnaire étymologique,*
the proper name of the girl Phrasikleia should be taken to mean
"famous-for-her-thoughts" or something of the kind.[22] The *Phrasi-*
element can be explained as an old dative plural of *phrén* (approximately rendered as "thought"), while the *-kleia* element is derived
from *kléos* 'fame'.[23] The name *Phrasíkleia* seems thus to be constructed in the same way as, for example, *Nausí-thoos* "swift-by-
means-of-his-ships", where the element *Nausi-* is the dative plural
of *naûs* 'ship'.

But the situation is more complicated. Chantraine mentions another proper name in which the *Phrasi-* element has assuredly nothing to do directly with *phrén* or *phrénes*. This name is *Phrasí-dēmos*,[24]
which, analogous to names like *Blepsí-dēmos,* means "he-who-pays-
attention-to-the-people". Here the *Phrasi-* element is derived from
phrásai/phrásasthai, aorist infinitives of the verb *phrázein/phrázesthai*
'to show/pay attention to'.[25] Now, if we consider the name *Phra-*

---

20. See the genealogical table by Lévêque and Vidal-Naquet, *Clisthène l'Athénien,* p. 56.

21. M. Foucault, *The Archaeology of Knowledge* (Tavistock, 1972), p. 139.

22. P. Chantraine, *Dictionnaire étymologique de la langue grecque* (Paris, 1968–
1980), pp. 1225, 1228.

23. In corroboration of this interpretation it would be possible to cite *Iliad*
24.201–202, which mentions the *phrénes* (dative) for which Priam "is renowned"
(verb: *kléomai*).

24. Chantraine, *Dictionnaire étymologique,* p. 1225.

25. I have chosen this translation rather than the more succinct 'to show/to
consider' to emphasize the logical articulation of the active and middle forms of the

síkleia within the framework to which it belongs, that is, the Attic onomastic system, it is clear that it should be included in the following list of women's proper names: *Dexí-kleia* (as in the adjective *dexí-mēlos* 'sheep-receiving'), *Erasí-kleia* (as in *erasi-khrḗmatos* 'money-loving'), *Mnēsí-kleia* (as in *mnēsí-theos* 'god-remembering'; also *Mnēsí-epēs* a man's proper name meaning '*épos*-remembering'), *Sōsí-kleia* (as in *sōsí-polis* 'city-rescuing').[26] Of these four women, the first "receives" *kléos*, the second "loves" it, the third "remembers" it, and the last "rescues" it. Each one, in her own manner, "cares for" the audible fame called *kléos*.

This excursion into the field of onomastic studies compels us to understand the proper name *Phrasíkleia* in a new manner.[27] It means 'she-who-draws-attention-to-*kléos*' or 'she-who-pays-attention-to-*kléos*', depending on whether we derive its first element from the active form *phrásai* 'to show', or from the middle form *phrásasthai* 'to pay attention to', an ambiguity that at first seems troubling but becomes, as we shall see, a key to our understanding the name.[28] To anyone whose profession was to make *kléos* resound and who was commissioned to write the epigram for the dead girl, this proper name must have possessed an extraordinary significance that presented a formidable challenge to all one's poetic skill.

For in truth, "fame" is not a very satisfactory translation for *kléos*. In the first place, *kléos* is the technical term for what the poet bestows on individuals who have accomplished something remarkable, as we know from the studies of Marcel Detienne and Gregory Nagy.[29] Second, *kléos* belongs entirely to the world of sounds. In the *Iliad*, Homer tells us about himself: "All that we hear is a *kléos*"; and the verb used for "hear" is *akoúein*.[30] If *kléos* is not acoustic, it is

---

verb, in which the notion of "attention"—both objective and subjective—is fundamental. Etymologically, *phrázein* is connected with *phrḗn* (see Chantraine, *Dictionnaire étymologique*, p. 1228), which can be translated as, precisely, "attention" (instead of "thought," which is the more general notion).

26. F. Bechtel, *Die attischen Frauennamen nach ihrem System dargestellt* (Göttingen, 1902), p. 21.

27. On *Phrasi-klēs* see A. Fick, *Die griechischen Personennamen nach ihrer Bildung erklärt*, 2d ed. (Göttingen, 1894), pp. 281–282.

28. See below, p. 18 and n. 47.

29. Detienne, *Les Maîtres de vérité dans la Grèce archaïque*; Nagy, *Comparative Studies in Greek and Indic Meter.*

30. *Iliad* 2.486; see also Nagy, *Comparative Studies*, pp. 244–246.

not *kléos*. This sonority of *kléos* is confirmed by etymology. In the Germanic languages, we find the following cognates of the word: the Icelandic *hljóð*, the Swedish *ljud*, the Danish *lyd*, and the German *Laut*, all meaning 'sound'.[31] In English, the adjective "loud" is another significant relative of *kléos*.

So much for *kléos*. But what is the precise meaning of the verb *phrázein?* Contrary to what we might expect (perhaps because of modern derivatives such as "phrase" or "phraseology," which are understood in a phonocentric manner), *phrázein* does not denote the act of speaking in its sonority. It does not cover the acoustic manifestation of the language performance. As Aristarchus, the great Alexandrian philologist, points out, in Homer *phrázein* is never a synonym for *eipeîn* 'to speak'.[32] Nor is it the equivalent of *légein* 'to say' in post-Homeric Greek.[33] The etymology of *phrázein* (related to *phrḗn* 'thought') seems to preclude such a meaning, which would be incompatible with the silent nature of mental activity.[34] That is why the Suda, the ancient lexicon, lists it as a synonym of *sēmaínein* 'to signify' and *dēloûn* 'to show'.[35] It is, of course, possible to *phrázein* 'to show' something in an oral statement, but the emphasis then is not on the acoustic character of the message. Consider a passage in the *Odyssey*, where Odysseus, disguised as a beggar, provides Penelope with the 'signs' (*sēmata*) that she is expected to recognize. Her eyes fill with tears "when she recognizes the signs that Odysseus has clearly shown [*péphrade*] her."[36] The nonacoustic nature of *phrázein* is abundantly clear in the expression *antì phōnês kheirì phrázein* "to show something with the hand instead of the voice", or rather "to show by gestures when the voice cannot be used." It is an expression used by Aeschylus in the *Agamemnon,*

31. E. Hellquist, *Svensk etymologisk ordbok*, 3d ed., 1 (Lund, 1980), p. 581.

32. K. Lehrs, *De Aristarchi studiis homericis*, 2d ed. (Leipzig, 1865), pp. 84–86.

33. J. H. H. Schmidt, *Synonymik der griechischen Sprache*, 1 (Leipzig, 1876), pp. 89–90.

34. H. Fournier, *Les Verbes "dire" en grec ancien*, thesis (Paris, 1946), seems less convinced by this etymology than Chantraine, *Dictionnaire étymologique*, p. 1228, but points out that it is implicitly accepted by Homer in the *Iliad*, in a line such as 9.423 (as it is, one might add, by Hesiod *Works and Days* 688), which provides a striking example of a *figura etymologica*. As for the silent nature of thought see Pindar *Nemean* 4.6–8, who contrasts sonorous speech (*rhêma*) with "deep" *phrḗn;* see also Plato *Sophist* 263e–264a, and *Theaetetus* 189e–190a.

35. *Suda*, s.v. *phrázousi: sēmaínousi, dēloûsi*.

36. *Odyssey* 19.250; see also 23.206, 24.346.

where Klytaimestra tells Kassandra (who does not speak Greek) to use the language of gestures: "Speak not, but make with your barbarian hand some sign [*phráze*]."[37] The same expression is also found in Herodotus, where an Amazon uses gestures to communicate with a Scythian: "Since they understood not each other's speech and she could not speak to him, she signed [*éphraze*] with her hand that he should come on the next day to the same place, bringing another youth with him."[38] Here too, *phrázein* is used in a context marked by linguistic alterity: it denotes the action of transmitting a message by means of a dumb show. *Phrázein* is accordingly just as appropriate as *sēmaínein*[39] to denote what is achieved by written signs. In Euripides' *Iphigenia in Tauris,* the heroine of the play says to Pylades, who is to carry her letter to Orestes: "If you preserve my writing [*graphḗ*], it will silently indicate [*phrásei sigôsa*] what I have written."[40] Writing "indicates" or "shows"; it does not itself speak (except metaphorically, a point to which we will return in Chapter 9). Nor does the stone on which it may be engraved speak in the strict sense of the word: stone is *áphthongos* 'voiceless'.[41] Inscribed or not, however, it may *provoke* speech, in the same way as the sepulchral monument (*sêma*) imagined by Hektor in the seventh book of the *Iliad:* " 'This is the barrow [*sêma*] of a man who died in olden days, whom, . . . in the midst of his prowess, glorious Hektor slew.' So shall someone say [*eréei*] one day; and my renown [*kléos*] will never die."[42] Inscribed or not, the *sêma* in itself is silent, but whoever recognizes it when passing by will speak. The stone will trigger speech.

37. Aeschylus *Agamemnon* 1061.

38. Herodotus 4.113. The reason Aeschylus and Herodotus use *phráze* and *éphraze* instead of the aorists *phráson* and *éphrase* is that the contexts require the "conative" force possessed by forms derived from the present infinitive *phrázein* '(to try) to show'.

39. Plato *Phaedrus* 275d.

40. Euripides *Iphigenia in Tauris* 762–763.

41. Theognis 568–569: "After my death," the poet declares, "I shall rest as a stone without a voice [*hôste líthos áphthongos*]." See Aristotle *De Anima* 2.8.420b5–6: "None of the inanimate beings is endowed with a voice." The fact that an object refers to itself as "I" in archaic Greek inscriptions does not make it a "speaking object," even in a metaphorical sense. As Chapter 2 will show, a voice is not constitutive of the first person (for even a mute man can refer to himself as "I").

42. *Iliad* 7.89–91.

Reminding us that the Indic *dhyāma* 'thought' is a cognate of the Greek *sêma*, Gregory Nagy has tried to resolve what seems at first sight to be a problem of meaning: How are we to understand the semantic relation between "thought" and "sign"?[43] Nagy's answer is that the Greek *sêma*, which he translates as "coded message," is associated with the idea of a *nóēsis*, an *anágnōsis*, or *anagnórisis*, key words that designate the mental processes of decoding signs, reading, and recognition. Such processes are to be found in the immediate contexts of the word *sêma*. There is no *sêma* without *nóēsis* 'decoding'. In Nagy's view this semantic link constitutes a linguistic reflex, as it were, in ancient Greek. A *sêma* remains *incomplete* without the "thought" implied in its decoding.

For a *sêma* to be decoded, it has first to be pointed out; attention must be drawn to it. *Sêma* is, in fact, used as the complementary direct object of *phrázein* 'to show', as when Odysseus shows the signs he expects Penelope to recognize.[44] But, as we have seen, the word *sêma* carries not only the general meaning of "sign" but also the more particular one of "funerary monument" or "tomb." In this sense, which of course does not exclude the other meanings of the word here, *sêma* is placed at the very beginning of the Phrasikleia epigram, immediately before the *Phrasi-* element of the girl's name:

σῆμα Φρασικλείας κούρη κεκλήσομαι αἰεί,
ἀντὶ γάμου παρὰ θεῶν τοῦτο λαχοῦσ᾿ ὄνομα.

[I, Phrasikleia's *sêma*, shall always be called girl [*koúrē*], having received this name from the gods instead of marriage.]

Through the word *sêma*, the inscription starts by confirming what we are already doing; the word is in fact an invitation to the kind

43. G. Nagy, "*Sêma* and *nóēsis*: Some Illustrations," *Arethusa* 16 (1983), pp. 35–55. I was privileged to attend the May 1982 lecture in which Nagy presented this article at the Centre de recherches comparées sur les sociétés anciennes in Paris. It has been reworked as chap. 8 in G. Nagy, *Greek Mythology and Poetics* (Ithaca, N.Y., 1990), pp. 202–222, under the title "Sêma and Nóēsis: The Hero's Tomb and the 'Reading' of Symbols in Homer and Hesiod."

44. If "attention" or "thought" is *phrēn* in Greek, this word in a sense translates the Indic *dhyāma;* that makes it easier to understand the connection between *sêma* and *phrázein* (which, as we have seen, is derived from *phrēn*).

of "recognition" called 'reading' (*anágnōsis*) in Greek. But for the Greeks, reading meant *reading aloud*. Not that they were incapable of silent reading, as one extreme view holds, but the normal way of reading a text in ancient Greece was, without any doubt, reading it out loud.[45] Their relation to the written word might perhaps be compared to our attitude to musical notation: not everyone can read music in silence, and the most common way to read it is by playing it on an instrument or singing it out loud to hear what it sounds like.

Therefore, whoever "recognizes" or "reads" Phrasikleia's *sêma* in the Greek way will read it out loud. And in doing so, the reader will immediately notice the emphatic alliteration in the first line of the epigram, where four *k*s are heard, the first and last followed by an *l*: [kl] [k] [k] [kl]. Four *s*s are also present. The "clicking" character of the line gives an important key to its interpretation, as it lends weight to the *kléos* contained in the name *Phrasíkleia*, the semantic value of which is thus reactivated.[46] The *kléos* to which *Phrasí-kleia* "pays attention" thus receives the attention of the reader too.[47] The semantic content of the words affected by the alliteration confirms this hypothesis: Phrasikleia's *kléos* depends precisely on the fact that she will be 'called' (*keklḗsomai*, as she says[48]) *koúrē* 'girl', 'daughter', 'virgin', '*kórē*'.[49] When people speak of Phrasikleia in the future,

45. B. M. W. Knox, "Silent Reading in Antiquity," *Greek, Roman, and Byzantine Studies* 9 (1968), pp. 421, 435.

46. I emphasize this point in order to avoid giving the impression that the Greeks always paid such attention to proper names. Of course they did not. But when they did, the nature of their onomastic system facilitated interpretation and reinterpretation, as most Greek proper names are composed of semantically identifiable elements.

47. Thus, the ambiguity of *phrásai/phrásasthai* "to draw attention to/pay attention to" mentioned above is altogether justified.

48. Although not etymologically linked with *kléos,* the verb *kaleîn* 'to call (someone by his/her name), to name', which Phrasikleia uses, is often associated with it. See Chantraine, *Dictionnaire étymologique,* pp. 485, 540–541. In fact, *kleîn* (derived from *kléos*) is sometimes the synonym of *kaleîn.* See Liddell-Scott-Jones, s.v. *kléō* (B). On *kaleîsthai* 'to be called', in the sense of *eînai* 'to be', see ibid., s.v. *kaléō,* 2.2.

49. For the formula that makes up the second half of the line, see *Iliad* 2.260; *Odyssey* 6.244; *Homeric Hymn to Aphrodite* 242; *Homeric Hymn to Apollo* 324. In these four passages it is used to define family relationships (father, husband, wife), a fact that suggests that, in the Phrasikleia epigram, *koúrē* means 'daughter'.

they will refer to her as a *koúrē*. That is the word that will be heard whenever she is talked about, for she has received this designation from the gods in exchange for, or instead of, 'marriage' (*antì gámou*). The designation *koúrē* is the lot assigned to her instead of that of a "married woman." Her lot thus consists of a single word, a designation, a 'name' (*ónoma*). In fact, she has sometimes been identified with Kore (that is, Persephone) herself, but in my opinion it is mistaken to do so, for, unlike Kore, Phrasikleia remains a *koúrē* 'forever' (*aieí*), whereas Kore became the wife of Hades and, as such, acquired a different name—Persephone.[50]

If there is an implied allusion here—and I believe there is—it is not to Kore but to another goddess, whose status and function are defined in the *Homeric Hymn to Aphrodite*. Of the three goddesses capable of resisting the power of Aphrodite, one is Hestia, who is explicitly referred to as a *koúrē* (line 21) and who swears to "remain a virgin forever."[51] The *Hymn* goes on to explain that "instead of marriage [*antì gámoio*], Zeus the Father grants her a fine *géras* [honorific portion or lot]."[52] This expression presents a perfect analogy with the second line of the Phrasikleia epigram. Like the verb *lankhánein* "to receive as one's lot", of which *lakhoûs(a)* is an aorist participle, the noun *géras* belongs to the vocabulary of division and distribution.[53] A *géras* may be an honorific portion of food or of booty or, as here, an honorific status.[54] Hestia's *géras* will be her place in the middle of the house, at the hearth. She is the goddess of domestic fire. Another *koúrē*, Antigone in Sophocles' tragedy, uses the same vocabulary when she describes herself as "unmarried, not

50. The identification of Phrasikleia with Kore is one of the questions at issue in the disagreement between Kontoleon (*Aspects de la Grèce pré-classique*, p. 54; "Περὶ τὸ σῆμα," pp. 3–12) and Daux ("Les Ambiguïtés du grec κόρη," pp. 386–388).

51. *Homeric Hymn to Aphrodite* 5.28: *parthénos éssesthai pánt' ḗmata*.

52. Ibid. 29. See J.-P. Vernant, *Myth and Thought among the Greeks* (London, 1983), p. 131 (See also Introduction, n. 7).

53. B. Borecký, *Survivals of Some Tribal Ideas in Classical Greek,* Acta Universitatis Carolinae. Philosophica et historica, 10 (Prague, 1965); G. Nagy, *The Best of the Achaeans,* p. 132; E. Benveniste, *Le Vocabulaire des institutions indo-européennes,* 2 (Paris, 1969), pp. 43–50.

54. See above for the *timḗ* 'honor' of the princess Phoinike (the verb used by Skamon is *aponémein* 'to attribute', which belongs to the same vocabulary of distribution).

having heard the nuptial song, not having received the portion of marriage [*oúte toû gámou méros lakhoûsan*]."[55] Having lost her brothers, Antigone will die without having given birth to a grandson for her dead father, which is what she is supposed to do as an 'heiress' (*epíklēros*) if the paternal hearth is to survive.[56] This is her unhappy lot, her *méros*. The participle *lakhoûsan* 'having received' is identical to the one used in the Phrasikleia epigram.

Like Antigone, Phrasikleia has not received the "lot" or "portion" of marriage. Her "portion" is instead an *ónoma*, the designation *koúrē*, received in place of marriage, which may also mean that this designation is equal in value to marriage. Normally the young girl is similar to a young plant (*neázon*), but will be called *gunē* 'woman' or 'wife' later in life.[57] Thus, in Sophocles' *Trachinian Women*, Deianeira says that the young woman is free from cares "until the moment when she will be called wife instead of girl."[58] The expression used by Deianeira is in fact symmetrically opposed to the one we have encountered in the Phrasikleia epigram. In Phrasikleia's case, the normal course of life has been "frozen" by death, which has crystallized her status as a *koúrē* forever. This status means that she will remain attached to her father's hearth forever, without any possibility of being carried off by a marriage that would bring her to another man's house, the house of a husband. She will never become the wife of a stranger but will always remain, like Hestia, the *koúrē* or daughter of her father, for whom she keeps the metaphorical fire of *kléos*.[59]

As represented by the sculptor, Phrasikleia carries a lotus flower-cup in her left hand, in front of her breast. She is displaying the lotus

55. Sophocles *Antigone* 917–918, 889 (*kórē*). See Borecký, *Survivals of Some Tribal Ideas*, p. 47.
56. *Antigone* 918. On the status of *epíklēros* see Vernant, *Myth and Thought*, pp. 142–146.
57. Sophocles *Trachinian Women* 144.
58. Ibid. 148–149: *héōs tis antì parthénou gunè klēthêi*. See, for example, pseudo-Theocritus 27.65–66.
59. Combined with the genitive of the name of the father, *koúrē* naturally takes on the meaning of 'daughter' or *thugátēr;* sometimes, as in the Phrasikleia epigram, the context on its own suggests it (see Liddell-Scott-Jones, s.v. *kórē*, 3). See above, n. 49. Given that *koúrē* can also mean "pupil of the eye" (Empedocles frag. B 84.8 Diels-Kranz), one is encouraged to think that Phrasikleia's father cherished his daughter "as the apple of his eye," as it were.

flower, paying attention to it (in Greek, what she does would be expressed as *éphrase* or *ephrásato*). But as we have already seen, *Phrasí-kleia* means "she-who-shows-*kléos*" or "she-who-pays-attention-to-*kléos*". That is what her name says she does. Thus, the lotus she shows (a visual sign) takes the place of the *kléos* (an acoustic sign). According to her name, Phrasikleia shows something that cannot be seen, only heard: *kléos*. But as a statue, she shows something that cannot be heard, only seen: a flower. In this interplay between word and image, Phrasikleia's *sêma* accomplishes a remarkable metaphorical operation, the principal implications of which I define below.

Like the fire in the hearth—the domestic fire, Hestia's fire—the lotus flower is said to open or "rekindle" in the morning and close or "die down" at nightfall. Theophrastus writes: "The flower is white, resembling in the narrowness of its petals those of the lily, but there are many petals growing close upon one another. When the sun sets, these close and cover up the 'head,' but with sunrise they open and appear above the water."[60] So this flower behaves like a domestic fire. It is, indeed, the metaphorical sign for fire, in short, a stylized fire and, as such, a well-known element of figurative art.[61] Homer speaks of the "flower of fire" (*puròs ánthos*). He does so in a well-attested variant of a line from the *Iliad* (9.212) cited by Plutarch: "but when the flower of fire had flown [*autàr epeì puròs ánthos apéptato*]."[62]

This metaphor using plant life has a suggestive parallel in the expression *spérma purós* "seed of fire".[63] The "seed of fire" means the

60. Theophrastus *Historia Plantarum* 4.8.9; see A. B. Cook, *Zeus: A Study in Greek Religion* 2 (Cambridge, 1925), p. 772. On the lotus, see also M. Guarducci, "Dioniso e il loto," *Quaderni ticinesi di numismatica e antichità classica,* 10 (1981), pp. 53–69.

61. Cook, *Zeus,* pp. 770 f.

62. Plutarch *Moralia* 934b; Aristarchus also knew of this line, but rejected it. For other examples of the same metaphor, particularly in Aeschylus *Prometheus Bound* 7, see Cook, *Zeus,* pp. 771–772.

63. *Odyssey* 5.490: *spérma puròs sôzon* "preserving the seed of the fire." See the proper name *Sôsí-kleia,* cited above, p. 14; see also J.-P. Vernant, "A la table des hommes," in *La Cuisine du sacrifice en pays grec,* ed. M. Detienne, J.-P. Vernant et al. (Paris, 1979), p. 64. The Greek word for 'spark' (used to light a fire) is *zópuron,* a compound of *zō(o)*= 'living', and *pûr* 'fire'. Plato calls the survivors from the Flood "little *zópura* of humanity" (*Laws* 3.677b).

precious and vulnerable embers that must not die during the night, for fear of having to borrow fire from another household in the morning. The continuity of the fire of the hearth symbolizes the autonomy and continuity of the house itself, which is why it is so important to watch over it carefully. If she has no brothers and her father dies, the girl who is in charge of the paternal fire must not marry into the house of another family. She becomes the 'heiress' (*epíklēros*) of the house. She must marry the next-of-kin of her dead father.[64] No stranger's seed must be admitted to keep the domestic fire alive. In fact, the son of the "heiress" will be considered not the grandson but practically the *son* of his biological maternal grandfather.[65]

We do not know whether Phrasikleia had any brothers capable of ensuring the continuation of the domestic cult of their father. What we do know is that her relationship to her father (dead or alive) is made all the closer by the fact that she has died a young girl (*koúrē* or *parthénos*). She will remain his daughter forever. But as she is dead, she cannot, of course, look after the real paternal hearth. The fire that she is in charge of is a metaphorical fire—a flower. At the same time, however, this fire is a *kléos* 'renown', her own renown as well as that of one or several ancestors: in short, the renown of her family. According to Proclus, "the names given to children by their fathers have the purpose of commemorating (something or someone) or of expressing a hope, or the like."[66] One illustration will

64. Vernant, *Myth and Thought,* pp. 142–146. See Plato *Laws* 11.924e–925c; Isaeus *Hagnias' Succession* 1–2 and 11; Demosthenes 43 [*Against Makartatos*] 51.

65. Vernant, *Myth and Thought,* pp. 143–144. As we will see in Chapter 5, the constellation of father/daughter/son-in-law/grandson (in which the grandson sometimes bears the name of his maternal grandfather) serves as a model for written communication. The place of the daughter is taken by the writing (*graphḗ*) of her father and that of the grandson is taken by the *lógos* pronounced out loud by the son-in-law, whose place is that of the reader (*entunkhánein* means both 'to read' and 'to have sex with'). This legitimate grandson should be compared with the bastard children that the Greeks were supposed to father eventually if they dreamed that they were writing from right to left. See Artemidorus *The Interpretation of Dreams* 3.25.

66. Proclus *Scholia to the Cratylus* 47, 88 Pasquali, cited by M. Sulzberger, "Ὄνομα ἐπώνυμον: Les Noms propres chez Homère et dans la mythologie grecque," *Revue des études grecques,* 37 (1926), p. 429 (hereafter cited as Sulzberger). We will return to the subject of onomatothesis, or name-giving in Chapter 4.

suffice. Achilles' son Neoptolemos is so named because his father was 'young' (*néos*) when he first went to 'war' (*pólemos*). At the same time, Neoptolemos is a suitable name for a boy who, like his father, was very young when he fought his first battle, thereby meeting the expectations attached to him in a culture of mimesis, as the son of his father, Achilles.[67]

In sum, Phrasikleia "shows" a lotus flower that may be identified as the domestic fire, which, in its turn, may be identified as her own *kléos* and that of her family. This series of homologies is less arbitrary than it may appear. In Greek one of the epithets of *kléos* is, precisely, *ásbeston* 'unquenchable', which means that *kléos* is considered a fire.[68] But again the "fire" vocabulary is wedded to "plant" vocabulary. For the Greeks, *kléos* is also, significantly, defined as *áphthiton* 'unwilting'; it is like a plant that never wilts.[69] Phrasikleia's *kléos* is an unwilting flower that no stranger will ever pluck.

Holding a flower in her hand, a flower unceasingly reborn, the flower of fire, the young girl thus enacts her *kléos* with a silent gesture. In fact, the gesture of her hand mimes her own name Phrasikleia. The entire *sêma* may be seen as the staging or representation of her name. Phrasikleia shows forth her *kléos,* she looks after it lest it should go out; and the *Phrasi-* element in her name suggests that she succeeds in doing so, as it derives more directly from the aorist *phrásai* than from the present *phrázein*. Phrasikleia sees to it that her family remains alive in the collective memory. She attracts the reader, triggers a reading aloud of the epigram and, in doing so, she may well be said to give birth to a son called *Lógos,* the sonorous, eagerly awaited descendant of her father.[70] Hers is a marvelously efficacious writing, which produces a resounding *kléos* whenever it is read aloud.

67. Sulzberger, pp. 389–390, citing Pausanias 10.26.4. The father/son relationship is normally one of resemblance for the Greeks: see *Odyssey* 4.141–144; Hesiod *Works and Days* 182; Aristotle *De Generatione* 4.3.767b3–4. On Neoptolemos, see P. Vidal-Naquet, "The Black Hunter Revisited," *Proceedings of the Cambridge Philological Society,* no. 32 (1986), p. 136.

68. *Odyssey* 4.584, 7.333.

69. *Iliad* 9.413. G. Nagy, *Comparative Studies,* p. 243. See Pindar *Pythian* 1.66: *kléos ánthēsen* "*kléos* flowers." See also the inscription in Pfohl, p. 48, no. 138: *zōòn dè phthiménōn péletai kléos* "our *kléos* lives, although we have withered away".

70. See above, n. 65.

The flower Phrasikleia holds in her hand is closed, not open, a significant distinction, as it suggests the mode of existence of the *sêma* itself, its double mode of existence.[71] Through the Night of Oblivion, Phrasikleia's *kléos* waits patiently, like a closed lotus flower, for the Day of Recognition—the day of 'reading' (*anágnōsis*), of 'truth' (*a-lḗtheia*), when its meaning will be realized in the reading aloud of the epigram.[72] Every reading aloud thus becomes an audible blossoming of meaning, in other words, true *kléos*. In fact, Homer uses the "blooming" of the voice as a recurrent metaphor, and in contexts in which a person is suddenly struck mute: "And her/his blooming voice was held back" goes the formula (*thalerḕ dé hoi éskheto phōnḗ*).[73] In Phrasikleia's case, the blooming of *kléos* is also held back, as long as the epigram remains without a reader. In fact, every period when the *sêma* must endure in darkness, without readers and without spectators, is a state of waiting, in which meaning is hardly more than a spark, reduced to a faint gleam—*zurückgeschraubt,* to use Rilke's very precise word[74]—a seed of fire or a flower cup ready to blossom. This veritable theory of the sign and its double mode of existence is already in the name *Phrasíkleia,* where the first element refers to the silent world of signs, while the second refers to the living world of sounds, of *kléos,* of reading aloud.

The contradiction contained in the name Phrasikleia was a challenge that the epigram writer and the sculptor accepted. They did so with such a zeal that even the categories of grammar are summoned to enact the passage from silent sign to vocal realization. The *sêma* of Phrasikleia, which designates itself in the first person, shifts imperceptibly from the neuter to the feminine gender (*sêma* is neuter, *lakhoûsa* is feminine), thereby anticipating its own "return to life"

71. In this perspective, a re-reading of R. Wellek and A. Warren, *Theory of Literature,* 3d ed. (New York, 1962), pp. 142–157 ("The Mode of Existence of the Literary Work of Art"), might prove interesting.

72. On 'truth' (*alḗtheia*) as opposed to 'oblivion' (*lḗthē*), see M. Detienne, *Les Maîtres de vérité,* pp. 22–25; J. Svenbro, *La Parole et le marbre. Aux origines de la poétique grecque* (Lund, 1976), pp. 146–149.

73. *Iliad* 17.696, 23.397; *Odyssey* 4.705, 19.472. See also *Iliad* 3.152.

74. Rainer Maria Rilke, "Archaïscher Torso Apollos," *Der Neuen Gedichte anderer Teil,* in *Gesammelte Gedichte* (Insel-Verlag, Frankfurt am Main, 1962), p. 313.

through the act of reading.[75] If we take this subtle movement into account, as well as the movement from silence to sound in the name *Phrasíkleia,* we may finally venture the following interpretation of the girl's crown, where closed and open lotus flowers alternate in an eternal circle.[76] The crown is an enactment of the very functioning of the sepulchral *sêma,* whose meaning blooms or rekindles whenever its inscription is read aloud.

75. The signature of the artist, engraved on the side of the base, emphasizes the first person: *Aristíōn Pári[os m' ep]ó[ē]se* "Aristion of Paros made me". The restoration is guaranteed by epigraphical as well as metrical factors. The regularity of the lettering (this is the earliest Attic example of an inscription that is completely *stoikhēdón,* that is to say, in which each letter occupies the same-sized space) rules out the restoration suggested by Jeffery, who suppresses the *m,* inserting [iē] instead of [ē] ("The Inscribed Gravestones of Archaic Attica," pp. 138–139). Yet it tallies perfectly with the restoration cited, which was first proposed by H. G. Lolling ("Der Künstler Aristion," *Mitteilungen des deutschen archäologischen Instituts. Athenische Abteilung,* 1 [1876], pp. 174–175, and "Zum Grabstein der Phrasikleia," *ibid.,* 4 [1879], p. 10) and was adopted by Mastrokostas, "Myrrhinous," p. 320. Another of Aristion's signatures has also come down to us: *Aristíōn m' epóēsen* "Aristion made me" (Pfohl, p. 12, no. 35). This inscription constitutes an enoplion (˘ ‒ ˘ ˘ / ‒ ˘ ˘ ‒ ˘), whereas *Aristíōn Páriós m'epóēse* forms a reizianum preceded by an iambic metron (˘ ‒ ˘ ‒ / ‒ ˘ ˘ ‒ ˘ ‒ ˘); without the *m'* the meter collapses (˘ ‒ ˘ ‒ / ‒ ˘ ˘ ˘ ‒ ˘). See M. Moranti, "Formule metriche nelle iscrizioni greche arcaiche," *Quaderni Urbinati di Cultura Classica,* no. 13 (1972), pp. 7–23.

For an analogous switch from neuter to feminine gender, see G. M. Richter, *The Archaic Gravestones of Attica* (London, 1971), p. 165 (with an epigraphical appendix by M. Guarducci: "I am (the stele) of Phanodikos, son of Hermokrates, of Prokonnesos; and I have given a krater." See also Pfohl, p. 8, no. 23, and (in the opposite direction) p. 45, no. 128, p. 49, no. 139, as well as Lazzarini, p. 315, no. 952.

I use the expression "return to life" with the work of Douglas Frame in mind: *The Myth of the Return in Early Greek Epic* (New Haven, 1978), followed by Nagy, "*Sêma* and *nóēsis.*" Frame derives *nóos* 'perception, sense', and *nóstos* 'return' from the verb *néomai* in the inherited metaphorical sense of "to return home (from darkness)".

76. On the "eternity" of the circular movement in Presocratic philosophy, see Alcmeon, frag. B 2 Diels-Kranz, and Parmenides, frag. B 5 Diels-Kranz.

CHAPTER 2

I Write, Therefore I Efface Myself:
The Speech-Act in the
Earliest Greek Inscriptions

In Book 9 of the *Iliad,* when Agamemnon seeks reconciliation with Achilles, he lists all the gifts that he intends to present to the hero if he will only return to the field of battle. This list—a genuine "catalogue of gifts"[1]—is first itemized for the three heroes who are to be sent to Achilles. It is then meticulously reproduced by one of them, namely Odysseus, in Achilles' presence. Odysseus relays the contents of the catalogue, introducing a few significant alterations on account of the difference in situation between the speech as delivered by Agamemnon to Odysseus, Ajax, and Phoinix and as delivered by Odysseus to Achilles. One quotation will suffice to illustrate the nature of these alterations. Agamemnon says: "And I will give you seven women whom, on the day when he himself took well-built Lesbos, I chose for me. . . . These I will give him and amid them shall be she that then I took away, the daughter of Briseus."[2] Odysseus repeats this, framing it as follows: "And he will give you seven women whom, on the day when you yourself took well-built Lesbos, he chose for himself. . . . These he will give you and amid them shall be she that then he took away, the daughter of Briseus."[3] Homer's hexameters adapt readily to this kind of alteration, which does not really affect the list that is to be passed

---

1. *Iliad* 9.262: *kataléxō* "I shall enumerate".
2. *Iliad* 9.128–132.
3. *Iliad* 9.270–274.

on. It is simply a matter of *dṓsō* becoming *dṓsei, hélen autós* becoming *héles autós,* and so on. All the words affected by the change of subject fulfill the same metrical function in the two versions of the list. Such is the flexibility of the formulaic system at the bard's disposal.[4]

In everyday speech, we have no difficulty in accomplishing similar operations, even if the messages that we pass on probably need to be briefer than Agamemnon's catalogue of gifts if they are being transmitted word for word to those for whom they are destined. On the level of grammar, we can do as Odysseus does: it is easy to replace a "tell him" with a "he wants you to know," which is appropriate to this new situation in which it is we who become the "I" in the speech.[5]

What happens when a message like that sent by Agamemnon to Achilles is set down in writing and read out to the person to whom it is addressed (or is read by that person)? That may seem an odd question, given that we learn of Agamemnon's message only through writing, so I should explain that I ask it here only in order to provide an example, one drawn from a fictitious narrative already set down in written signs. Now another question presents itself. What happened when the bard's narrative was committed to writing and was thereby immutably fixed? I would say that, from the point of view of the speech-act, the *egṓ* that was pronounced out loud by the bard and that referred to himself[6] was written down so that it could be repronounced by the reader (the reciter of the narrative) who, for his part, could not lay claim to that *egṓ* despite the linguistic definition according to which "the *ego* is the one who *says* 'ego'."[7] In truth, transcription produces paradoxes that are

---

4. See also *Iliad* 4.193 f., 204 f.; 12.343 f., 354 f.

5. On the theory of the 'speech-act' (*énonciation*), see in the first instance E. Benveniste, *Problèmes de linguistique générale,* vol. 1 (Paris, 1966), chaps. 18, 20, and 21, and vol. 2 (Paris, 1974), chap. 5. See also C. Calame, "Entre oralité et écriture: Énonciation et énoncé dans la poésie grecque archaïque," *Semiotica,* 43 (1983), pp. 245–273.

6. See, for example, *Odyssey* 1.1: "O Muse, tell me," and, in the invocation preceding the Catalogue of Ships, *Iliad* 2.493: "I shall enumerate the commanders of the ships."

7. Benveniste, *Problèmes de linguistique générale,* 1:260. As it stands, Benveniste's theory applies only to oral communication.

sometimes difficult to resolve, perhaps particularly in the case of the Homeric epic, which is known to us through writing but without doubt had a long oral prehistory. The end product of that prehistory was the Homeric text with which we are familiar, even if we know nothing at all of the exact conditions in which it was produced.[8]

Rather than return to that daunting problem, I have chosen to examine another corpus, that of funerary and votive inscriptions.[9] Whereas the epic has the air of a *transcription* of a voice, many of these texts can claim to be *inscriptions* in a very emphatic sense of the word. Why "in a very emphatic sense"? Because they were conceived and designed for the very written signs through which we come to know them. Of course, sometimes they make use of the formulaic language of the bards, but it is certainly impossible to regard them as oral statements committed to writing only at some later date.[10] As we shall see, the form in which these texts are cast, indicative as they are of the speaker's identity, confirms that impossibility.

But let us return to our initial question: what happens when a message such as Agamemnon's is set down in writing? The base of a little bronze statue found on the Acropolis of Athens and dating from the end of the sixth century bears the following inscription, which provides us with a ready answer: "To whoever asks me, I reply [*hupokrínomai*] with the same [*ísa*] answer, namely that Andron, the son of Antiphanes, dedicated me as a tithe."[11] The written text "replies with the same answer" to all those who question it. It is inflexible. Its message always reaches the one to whom it is addressed—the abstract reader—in the same unchanging form, as the inscription itself triumphantly proclaims. That triumphant confi-

8. See J. Svenbro, *La Parole et le marbre. Aux origines de la poétique grecque* (Lund, 1976), pp. 11–45, esp. 14 and 42–44.

8. See J. Svenbro, *La Parole et le marbre. Aux origines de la poétique grecque* (Lund, 1976), pp. 11–45, esp. 14 and 42–44.

9. The two basic works on the subject are G. Pfohl, *Greek Poems on Stones,* vol. 1, *Epitaphs: From the Seventh to the Fifth Century B.C.,* Textus minores, 36 (Leiden, 1967); and M. Lazzarini, *Le formule delle dediche nella Grecia arcaica,* Atti della Accademia nazionale dei Lincei. Memorie. Classe di scienze morali, storiche e filologiche, 8th ser., 19:2 (Rome, 1976). Hereafter I refer to both of these works by the names of their authors.

10. See A. E. Raubitschek, "Das Denkmal-Epigramm," *L'Épigramme grecque,* Fondation Hardt, Entretiens, 14 (Vandoeuvres-Genève, 1968), p. 5.

11. Lazzarini, no. 658. We will return to this at greater length in Chapter 9.

dence was, as we know, to be challenged by the Socrates of the *Phaedrus,* at the point where he draws a comparison between writing and painting: "The creatures of painting stand like living beings, but if we ask them a question, they preserve a solemn silence. And so it is with written words; you might think they spoke as if they had intelligence, but if you question them, wishing to know about their sayings, they *always say one and the same thing.*"[12] In other words, for Socrates, writing has no internal life. And in the same spirit, one might add that even if reading aloud gives the impression of being a direct speech-act, in reality it is not. For the speech-act has already taken place, before the eye, in the writing—writing that, unlike tattooing,[13] can be separated from its "father" and go off "to roll to the right and to the left," to borrow Socrates' expression.[14]

This inflexible character of the written word, which the inscription of Andron, son of Antiphanes, vaunts in an almost democratic spirit ("To whoever asks me, I reply with the same [*ísa*] answer"), is particularly marked in the earliest Greek inscriptions, since, like the Andron inscription, they use the first person to refer to the object to which they belong.[15] These inscriptions are thus not only autodeictic but forthrightly egocentric, to use the etymologically correct word (although not with its current, general meaning). They assume the *egố* of the speech-act. Over twenty years ago, Mario Burzachechi devoted a classic study to these inscriptions on what he called "speaking" objects.[16] These are not statements that might

12. *Phaedrus* 275d (my emphasis). See *Protagoras* 329a, *Hippias Minor* 365c–d (and *Republic* 378d), *Laws* 12.968d–e, *Letters* 7.343a.

13. I return to the subject of tattooing in Chapter 7.

14. *Phaedrus* 275e. The verb is *kulindeîsthai*.

15. The date and the place of origin of the inscription suggests the idea of *isonomía,* a word with antityrannical or even democratic associations. See P. Lévêque and P. Vidal-Naquet, *Clisthène l'Athénien* (Paris, 1964), pp. 25–32; and G. Vlastos, "Ἰσονομία πολιτική" in *Isonomia,* ed. J. Man and E. G. Schmidt (Berlin, 1964), pp. 1–35. Furthermore, the verb *némein,* from which both *-nomía* and *nómos* 'law' are derived, can also mean 'to read' (Sophocles frag. 144 Nauck²): see below, Chapter 6, n. 3.

16. M. Burzachechi, "Oggetti parlanti nelle epigrafi greche," *Epigraphica,* 24 (1962), pp. 3–54. See H. Häusle, "Ζωοποιεῖν-ὑφιστάναι. Eine Studie der frühgriechischen inschriftlichen Ich-Rede der Gegenstände," in *Serta Philologica Aenipontana,* ed. R. Muth and G. Pfohl, Innsbrucker Beiträge zur Kulturwissenschaft,

have been pronounced by a speaker in an oral situation. That becomes quite clear as soon as one reads a few of the inscriptions. For
example, a very ancient bronze statuette tells us, "Mantiklos dedicated me"; on another equally ancient object, one reads, "I am the
kylix of Korakos."[17] Funerary monuments refer to themselves in
similar fashion: "Eumares set me up as a monument"; "I am the
memorial [mnêma] of Glaukos."[18] Clearly these assertions are not
transcriptions of something declared in an oral situation and then
inscribed upon the object. It is hard to imagine a situation in which
anyone would make such pronouncements with himself in mind. In
fact, quite the opposite seems to be the case. Assertions such as these
are, in a sense, peculiar to writing, for writing makes it possible for
inscribed objects to refer to themselves in the first person despite
their being just objects, not living, thinking beings endowed with
the power of speech.

On the other hand, while these assertions may be peculiar to
writing and represent a kind of speech-act that would be virtually
unimaginable without writing, or, more concretely, although it is
only thanks to writing that they have been conceived and have
come into being, that does not mean to say that they are their own
authors. Egocentric inscriptions are staged by an author who is
systematically considered absent. "Kleimachos made me and I am
his [eimì keínou]" is the message written on one sixth-century Athenian amphora.[19] Here, the absence of the director of what is being
staged, namely Kleimachos, is indicated by the third-person demonstrative pronoun (e)keînos, which refers precisely to the absent
man.[20] Kleimachos is not here; he is elsewhere, "far away" (ekeî).

---

20 (Innsbruck, 1979), pp. 23–139. See also the works of two Italian scholars:
L. Agostiniani, Le "iscrizioni parlanti" dell'Italia antica, Lingue e iscrizioni dell'Italia
antica, 3 (Florence, 1982); and G. Colonna, "Identità come appartenza nelle iscrizioni di possesso dell'Italia preromana," Epigraphica, 45 (1983), pp. 49–64.

17. Lazzarini, no. 795 (Thebes, late eighth century); Lazzarini, "I nomi dei vasi
greci nelle iscrizioni dei vasi stessi," Archeologica classica, 25–26 (1973–1974), p. 346,
no. 7 (Rhodes).

18. Pfohl, nos. 158 (Methana) and 15 (Thasos).

19. M. Guarducci, Epigrafia greca, 3 (Rome, 1975), p. 482. The inscriber did not
write "I made it and it is mine. Kleimachos," which from our point of view would
have been normal (i.e., a "transcription").

20. See E. Schwyzer and A. Debrunner, Griechische Grammatik, 2d ed., 2 (Munich, 1959), p. 209. See also Benveniste, Problèmes de linguistique générale, vol. 1,
chap. 18.

His amphora, on the other hand, refers to itself in the first person. The presence of the amphora, standing before the person reading the inscription, is as emphatic as the absence of the author who, at the moment when his inscription is read, is no longer there.

Let us look at the matter in a more methodical fashion, starting with the earliest funerary inscriptions and limiting ourselves, in the first instance, to seventeen that date from the seventh century, virtually the entire collection of funerary inscriptions from before 600 B.C. Among them, the memorial to Glaukos, mentioned above, uses both *eimí* 'I am', and *me* 'me', to establish its first-person status. Androkles' *sêma,* also mentioned above, settles for one *me* to accomplish the same operation, as does Praxilas' tomb, while Polynoe's stele refers to itself as *egố*.[21] Seven inscribed monuments refer to themselves using the demonstrative *tóde* (qualifying *sêma*) or *hóde* (qualifying *oîkos* or *thôkos*).[22] In six cases, there is neither an explicit first person nor any form of the demonstrative pronoun *hóde*.[23]

Remarkably, not one of these monuments refers to itself explicitly in the third person. Each refers to itself using either the first-person *egố, me,* or *eimí,* squarely establishing them at the center of the speech-act, or by means of *hóde* or *tóde*. When we translate the inscriptions in the latter group, we usually infer a verb in the third person: *sêma tóde toû deînos* "this [is] the tomb of so-and-so". One tends to accept this translation spontaneously, for it seems difficult, if not impossible, to regard *sêma tóde toû deînos* as an expression in which the first person is implicit. The demonstrative *tóde* 'this' seems to rule that out, at least it does if we look at it from the perspective of modern languages such as English, French, or Italian. But if we adopt the linguistic standpoint of the ancient Greeks, the third person is not necessarily implied. On the contrary, for in ancient Greek it is perfectly normal to have the demonstrative *hóde* agree with a personal pronoun in the first person or with a verbal form in the first person, as plenty of examples demonstrate. Upon

21. Pfohl, nos. 158 and 15; Guarducci, *Epigrafia greca,* p. 178 (Thera); Pfohl, no. 9 (Corfu).

22. With *tóde:* Pfohl, nos. 13, 10, 22 (corrected by C. Gallavotti, "L'iscrizione arcaica di Sicino e la metrica stesicorea," *Quaderni Urbinati di Cultura Classica,* no. 25 [1977], p. 76), 5, and 11. With *hóde:* Pfohl, no. 1; L. H. Jeffery, *The Local Scripts of Archaic Greece* (Oxford, 1961), pl. 62.26.

23. Pfohl, no. 129; Jeffery, *The Local Scripts of Archaic Greece,* pls. 2.8, 61.3 (i, ii, and iii), 61.5.

his return to Ithaca, Odysseus exclaims, "*hód' egṓ . . . ḗluthon,*" which we are bound to translate as "Here I am, home again." Similarly, Zeus declares to the assembly of the gods, "All of us present here [*hēmeîs hoíde*], let us decree. . . ." In Herodotus, Cyrus says to Astyages, "Here I am, at your disposal [*hóde toi páreimi*]." In Euripides, Orestes uses a similar expression: "Here I am, the Orestes whom you seek [*hód' eim' Oréstēs*]."[24] Further examples are unnecessary except to show that inscriptions, too, employ this kind of syntax. "Here I am, the tomb of Krites [*sêma tód' eimì Krítou*]" declares a *sêma* from the plain of Marathon, dating from 500 B.C.[25] We must reject L. H. Jeffery's comment: "The author is clearly confusing two different expressions: *sêma tód' estì toû deînos* (this is the tomb of so-and-so) and *toû deînós eimi mnêma* (I am the funerary monument of so-and-so)."[26] And for the same reason, it is not possible to follow Mario Burzachechi who considered this inscription an example of contamination.[27] In truth, what we have here is not a contamination or a confusion of two constructions, but perfectly normal syntax.

The same goes for another type of formula which occurs in funerary inscriptions and, above all, in dedications.[28] According to Burzachechi, a phrase such as *Alkímakhós m' anéthēke Diòs koúrēi tód' ágalma* "Alkimakhos dedicated me to the daughter of Zeus—me, this statue" should also be considered as a contamination between two formulas, namely *ho deîna me anéthēken* "so-and-so dedicated me" and *ho deîna anéthēke tóde ágalma* "so-and-so dedicated this statue."[29] Problems arise when we try to translate *ho deîná me anéthēke tóde ágalma,* because French and English, as well as other modern languages, do not coordinate first-person personal pronouns with demonstrative ones. In ancient Greek, however, such a

24. *Odyssey* 16.205–206, 1.76; Herodotus 1.115; Euripides *Orestes* 380.

25. Pfohl, no. 115.

26. L. H. Jeffery, "The Inscribed Gravestones of Archaic Attica," *Annals of the British School at Athens,* 57 (1962), p. 134.

27. Burzachechi, "Oggetti parlanti nelle epigrafi greche," p. 38. Both this article and Jeffery's article appeared in 1962.

28. Pfohl, no. 152; see also no. 139. Lazzarini, nos. 678, 679, 681, 686, 725, 732, and 748.

29. The phrase is found in Lazzarini, no. 732. Burzachechi, "Oggetti parlanti nelle epigrafi greche," pp. 22, 53.

coordination poses no problems: *hód' egó* and *tónde me* are perfectly grammatical expressions.[30] Therefore, we cannot follow Maria-letizia Lazzarini when she suggests that the *me* in the formula *ho deînā me anéthēke tóde ágalma* is a "pleonasm," chiefly justified by the meter.[31] If there is any pleonasm here, it is, in truth, only to the extent that *tóde* already contains a reference to the first person.

The fact is that in ancient Greek, *hóde* is precisely a first-person demonstrative pronoun.[32] Consequently, *hóde* situates the object or person that it qualifies in the immediate sphere of the speaker as opposed to that of the person addressed. "Take off those clothes [= your clothes, the clothes that you are wearing; *heímata taûta*] and put on this veil [= my veil, the veil that I have here; *tóde krêdemnon*]," says Leukothea to Odysseus.[33] In this example, *hóde* seems to act as a first-person possessive pronoun. Furthermore, as we have already noted, *hóde* is sometimes even more egocentric. In Homer, Odysseus can say, "Here I am, home again [*hód' egò éluthon*]." And *hóde, (ho) anèr hóde,* and *hóde (ho) anér* (literally, "this one," "this man") are quite frequently used by the dramatic poets and in fifth- and fourth-century prose as equivalents for *egó*.[34] The speaker can thus refer to himself using *hóde:* "with me [*têsde*] still alive"; "you who have done me [*tòn ándra tónde*] an injustice"; "you are aiming your arrows at me [*andròs toûde*]"; "do not die for me [*toûd' andrós*]"; "never until this day can you have seen in me [*andrì tôide*] anything to displease you."[35] As early as Homer, the demonstrative pronoun

30. *Odyssey* 16.205; Hesiod *Theogony* 24. See *hēmeîs hoíde* and *hēmâs toúsde* "we here": *Odyssey* 1.76 and Thucydides 1.53.2.

31. Lazzarini, pp. 74–75. In M. Moranti, "Formule metriche nelle iscrizioni," *Quaderni Urbinati di Cultura Classica*, no. 13 (1972), pp. 11–15, nos. 2, 4, 5, 8, 15 (?), 18, 19, and 20 all contain the word *me* even though it has no metrical function; in nos. 12, 14, 16, 17, 21, 25, and 26 the word *me* that they contain does have a metrical function. These are votive inscriptions of the *ho deîna (me) anéthēke* type: "So-and-so dedicated (me)," and this should set us on our guard against Lazzarini's attempt to discount the importance of *me* here.

32. R. Kühner and B. Gerth, *Ausführliche Grammatik der griechischen Sprache,* 3d ed., part 2, 1 (Hanover, 1898), p. 641.

33. *Odyssey* 5.343 and 346; see 8.403 and 415.

34. Kühner and Gerth, *Ausführliche Grammatik der griechischen Sprache,* pp. 630, 643.

35. Sophocles *The Trachinian Women* 305, *Philoctetes* 1036, and *Antigone* 1035; Euripides *Alcestes* 689; Herodotus 1.108.

ho is used in this way. "It is . . . for me . . . to speak," Telemakhos tells Odysseus in the *Odyssey,* and he adds, "for authority in this house belongs to me [*toû gàr krátos ést' enì oíkōi*]."[36]

Clearly we must take the syntax of *hóde* into account when we consider the speech-act situation in the seventh-century funerary inscriptions. As we have noted, four of the seventeen monuments are explicitly egocentric, and seven make their position clear by using forms of *hóde;* the remainder contain neither personal pronouns nor demonstrative pronouns nor verbs that refer to the monument itself. It seems reasonable, then, to imply a first person even where it is not made explicit by *egṓ, me,* or *eimí,* certainly in the seven inscriptions where *hóde* appears, but likewise in the six "zero degree" cases.[37]

In Greek syntax there is nothing to stop the demonstrative *hóde* from being linked with a verb in the third person. That goes without saying. And from 540 B.C. on, we come across monuments that, although autodeictic, are no longer egocentric. The first inscription to make the third person explicit after a *tóde* seems to be the one that appears on the *sêma* of Archias and his sister, discovered in Attica and dating from 540: "This is the *sêma* of Archias [*tód' Arkhíou 'sti sêma*] and his sister Phile. Eukosmides, its maker, made it [*toût'*] beautiful. Upon it [*ep' autôi*] the skillful Phaidimos set the stele."[38] The choice of the trimeter rather than the hexameter in this inscription is, in itself, probably a sign of modernity. But from our present point of view, the fact that it uses the third person *estí* after a *tóde* constitutes a break with tradition. It is followed in this by another Attic inscription dating from 525, and by one from Eretria dating from the last quarter of the sixth century.[39] Gerhard Pfohl's collection contains a total of nine inscriptions that explicitly link *tóde* with *estí* (or an equivalent term).[40]

In another group of inscriptions, the form of the statement more

36. *Odyssey* 1.358–359.

37. The nominatives in one of the inscriptions (Jeffery, *The Local Scripts of Archaic Greece,* pl. 61.5) are not necessarily incompatible with this interpretation, as Prokleidas' epitaph shows (see below, p. 36).

38. Pfohl, no. 62. The translation might run "his dear sister," rather than "his sister Phile."

39. Pfohl, nos. 42 and 125.

40. Pfohl, nos. 62, 42, 125, 116, 96, 91, 117, 180 (chronological order, from 540 to "fifth-fourth century"). On Pfohl, no. 164, see below.

or less excludes the possibility of considering the *sêma* as an ego-centric object. Let us study an inscription from Thasos, dating from 500–490 B.C. "To the deceased Learete her father raised this fine memorial, yes fine [*ê kalòn tò mnêma*]: for nevermore shall we see her alive."[41] Although a change of grammatical subject within even a very short space is not unknown in inscriptions,[42] here we have an inscription in which *tò mnêma* cannot be regarded as being in the first person, for that position is taken by the "we" of the family and the passersby whose voices are, as it were, transcribed on to the stone. Half a century later, another inscription performs a similar operation: "Here rests Aristylla, the daughter of Ariston and Rho-dilla: you were sweet, o daughter [*ô thúgater*]."[43] First the third person: "she rests" (*keîtai*), as if the stone were addressing the passersby. This verbal form does not in itself exclude the possibility of an egocentric *sêma*. But when the vocative is used—implying a change in the speech-act situation, in which Aristylla, having started as "she" becomes "you"—the meaning of the word *thugátēr* eliminates the possibility of including the *sêma* in the "we" that con-stitutes the subject of the speech-act, namely the two parents, and them alone. Pfohl's collection contains about a dozen inscriptions in which the form of the allocution, rather than the use of *estí,* seems to exclude the possibility of an egocentric *sêma.*[44] We should note, however, that none of these inscriptions is earlier than 550 and that the text of the most ancient, dating from 550–530, is largely a mat-ter of guesswork.[45] We should also note the existence of three other inscriptions that, despite addressing either the deceased or the pas-serby, do belong to the group of explicitly egocentric inscriptions.[46]

For a Greek reading *aloud* (as the verbs meaning 'to read' them-selves suggest),[47] the change in perspective, of which the *sêma* to

41. Pfohl, no. 20. Wherever, as in this case, the definite article *tó* retains its deictic force, it has practically the same meaning as *tóde.*

42. See, for example, Pfohl, no. 96.

43. Pfohl, no. 113 (Piraeus, ca. 440).

44. Pfohl, nos. 14, 20, 30, 36, 86, 90, 113, 122, 135, 146, and 169. Inscriptions in which the deceased use(s) the first person provide an analogous case (nos. 7, 8, 54, 96, 104, 118, 151, 154, 184, and 191).

45. Pfohl, no. 30.

46. Pfohl, nos. 75, 128, and 192.

47. That is to say *némein* (see above, n. 15), *ananémein, ananémesthai, légein* (Plato *Theaetetus* 143c), *analégesthai, epilégesthai,* and *anagignóskein,* whose "vocal" implica-

Archias and his sister seems to constitute the earliest example, is of considerable importance. If the reader proclaims aloud, "I am the *mnêma* of Glaukos," his lips serve an inflexible *egô* that is not his own. In contrast, "This is the *sêma* of Archias" is a phrase that does not for an instant dispossess the reader of his own *egô*. In fact, he might well have made that announcement himself if he already knew that the monument in question was that of Archias. In other words, the inscription takes on the form of a transcription. The reader of a nonegocentric *sêma* can occupy the position of the writer without clashing with another *egô* that the latter has staged.

In the inscriptions dating after 550, the demonstrative pronoun *hóde* may thus be supposed to refer to a third person, even if the reference is not made explicit by an *estí* (or its equivalent). The meaning of *sêma tóde estì toû deînos* must, it seems, be "This is the *sêma* of so-and-so." But consider the *sêma* of Prokleidas, discovered in Acarnania and dating from the second quarter of the fifth century: "This *sêma* [*tóde sêma*], close to the path, will be called [*kek-léstai*] 'Prokleidas', who died fighting for his country."[48] What is the force of *tóde* here? In inscriptions of the *sêma tóde estì toû deînos* type, *tóde* seems to refer to the position of the reader (standing in for the writer), so that the meaning is "the *sêma* that I have before me." Having first been used as the equivalent of *egô*, to refer to the *sêma* itself—if, that is, my hypothesis is correct—*tóde* here refers to the immediate sphere of a different *egô*, that of the reader. That, at any rate, is the only way to make sense of the inscription on Archias. But in the case of Prokleidas' *sêma*, the interpretation is not so simple. Readers of Aeschylus' *Persians* will no doubt recall the opening lines of the play, where the chorus introduces itself saying, literally "These are called the Faithful [*táde . . . pistà kaleîtai*]," the sense being "We, who are here before you, are the Famous Faith-

---

tions I analyze in Chapters 3, 6, and 9. On reading aloud, see B. M. W. Knox, "Silent Reading in Antiquity," *Greek, Roman, and Byzantine Studies*, 9 (1968), pp. 421, 435.

48. Pfohl, no. 164. On the ambiguity of "Prokleidas" here—at once a memorial and a man—cf. the stele of Phanodikos, cited above, Chapter 1, n. 75. On the nominative *Prokleídas*, see A. Morpurgo, "Il Genitivo maschile in = ας," *Glotta*, 39 (1960), p. 95 n.1. Cf. H. Häusle, *Das Denkmal als Garant des Nachruhms. Eine Studie zu einem Motiv in lateinischen Inschriften*, Zetemata, 75 (Munich, 1980), p. 126 n.286.

ful."[49] In these lines, the egocentric force of *táde* (the plural of *tóde*) is stronger than the third person of the verb *kaleîtai*. Even with a verb in the third person, a statement using *táde* may thus refer to the speakers who are the subject of the speech-act. The following translation of Prokleidas' epigram might thus be justified: "Close to the path, I shall be the famous *sêma* 'Prokleidas', who died fighting for his country." So this *sêma*, the isonym of the deceased, could in fact be an egocentric *sêma*. Indeed, it makes use of the verb *kaleîsthai* in the same way as another egocentric *sêma*, as we saw in Chapter 1: "I shall always be called [*keklḗsomai*] a girl," Phrasikleia's *sêma* forthrightly announces, removing all ambiguity about the first person.[50]

As I have noted, however, from 550 on, inscriptions using *tóde*, which do not make the verb explicit, may refer to the immediate sphere of an *egṓ* that is not of the monument but of the reader. Here, there is a real ambiguity, one to which univocal translations seldom do justice. No doubt that ambiguity, produced by the introduction of the formula *sêma tóde estì toû deînos* in the mid-sixth century, was perceived by the Greeks themselves, for about one generation after the *sêma* of Archias and his sister, inscriptions begin to appear that—with perfect grammar—overcome that ambiguity by specifying the egocentric status of a *sêma tóde* with *eimí* or *me*. The first *sêma* of this type is that of Krites, discovered on the plain of Marathon and dating from 500, to which I have already briefly referred. Another, this time from Aegina and dating from the fifth century, runs as follows: "I am the *sêma* of Gleukitas [*Gleukíta tóde sêma*], the son of Kyprios of Salamis. Diotimos set me up [*me epéthēke*]."[51] A third, the *sêma* of Partheneia from Sinope, dating from the early fifth century, begins as follows: "I am the *sêma*, [*tóde sêma . . . eimí*] of the daughter of Nadys, the son of Kares. You, who are passing, stop and weep for me."[52] The same concern to specify the egocentric

49. *Persians* 1–2 (see P. Groeneboom, *Aischylos' Perser*, Studientexte griechischer und lateinischer Schriftsteller, 3 [1930; rpt. Göttingen, 1960], 2:7–8). Cf. Thucydides 6.7.1: *ouk Íones táde estín* "We who are here, we are not Ionians". On *kaleîtai* in Aeschylus and on *keklḗsetai* in the epitaph of Prokleidas, see the discussion above, p. 18, on the subject of the affinities between *kaleîn* and *kléos*.

50. Pfohl, no. 61. See above, Chapter 1, pp. 17 and 25, n. 75.

51. Pfohl, no. 152.

52. Pfohl, no. 192.

status of the demonstrative pronoun *hóde* is detectable in the epitaph to the little girl Thessalia: "Kleodamos, the son of Hyperanor and Korona, set me up as a monument here [*mnêma . . . têide . . . stāsé me*] for their daughter Thessalia."[53] In this inscription, the presence (*têide* 'here') of the *mnêma* is the presence of an *egṓ*.

Let us now move to the set of votive inscriptions meticulously collected by Marialetizia Lazzarini. There are five times as many of these as of the funerary inscriptions collected by Pfohl—about one thousand in all.[54] They date from the eighth century B.C. (and so are rather earlier than the funerary inscriptions) to the end of the fifth century (the date at which Pfohl's collection also stops).[55]

In these thousand inscriptions, the speech–act situation seems, by and large, more homogeneous than that which I have attempted to analyze in the case of the funerary inscriptions. A typical one would contain the name of the dedicator, the verb dedicating it, and the name of the deity, using the formula *ho deîná me anéthēke tôi theôi* "so-and-so dedicated me to the god," which might be reduced to "so-and-so dedicated me," "so-and-so dedicated," "so-and-so to the god," or simply "so-and-so" or "to the god." Alternatively, some feature the genitive of a proper name, either that of the dedicator or that of "the god." In the latter case, the name of the god is accompanied by *eimí: toû thoû eimi* "I belong to the god" (with a

53. Pfohl, no. 139 (Oloosson, Thessaly, early fifth century).

54. In reality, there are just over one thousand, because the duplicated numbers (as marked with *bis*) should be included. Pfohl's collection contains exactly 198 inscriptions.

55. Of course, other egocentric objects exist in addition to stelae and objects bearing a dedication. The so-called Nestor's cup, for instance, bears this inscription: "I am Nestor's cup, well made for drinking" (Pithecussae, second half of the eighth century). The restoration of *e[im]i* seems inevitable (Jeffery, *The Local Scripts of Archaic Greece,* pl. 47.1). See the contemporaneous inscription, also from the Pithecussae islands: "(. . .)inos made me," which is the most ancient signature of a potter to have come down to us (Guarducci, *Epigrafia greca,* 3:476). Among other egocentric objects, gems and coins (Burzachechi, "Oggetti parlanti nelle epigrafi greche," pp. 24, 40), boundary markers ("I am a boundary post for the Agora," Athens, 500 B.C. Guarducci, *Epigrafia greca,* 2 [1970], p. 435), and perhaps above all the written signs that refer to themselves as "we" in the Abu Simbel inscriptions (590 B.C., Burzachechi, "Oggetti parlanti nelle epigrafi greche," p. 42) are worth noting. My own purpose is rather different from Burzachechi's, which was to study "speaking objects" as a whole. My aim is to contrast egocentric objects with nonegocentric ones. Accordingly, it seems better, in the main, to limit myself to the collections of Pfohl and Lazzarini.

number of variants).[56] Such is the range of the formulas that elliptically (some more, some less) define the speech-act status of these
votive objects. In some cases, such as that of the above-cited inscription by Alkimakhos, the formula is quite lengthy: "Alkimakhos dedicated me to the daughter of Zeus—me, this statue"
(Athens, 525–500). In others it is elliptical in the extreme, as in the
case of a shield from Olympia, *Dí,* "to Zeus" (fifth century). The
difference in the length of these dedications, however, does not
necessarily indicate that they are different in kind.[57]

Over two hundred of these thousand inscriptions make the first
person explicit, so that the objects that bear them become explicitly
egocentric. More than 20 percent of the inscriptions in Lazzarini's
collection belong to this category, as opposed to just under 20
percent in Pfohl's collection (25 percent of the seventeen inscriptions from before 600). Of the thousand votive inscriptions, only
one uses *estí* to make the third person explicit: the dedication by
Praxiteles, inscribed on a votive base discovered at Olympia and
dating from the first half of the fifth century. "Praxiteles, a citizen of
Syracuse, dedicated this statue [*tód' ágalma*]," it begins, ending three
lines later with "and this is the monument [*mnâma tód' est'*] commemorating his virtue."[58] As we have seen, however, using the
third person singular of the verb "to be" in Greek is not the only
way to make the nonegocentric nature of an object explicit. An
inscription from Miletus, dating from 550, provides the earliest
example of a nonegocentric dedication in Lazzarini's collection:

56. Lazzarini, pp. 58–60.

57. Lazzarini, no. 429a. According to Agostiniani, *Le "iscrizioni parlanti"
dell'Italia antica,* pp. 33–36, there are no grounds for considering such an inscription
to be an ellipse of a complete formula of which the reader would be more or less
aware. The proof, he claims, is that an inscription such as *Héra* could not possibly
evoke any complete formula (p. 35; he is referring here to graffiti on a vase dedicated
to Hera and discovered at Gela, dating from about 550 B.C.; see Jeffery, *The Local
Scripts of Archaic Greece,* p. 278, no. 47). To be convinced of the contrary, one has
only to read the inscription on the statuette dedicated by Mantiklos (Lazzarini, no.
795), where the dative "to the god" is followed by a vocative, "O Phoibos." By
analogy, *Héra* could be considered as the vocative of the name of the goddess to
whom the vase is dedicated.

58. Lazzarini, no. 723 ("before 484"). See also Jeffery, *The Local Scripts of Archaic
Greece,* pp. 160–161 ("between 484 and 461") and p. 211 n. 3. My observations on the
expression *tóde sâma keklḗsetai* in Prokleidas' epitaph (above, p. 36) could be equally
valid for the formula *mnâma tód' est'*.

"Aristolochos and Thrason dedicated to Apollo these *agálmata* [*táde tagálmata*] as a tithe of their booty. Isikles, the son of Kydimandros, melted them [*autá*] down."[59] Where "us" could have been used, the inscription has *autá*, which seems to exclude the possibility that *táde* might refer to an "us."[60] From 550 on, the demonstrative pronoun *tóde* may thus be ambiguous in votive inscriptions, which is no doubt why, from that date on, we come across a handful of examples (most of them from the last years of the century) in which *tóde* is made explicitly egocentric.[61] This development is similar to that already noted in the case of the funerary inscriptions. The undermining of the egocentric status of *tóde* by an explicit *estí* (or an equivalent) provokes a reaction that only reaffirms the inherent association of *tóde* with the first person.

From 550 on votive inscriptions may thus be differentiated as to their speech-act situation, although possibly less frequently than funerary inscriptions. Nevertheless, the egocentric inscription remains fundamental, constituting in its explicit form 20 percent of the entire body of funerary and votive inscriptions. That is a high enough percentage to warrant our pondering the reasons that may have prompted the choice of the first person to denote an inscribed object.

In drawing attention to a number of grammatical points, my purpose has also been to call into question certain of our linguistic habits that predispose us to understand the demonstrative pronoun *tóde* as referring exclusively to the third person, to a "he" rather than an "I," so that we tend to translate *sêma tóde toû deînos* not as "I am the *sêma* of so-and-so," but as "this is the *sêma* of so-and-so," as if the earliest inscribed objects referred to themselves sometimes in the first person, sometimes in the third.[62] But they did not. Only the first person is made explicit in inscriptions dating before 550. Actually, our way of understanding *tóde* matters above all for funer-

59. Lazzarini, no. 693.
60. Two other inscriptions seem to exclude the possibility of the object's being egocentric: Lazzarini, nos. 585 (Posidonia, 550) and 811 (Olympia, 500–450).
61. In chronological order, Lazzarini, nos. 726 (Paros, 550), 732 (Athens, 525–500), 679, 681 (Athens, late sixth century), 686 (Delos, late sixth century), 678 (Athens, 475–450), 725 (Thessaly, fifth century), 748 (Epidauros, late fifth century).
62. In the inscriptions dating before 550, a *tóde* has the same force as an *egṓ*, a *me*, or an *eimí* when used to indicate the speech-act situation; none of these words, however, possesses the same metrical value.

ary inscriptions, since over 20 percent of these express themselves through that demonstrative pronoun (the corresponding figure for votive inscriptions is only 7 percent). Now, the fact that the use of an *estí* or an *autó*, or of a number of other ways of defining the object in the third person, is exceptional suggests that the first person is implicit in even the most elliptical inscriptions, such as *Epikharídou*, an Attic funerary inscription possibly dating from the seventh century, which I am inclined to translate as "I am the *sêma* of Epicharides," or *Méga* "I am the *ex-voto* of Megas," or *Dí* "I was dedicated to Zeus."[63]

Why the choice of the first person? Why did the Greeks not choose another way of expressing themselves when they began to write on votive objects and on their tombstones? Why did they prefer an "inscription" to a "transcription"? To answer these difficult questions, Burzachechi proposes an animist or even "vitalist" explanation for the phenomenon. He suggests that attributing a soul to objects and endowing them with speech is typical of primitive civilizations and that only in the second half of the sixth century do we "begin to notice a certain rationalization of the statue, which now loses its old magic halo."[64] But the principle behind Burzachechi's explanation is found at a different level, in the relationship that he establishes—at the outset, in his very title, "Oggetti parlanti" (with no quotation marks for parlanti)—between the "voice" and the first person used to refer to the inscribed object (which is the sole criterion determining the choice of the inscriptions included in his collection). The object is endowed with speech simply because it refers to itself as *egó*.

In place of this animist interpretation, which is indemonstrable and at odds with the facts (for the Greeks did not believe in writing that spoke—except in a metaphorical sense—conscious as they were that it is the reader who must lend his voice to the mute stone[65]), I suggest a linguistic explanation that takes account of the

63. For Epicharides see Jeffery, "The Inscribed Gravestones of Archaic Attica," no. 39; for Megas see Lazzarini, no. 420d (Gela, sixth–fifth century); for Zeus see Lazzarini, no. 429b (Olympia, fifth century).

64. Burzachechi, "Oggetti parlanti nelle epigrafi greche," p. 53.

65. The "letters that speak" metaphor is extremely rare in the inscriptions that I am studying here (the only definite example is Lazzarini, no. 658, "I answer *ísa* to all," cited above and analyzed below), although it is not uncommon in inscriptions

speech-act situation inherent in egocentric inscriptions. Is not the ploy of setting up an object that is designed to carry the message, an object that must not or cannot be physically separated from the first person statement that it bears, the most "economical" way of drawing attention to the presence of the object before its beholder?[66] This use of the first person, of course, should not run up against a metaphysical conviction on the part of the receivers of the message, namely the conviction that the first person necessarily implies an inner life and a voice. The very action of reading these egocentric objects encourages us to deconstruct that conviction—in other words, to remove the link between the *egó* and the voice.[67]

In his book on demonstrative pronouns in Indo-European languages, Karl Brugmann accepts the hypothesis that the Greek *egó* is descended from an Indo-European neuter noun, *eḡ(h)om,* meaning *Hierheit* or "hereness," if such a word can be imagined in English.[68] Whether or not the hypothesis is correct from the point of view of linguistics, it suggests a perspective that seems to me singularly true. By denying the *egó* any psychological depth, one can understand why, when the earliest inscriptions were produced, the first person was chosen to refer to the object bearing the inscription. For as long as the inscription can be read, the object will be there. No one could lay greater claim than the object itself to the *Hierheit* of the written speech-act. Soon the writer would no longer be there; he became the third person by virtue of the fact that *he wrote.* *Anéthēke, epéthēke/éstēse, epoíēse, égrapse:* it is precisely in the third person that all these verbs denoting dedicating, setting up, making,

---

of the Hellenistic and Roman periods. If we exclude the epigraphic evidence, it does not appear until the fifth century (see, for example, Herodotus 1.124: *tà grámmata élege,* literally, "the written signs said"). We will return to this problem in Chapters 3 and 9.

66. "Economical" is the term used by Pietro Pucci in this connection, in his lecture delivered at the Centre de recherches comparées sur les sociétés anciennes, Paris, June 1984. Pucci's point of view, however, is rather different from mine.

67. For a critique of what might be called the metaphysics of the voice in the western tradition, see the fundamental work by J. Derrida, *La Voix et le phénomène* (Paris, 1967).

68. K. Brugmann, *Die Demonstrativpronomina der indogermanischen Sprachen. Eine bedeutungsgeschichtliche Untersuchung,* Abhandlungen der philologisch-historischen Klasse der Königl. Sächsischen Gesellschaft der Wissenschaften, 22:6 (Leipzig, 1904), p. 71.

and writing appear in these inscriptions.[69] If that third person is to be made explicit, *ekeînos* "that one," is probably best suited.[70] In relation to the object, present because it stands before a passerby (the reader, the addressee), the person who made it or inscribed it finds himself in a kind of "beyond," in an *ekeî* "over there" that stands in contrast to the *entháde* or *têide* 'here' of the inscribed object.[71] The way that the earliest inscriptions were devised thus presents us with a speech-act subject that, albeit without voice or inner life, has more claim than any other to the Hierheit of the first person, that Hierheit that the demonstrative pronoun *tóde* may convey with no less deictic force.

69. An extremely difficult inscription from Rhodes dating from 600–575 appears to be the sole exception: Jeffery, *The Local Scripts of Archaic Greece,* pl. 67.5 (verb: *poieîn* 'to make, to fabricate').

70. See Lazzarini, nos. 719, 786, 797, and 870.

71. The pronoun *ekeînos* is sometimes used in prose to refer to someone who is dead, someone who is now among *hoi ekeî* "the people beyond", in other words, the dead. See above, p. 30 and n. 20.

CHAPTER 3

The Reader and the Reading Voice: The Instrumental Status of Reading Aloud

What is written is present, the writer is absent: those are two facts essential to reading as envisaged by the inscriptions we have been studying. At the moment of reading, the reader finds himself before a written word that is present in the absence of the writer. Just as he foresees his own absence, the writer foresees the presence of his writing before the reader. The reading constitutes a meeting between the reader and the written marks of someone who is absent. The writer foresees that meeting, plans it carefully. He counts on the reader and the reading aloud that the reader will accomplish, for in a culture in which *kléos* has a fundamental part to play, what is written remains incomplete until such time as it is provided with a voice. As we noted in Chapter 1, the written *sêma* is incomplete without the sonorous *anágnōsis* 'reading' effected by the reader. From the point of view that we have adopted, an important consequence stems from Gregory Nagy's theory on the close link between *sêma* and *nóēsis,* between the "sign" and its "decoding."[1] If the *sêma* is incomplete without *nóēsis* or *anágnōsis,* then *nóēsis* or *anágnōsis* is a part of the *sêma.* In other words, the reading is part of the text. In precisely these terms Michel Charles defines his point of departure in *Rhétorique de la lecture:* "Let us concentrate on this

---

1. G. Nagy, "*Sêma* and *nóēsis*: Some Illustrations," *Arethusa,* 16 (1983), pp. 35–55 (reworked as chap. 8 in G. Nagy, *Greek Mythology and Poetics* [Ithaca, 1990], pp. 202–222).

essential fact: the reading is part of the text, an integral part."[2] That relationship is also my own point of departure, with the qualification that the word "reading" must be given the sense of "reading aloud." If it is, the expression takes on a meaning that is at once more limited and wider than in Charles's book—more limited because it extends only to the technical act of "reading" (leaving aside that of critical or interpretative reading) and wider because it brings the voice into play.

The reading aloud is a part of the text, an integral part of it, then. At first sight, that may seem a paradoxical statement, for how can this sonorous action be a part of the mute text? How can the one be understood to include the other? One immediate technical observation seems appropriate at this point: the Greeks concerned here used to write in *scriptio continua,* that is to say, leaving no spaces between the words, a practice that, as experience shows, makes reading aloud a virtual necessity.[3] So the reading aloud is indeed a part of the text, which is incomplete without it. The text is thus more than the sum of the alphabetic signs of which it is composed. These signs will guide the voice that will permit the vocalization of the text, its sonorous realization. This, then, is the way in which the text includes the voice that its mute signs are lacking. If the text is to find total fulfillment, it needs the voice of the reader, the reading voice.[4]

The writer, who is present only at the action of producing the written statement and soon disappears for good, has foreseen the vocalization of his writing. Absent as he is, he depends on the voice that the reader will lend him. By writing, he deferred the production of his speech in sound. One might say that he held his own breath so that the reader can breathe his into the writing that meets his eyes. For on its own this writing is voiceless. It is *sigôsa* 'silent'; it keeps quiet. It "indicates," "signals."[5] The most it can do is *provoke* a reading, prompt its own rendering in sound, get the reader's voice going—the voice that, as has been argued, is part of the text. For the text to achieve complete fulfillment, the reader must lend his voice

2. M. Charles, *Rhétorique de la lecture* (Paris, 1977), p. 9.
3. We will return to this problem in Chapter 9.
4. It is as if this "fabric" of the text were woven with a written warp and a vocal weft.
5. Euripides *Iphigenia in Tauris* 762–763; Plato *Phaedrus* 275d.

to the writing (or, in the last analysis, to the writer). At the moment of reading, the reading voice does not belong to the reader, even though he is the one using his vocal apparatus to ensure that the reading takes place. If he lends his voice to these mute signs, the text appropriates it: his voice becomes the voice of the written text. So the "I" that denoted the funerary *sêma* ("I am the *sêma* of so-and-so") does not have to be changed to "it" at the moment of the reading, for while he is reading, the reader is not speaking *en idíois lógois* "with his own words" or as the subject of the statement.[6] He has lent his voice, relinquished it. His voice is not regarded as his own as he reads. It belongs to what is written: the reading is part of the text. And that remains true even when, from 550 or 540 B.C. on, some inscriptions begin to use the third person instead of the first in order to refer to themselves. "This is the *sêma* of Archias" is what we read on the monument already mentioned;[7] and this inscription does not for a moment dispossess the reader of his "I," for he could have made that pronouncement without reading it, provided that he knew that it was indeed Archias' monument. As the one lending his voice to the mute inscription, however, the reader is still an instrument, even if he does not clash with an "I" that is not his own. The reader is the instrument necessary for the text to be realized. His voice is instrumental. Either he can refuse to read, which is certainly a possibility, or he agrees to do so—and by agreeing, he is instantly defined as the sonorous instrument of what is written.

A number of consequences ensue from the act of reading aloud, making it a different act from the silent reading of today; and the instrumental nature of the reader in this act is one of the more important of these consequences. The writing is there to produce speech destined for the ear. The text's "listeners," from the ancient Greeks' vantage point, are not—as the dictionaries hold—its "readers" in the true sense of that word; they are individuals who are listening to the reading.[8] Thanks to the instrumental voice of the

6. The expression is borrowed from Plato *Republic* 2.9.366e: see J. Svenbro, *La Parole et le marbre. Aux origines de la poétique grecque* (Lund, 1976), pp. 210–212.

7. G. Pfohl, *Greek Poems on Stones,* vol. 1, *Epitaphs: From the Seventh to the Fifth Centuries B.C.,* Textus Minores, no. 36 (Leiden, 1967), no. 62 (hereafter referred to as "Pfohl"). See above, Chapter 2.

8. See Liddell-Scott-Jones, s.v. *akoúō,* 1.4 (*hoi akoúontes* "readers of a book") and *akroatḗs,* 2 ('reader').

reader, they can listen to the text. The written word uses that voice to communicate its contents. The reading thus becomes a veritable "question of power," as Pierre Bourdieu puts it—in this case, power over the voice of the reader.[9] Ancient reading indeed takes the specific form of an exercise of power over the voice of the reader. The voice has to submit to the written word. It is crucial in the confrontation that takes place through the medium of the writing, between the writer and the reader. The writer, who is absent, cannot raise his own voice; the writing, which is present, remains mute, silent, voiceless. But the writing knows how to remedy the absence of a voice: like a *sêma* demanding *nóēsis,* it asks to be read aloud. In these circumstances, the reader has but one means of resistance: he can refuse to read.

Reading aloud leads to consequences that may not be immediately apparent if one is conditioned by a culture that depends chiefly on silent reading (and for which the "question of power" takes different, less basic forms[10]). But as we saw in the last two chapters, the idea of a reader dispossessed of his own voice is implicit. Both chapters take off from a postulate that is simply an extrapolation from what we believe we know about Greek reading in the classical and postclassical periods.[11] So far as the archaic period is concerned, we do not, to date, have any positive evidence at our disposal, so we must content ourselves with a basically reasonable hypothesis, namely, if the Greeks of the classical period read aloud, presumably their archaic ancestors did likewise. It seems logical to assume that reading aloud was the basic form of reading and that silent reading was derived from it at a later date.

The following pages set out, not to cast doubt upon that hypothesis but to verify it and, through its verification, to flesh out the (so far) very abstract figure of the archaic reader, the vocal instrument of the writing that cannot do without it. This introduction has relied somewhat heavily on a priori arguments, as I set out to establish the terms of a problem that is essential to Greek reading. I intend, however, to prove the possibility of distinguishing those

9. In his discussion with R. Chartier, "La Lecture: Une pratique culturelle," in *Pratiques de la lecture,* ed. R. Chartier (Paris, 1985), p. 235.

10. Bordieu, ibid.

11. See B. M. W. Knox, "Silent Reading in Antiquity," *Greek, Roman, and Byzantine Studies,* 9 (1968), pp. 421–435.

factors in concrete form in the archaic inscriptions themselves. So let us now pass from an abstract to a concrete level for a reading of two epigrams, one a funerary inscription, the other a votive one. The former presents us with the figure of the reader; the latter with the reading voice.

The first inscription is engraved on a rough-hewn limestone rock seventy-four centimeters high, resting on a base twenty-two centimeters high: the stele of Mnesitheos.[12] It was discovered at Eretria, in Euboea, and, according to L. H. Jeffery, it dates from the first half of the fifth century.[13] First, let us read it in the version given by Werner Peek (supplemented by Gerhard Pfohl):

> χαίρετε τοὶ παριόντες, ἐγὸ δὲ θανὸν κατάκειμαι·
> δεῦρο ἰὸν ἀνάνεμαι, ἀνὲρ τίς τέδε τέθαππται·
> ξένος απ Αἰγίνες, Μνεσίθεος δ᾽ ὄνυμα·
> καί μοι μνêμ᾽ ἐπέθεκε φίλē μέτēρ Τιμαρέτε
> τύμοι ἐπ᾽ἀκροτάτοι στέλεν ἀκάματον,
> hάτις ἐρεῖ παριôσι διάμπερες ἄματα πάντα·
> Τιμαρέτε μ᾽ ἔσστεσε φίλοι ἐπὶ παιδὶ θανόντι.

Salutations, O passersby! I rest, dead, under here. You, who draw near, read out who is the man buried here: a stranger from Aegina, Mnesitheos by name; and my own mother Timarete has set up for me, as a monument on top of the mound, an inextinguishable[14] stele, which will tell passersby for all eternity: Timarete set me up for her dear deceased son.

One is immediately struck by the presence of the metaphor of the speaking object which, as I have noted above, is extremely rare in inscriptions dating from before 400 B.C. and accordingly attracts our undivided attention.[15] When we look into the matter, however, we notice that line 6 ("which will tell passersby for all eternity")

12. For the dimensions, see K. Kourouniotis, "'Επιγραφαὶ 'Ερετρίας," 'Εφημερὶς 'Αρχαιολογική (1897), col. 153.
13. Pfohl, no. 128 (no. 1210 in W. Peek, Griechische Vers-Inschriften, 1 [Berlin, 1955]). See also C. Karousos, "Perikalles agalma," in Inschriften der Griechen, ed. G. Pfohl (Darmstadt, 1972), pp. 136–137. For the dating of this stele see L. H. Jeffery, The Local Scripts of Archaic Greece (Oxford, 1961), pp. 85–86.
14. We will return to this translation of akámatos.
15. See Chapter 2, n. 65.

contains two anomalies from the point of view of dialect: the Dorian forms *hâtis* and *ámata,* in an epigram certainly not written in the Dorian dialect. Except for the form *ónuma* in line 3, which is Aeolian or Dorian (unless it is simply a mistake for *ónoma*), the epigram is written in the Ionian dialect, the dialect spoken in Euboea.[16] In this dialect, the original *ā,* preserved in Dorian, has become *ē.* The author of the epigram writes *Aigínēs* (not *Aegínās*), *Mnēsítheos* (not *Mnāsítheos*), *mnêma* (not *mnâma*), *phílē* (not *phílā*), *mḗtēr* (not *mâtēr*), *Timarétē* (not *Timarétā*), *stḗlēn* (not *stálān*), *éstēse* (not *éstāse*). In line 6, one would consequently expect to find the forms *hḗtis* (not *hâtis*) and *ḗmata* (not *ámata*). The text is therefore suspect, and we must look at the stone itself, which I transcribe below, from the photograph published by Hermann Diels:[17]

```
    ΧΑΙΡΕΤΕΤΟΙΠΑΡΙΟ
    ΝΤΕΣ:ΕΓΟΔΕΘΑΝΟΝ
    ΚΑΤΑΚΕΙΜΑΙ:ΔΕΥΡ̣
    ΟΙΟΝΑΝΑΝΕΜΑΙΑΝ̣
5   ΕΡΤΙΣΤΕΔΕΤΕΘΑΠ
    ΠΤΑΙ:ΞΕΝΟΣΑΠΑΙΓ
    ΙΝΕΣΜΝΕΣΙΘΕΟΣΔΟΝ
    ΥΜΑΚΑΙΜΟΙΜΝΕΜΕΠΕ
    ΘΕΚΕ̣ΦΙΛΕΜΕΤΕΡΤΙΜ
10  ΑΡΕΤΕ Τ̣ΥΜΟ̣ΙΕΠΑΚΡΟΤ
    ΑΤΟΙΣΤΕΛΕΝΑΚΑΜΑΤΟΝ̣
    ΗΟΤΙΣΕΡΕΙΠΑΡΙΟΣΙΔΙΑ
    ΜΠΕΡΕΣ̣ΕΜΑΤΑΠΑΝ̣ΤΑΤ̣
    ΙΜΑΡΕΤΕΜΕΣΣΤΕΣΕΦΙΛ
15  ΟΙΕΠΙΠΑΙΔΙΘΑΝΟΝΤ̣Ι̣
```

The photograph of the stone rules out the possibility that the second letter of line 12 (line 6 of the poem) is an "A." It is an "O." We can compare it to the "O" of the preceding word (ΑΚΑΜΑΤΟΝ) or the "O" that occurs a little farther on in ΠΑΡΙΟΣΙ. The three "O"s

16. C. D. Buck, *The Greek Dialects* (Chicago, 1955), p. 10. On the form *ónuma* see M. Lazzarini, *Le formule delle dediche votive nella Grecia arcaica,* Atti della Accademia nazionale dei Lincei. Memorie. Classe di scienze morali, storiche e filologiche, 8th ser., 19:2 (Rome, 1976), no. 719 (Aegina, 500–475) (hereafter Lazzarini).

17. H. Diels, "Die Stele des Mnesitheos," *Sitzungsberichte der Akademie der Wissenschaften zu Berlin* (1908), pp. 1040–1046, pl. 12.

are almost identical. The first scholar to publish the inscription, K. Kourouniotis, transcribed the first four letters of line 12 (line 6 of the poem) as "HOTI," and he was followed in this by Diels.[18] As in ΠΑΡΙΟΣΙ (*parioûsi*), which immediately follows, this "O" may represent *ou*, which leaves us with *hoû*, the equivalent of *hópou* 'where', the equivalent of the Latin *ubi*.[19] Once we have changed *hátis* to *hoû tis*, there is no need to "Doricize," and we can simply change the word *ámata*, whose first *a* is not certain in the stone inscription, to *émata*.

Here, then, is the text of Mnesitheos' epigram in normalized spelling:

> χαίρετε τοὶ παριόντες, ἐγὼ δὲ θανὼν κατάκειμαι·
> δεῦρο ἰὼν ἀνάνειμαι, ἀνὴρ τίς τῇδε τέθαπται·
> ξεῖνος ἀπ' Αἰγίνης, Μνησίθεος δ' ὄννμα·
> 4 καί μοι μνῆμ' ἐπέθηκε φίλη μήτηρ Τιμαρέτη
> τύμβῳ ἐπ' ἀκροτάτῳ στήλην ἀκάματον,
> οὗ τις ἐρεῖ παριοῦσι διαμπερὲς ἤματα πάντα·
> Τιμαρέτη μ' ἔστησε φίλῳ ἐπὶ παιδὶ θανόντι.

I would translate lines 4–6 as follows: "And my own mother Timarete set up for me, as a monument on the top of a mound, an inextinguishable stele, where through all the days to come, someone will tell the passersby. . . ."

The reading that I propose for line 6 is in agreement with the dialect and the stone, as well as the contents of the epigram. The metaphor of the speaking object implicit in the *hátis ereî* reading contradicts line 2, in which the inscription commits the task of reading to whoever approaches the stone. If it were the stone speaking, as Peek and Pfohl suggest, the reading mentioned in line 2 would become superfluous and could be replaced by listening on the part of passersby. Once *hátis ereî* is replaced by *hoû tis ereî* "where

18. Kourouniotis, "'Επιγραφαὶ 'Ερετρίας." Note the prudence of B. Leonardos, "*IG* 12.285," 'Εφημερὶς 'Αρχαιολογική (1919), p. 88, who prints *h[á]t[i]s* and *[ám]ata*.

19. See Liddell-Scott-Jones, s.v. *hós*, B, Ab, I, 1 ("gen. sg. οὗ, of Place, l. like ὅπου, *where*"), citing Aeschylus *Persians* 486. See the remark made by Buck, *The Greek Dialects*, p. 102: "-ου. Place 'where'. . . . These . . . are specifically Attic-Ionic."

someone will tell", that contradiction disappears. It is not the stele that speaks; the reader lends it his voice by reading the inscription to the *parióntes* 'passersby' of lines 1 and 6. This repetition of the word *parióntes* toward the end of the epigram is not an isolated phenomenon. If we look closely, we notice that lines 2 and 6, which are arranged symmetrically, start in an exactly analogous fashion: the *deûro iồn anáneimai* "you who approach, read" of line 2 is picked up by the *hoû tis ereî* "where someone will tell" of line 6, in the sense that *deûro* 'here' and *hoû* 'where' refer to the place of the reading, *iồn* and *tis* to the reader, *anáneimai* and *ereî* to the act of reading that the inscription anticipates (with an imperative and a future tense, respectively). The plural *parióntes* (line 1 and line 6), which refers to those to whom the reading will be addressed, is thus balanced by the singular forms *iồn* 'going, coming' and *tis* 'someone, one', which refer to the reader.

The reader conjured up by the inscription thus makes two analogous appearances in the text. In the first, his activity is denoted by the verb *ananémesthai*. The use of this verb is extremely telling, indeed decisive: its literal meaning is "to distribute." The reading is thus a "distribution." And the only things that the reader can "distribute" to the passersby are the words that he pronounces. As early as the archaic period, the idea of reading aloud was thus implied in one of the verbs meaning "to read." Whoever approaches the stone is expected to "read" the name of the deceased, making it resound. He must "read aloud" (*ananémesthai*). The same verb is used by Herodotus with the meaning "to recite from memory," that is to say, "to distribute" orally, by appealing to the memory. (In Herodotus it is a matter of reciting genealogies[20]). Unlike the reciter, however, the reader follows written, tangible signs that guide his voice. The same verb *ananémesthai* is also known in Dorian, with the meaning "to read," but with one important difference: the Dorians used the active form, *ananémein*.[21] In our epigram, the mid-

20. Herodotus 1.173.
21. Theocritus 18.47–48: "And an inscription will be engraved on the back so that the passerby [*hōs parìon tis*] can read it [*anneímēi*], as we say in Dorian [*dōristí*]." This translation of *dōristí* is suggested by A. S. F. Gow, *Theocritus*, 2 (Cambridge, 1952), pp. 359–360. See also Epicharmus frag. 224 Kaibel, and the Dorian epigram from Gela (in C. Gallavotti, "Letture epigrafiche, 2. Epigramma dorico di Gela,"

dle form *ananémesthai* is used, which seems to imply that the reader, by "distributing" what he sees, by means of his voice, includes himself in the distribution. The message that he pronounces is not just for other people, but for himself as well.[22] His voice is the instrument that distributes to passersby and to himself the contents of the text. In an extreme situation, the solitary reader can thus "distribute" the contents of the written text to himself alone. Thanks to his voice, he will distribute the words of the inscription to his own ears.[23]

On Mnesitheos' stele, the first verb meaning "to read" is *ananémesthai*. The second instance of a "to read" is less obvious, but is implied by the text: *hoû tis ereî purioûsi* "where someone will tell the passersby" (line 6). *Ereî,* the future of *légein* 'to say, tell', in a practical sense here means "someone will read" (whatever some dictionaries, which deny that possibility, may say[24]). After all, consider a formula such as *lége tòn nómon* "read out the law," or the passage in Plato's *Theaetetus,* where we read, "Well, slave, take the book and read! [*allá, paî, labè tò biblíon kaì lége*]."[25] In this sentence it is hard to see how *lége* could possibly mean anything but "read." Justifiably, then, we can translate *hoû tis ereî parioûsi* as "where someone will read to the passersby," for, as we have just seen, the verb *légein* can take on the meaning "to read" where the context shows quite clearly that it is a matter of reading in the strict sense of the word. Furthermore, I believe this meaning is more in keeping with what precedes the word in the epigram, because it allows a closer link between *hoû* and *stélēn akámaton:* the "inextinguishable stele" (rather than the mound) is the place "where someone will read to the passersby."

Quaderni Urbinati di Cultura Classica, no. 20 [1975], pp. 172–177), to which we will return in Chapter 10. See also Hesychius, s. v. *annémein,* and *scholia to Pindar* 3.222, 16–17 Drachmann (*ánneme = anágnōthi* 'read!' in Parthenios).

22. On the force of the middle form, see E. Benveniste, *Problèmes de linguistique générale,* 1 (Paris, 1966), pp. 171–172. The active form used in Dorian thus implies a more instrumental attitude, to the extent that it is irrelevant whether the reader himself receives the message that he distributes to others.

23. See below, pp. 63 and 166. See also Aristophanes *Frogs* 52–53.

24. As does Liddell-Scott-Jones, s.v. *légō,* 3.13; but see H. Fournier, *Les Verbes "dire" en grec ancien* (Paris, 1946), p. 67.

25. "Read out the law" is an expression frequently used by the orators, for example, in Demosthenes 21 *Against Meidias* 8 and 10; Plato *Theaetetus* 143c.

In its Greek form, this phrase calls to mind another phrase, one we considered in Chapter 1. In the *Iliad* Hektor imagines the *sêma* that will be erected over an Achaean whom he has not yet slain. In the future, he thinks, when this *sêma* is seen, people will say: "This is the barrow of a man who died in olden days, whom, in the midst of his prowess, glorious Hektor slew." And he adds, "So shall it be said one day [*hốs poté tis eréei*]; and my *kléos* will never die."[26] The half-line *hốs poté tis eréei* might well be considered as the model for *hoû tis ereî,* for once the author of the epigram has used *diamperès êmata pánta* "for all the days to come", another Homeric half-line, *poté* 'one day,' becomes impossible.[27] For metrical reasons, *eréei* must be changed to *ereî,* and for semantic reasons *hốs* must become *hoû.* In other words, the author of the epigram has reworked an identifiable Homeric half-line, tacking on another ready-made one.

Another important consequence stems from this allusion to Homer. The beholder, faced with the blank, uninscribed *sêma* of the hero slain by Hektor, himself pronounces what might well have been a funerary inscription ("This is the barrow of a man who died in olden days") and thereby helps to make Hektor's *kléos* resound.[28] The commemorative speech, pronounced aloud, in fact constitutes the *kléos*. The readers of Mnesitheos' stele will also pronounce a commemorative speech, programmed by the inscription: they will guarantee Mnesitheos' *kléos,* by "distributing" it aloud to the passersby. In the case of the Homeric *sêma,* there is no writing. To Hektor's mind, "people will know," quite simply, that such-and-such a hero, slain by Hektor, is buried beneath the *sêma.* The voice of whoever speaks aloud that shared knowledge has no need of written signs to guide him; his "distribution" of the *kléos* depends on memory, on an unwritten tradition. But in the case of both the Homeric *sêma* and the memorial to Mnesitheos, the *kléos* will live forever among people—like an eternal flame, in fact. For as we have seen in Chapter 1, the *kléos* is like a fire that never dies: it is *ásbeston*

26. *Iliad* 7.89–91.
27. For the half-line *diamperès êmata pánta* see *Odyssey* 4.209; *Homeric Hymn to Apollo* 485; *Homeric Hymn to Aphrodite* 209 (also 248 and *Iliad* 16.499).
28. Once again, we should remember the link between *kaleîn* 'to call [someone by name], to name' and *kléos* (the derivative from which, *kleîn,* is sometimes the synonym of *kaleîn*). See above, Chapter 1, p. 18 and n. 48; Chapter 2, p. 37 n. 49.

'inextinguishable', 'unquenchable'.[29] That is how I also translated *akámaton* in line 5 of Mnesitheos' epigram. The literal meaning of *akámaton* is 'indefatigable', but in view of the fact that this adjective is the traditional epithet for *pûr* 'fire', it can transfer the properties of fire to the commemorative stele, which is what my translation "inextinguishable stele" was supposed to convey.[30] Thanks to the readers of the stele, which is "inextinguishable," the *kléos* of Mnesitheos will be like a flame: the inscription on the stele will provide the spark.

Although the author of the epigram has tried to endow the text with a certain symmetry (the essential elements of which we have analyzed above), his writing does not possess the formal elegance found in other versified inscriptions of the period. I am thinking in particular of the line right in the middle of this symmetrical poem which contains a remarkable fault in the versification: a hexameter cannot end with *Tīmarétē,* ‾ ˘ ˘ ‾ (the same name is correctly used at the beginning of line 7). Now, to us, this mistake is extremely precious, for it sets us on the track of the writer who is engaged in reading himself. In fact, we can reconstruct the precise way in which this mistake came about. Having written the word *mḗtēr,* the author of this epigram reread the line before finishing it off, but instead of starting to read at *kaí,* he began at *mnêm',* thereby forming the impression that he had written a pentameter, which he proceeded to complete by adding *Timarétē:*

mnêm' epéthēke phílē mḗtēr Timarétē
‾ ˘ ˘ | ‾ ˘ ˘ | ‾ || ‾ ‾ | ‾ ˘ ˘ | ‾

Admittedly, he ought to have avoided the spondaic *mḗtēr,* but the very same anomaly appears again in the next line, which ends with *stélēn akámaton,* ‾ ‾ | ‾ ˘ ˘ | ˘ . The slow pace at which he writes-as-he-reads-himself is probably the explanation for this error of versification. It breaks the automatic progression of oral composition.[31]

---

29. Above, Chapter 1, p. 23 and n. 68.
30. In the *Iliad* the hexameter ends with *akámaton pûr* seven times.
31. On which topic see A. B. Lord, *The Singer of Tales* (Cambridge, Mass., 1960), pp. 126–127. If the author of this epigram had first composed it orally and only then transcribed it, the mistake would not have occurred. That is not to

The only way to ensure metric correctness under such conditions is to be conscious of metrical theory.

The reader conjured up by our epigram is the distributor of Mnesitheos' *kléos*. He will speak the name of the deceased aloud. He will distribute his *kléos* to the passersby who, for their part, will not need to read the inscription, for they will hear it from the reader. They will be the "listeners" to the text, not its readers (whatever the claims of dictionaries that translate *akoúontes* and *akroataí* as "readers"). The reading is ensured by an individual who, unlike most of the passersby, it may be supposed, knows how to read. In the absence of statistics on the level of literacy among fifth-century Greeks, the most we can do is hypothesize on this point, but the impression is that the distinction between reader and listeners in this epigram reflects a situation of semiliteracy, that is to say, an uneven distribution of the ability to read and write. An episode that happened during the siege of Potidaea in 479 B.C.—roughly at the time when Mnesitheos' stele was set up—would appear to indicate a similar level of literacy.[32] (We should keep in mind that neither Potidaea nor Eretria are Athens.) The episode is recounted by Herodotus.[33] Artabazos was laying siege to Potidaea. In the town he had a collaborator, Timoxenos, who was willing to betray the other Greeks. Artabazos and Timoxenos communicated by sending each other messages concealed in arrows. One day, an arrow intended for Timoxenos struck the arm of a citizen of Potidaea. A crowd assembled and "straightaway they took the arrow and found the letter and carried it to their generals. . . . The generals read the letter and perceived who was the traitor." Admittedly, the behavior of the people who discovered the message may have been prompted by

---

suggest that he wrote directly on the stone. He probably first wrote his epigram on a *déltos* and the text was then reproduced on the stone, either by himself or by someone else. For a different view of the role of writing in the archaic composition of inscribed poetry, see G. Nagy, *Pindar's Homer: The Lyric Possession of an Epic Past* (Baltimore, 1990), pp. 18–19n.7; also 168n.95, 171–172, 219–220.

32. On the degree of literacy in fifth-century Athens see A. Burns, "Athenian Literacy in the Fifth Century," *Journal of the History of Ideas*, 42 (1981), pp. 371–387. See also O. Longo, *Techniche della communicazione nella Grecia antica* (Naples, 1981), pp. 119–120.

33. Herodotus 8.128. I am indebted to Joseph Russo for this reference ("The Persistence of Oral Culture in Classical Greece," typescript).

their respect for their leaders, but it seems more likely that they handed the written message over to them because only the leaders could read.[34]

Because he can read, the reader will become the instrument of Mnesitheos' posthumous renown. An analogous situation obtains in the second epigram that I discuss. An inscription on the plinth of a bronze statue now lost, the epigram must be roughly contemporary with Mnesitheos' epigram.[35] It was discovered at Halikarnassos and published in 1920 by Ulrich von Wilamowitz-Moellendorff, whose interpretation has essentially been followed by H. J. Rose, by the editor of the *Supplementum Epigraphicum Graecum,* and by Maria-letizia Lazzarini.[36] Here is the text published by Lazzarini, followed by her interpretation.

$$\alpha \dot{v} \delta \dot{\eta} \ \tau \epsilon \chi \nu \dot{\eta} \epsilon \sigma \sigma \alpha \ \lambda i \theta o \ \lambda \acute{\epsilon} \gamma \epsilon, \ \tau i \varsigma \ \tau \acute{o} \delta' \ [\ddot{\alpha} \gamma \alpha \lambda \mu \alpha]$$
$$\sigma \tau \hat{\eta} \sigma \epsilon \ ' A \pi \acute{o} \lambda \lambda \omega \nu o \varsigma \ \beta \omega \mu \grave{o} \nu \ \dot{\epsilon} \pi \alpha \gamma \lambda \alpha i [\hat{\omega} \nu];$$
$$\Pi \alpha \nu \alpha \mu \acute{v} \eta \varsigma \ v \acute{\iota} \grave{o} \varsigma \ K \alpha \sigma \beta \acute{\omega} \lambda \lambda \iota o \varsigma, \ \epsilon \ddot{\iota} \ \mu \epsilon \ \kappa [\epsilon \lambda \epsilon \acute{v} \epsilon \iota \varsigma]$$
$$\dot{\epsilon} \xi \epsilon \iota \pi \epsilon \hat{\iota} \nu, \ \delta \epsilon \kappa \acute{\alpha} \tau \eta \nu \ \tau \acute{\eta} \nu \delta' \ \dot{\alpha} \nu \acute{\epsilon} \theta \eta \kappa \epsilon \ \theta \epsilon [\hat{\omega} \iota]$$

[O voice, issuing from the stone, tell, who set up this votive gift to adorn the altar of Apollo? Panamyes, son of Kasbollis, if you ask me to tell, dedicated this tithe to the god.]

There are two immediate comments to make, one concerning the Greek text, the other concerning the translation. At the end of line 2, Lazzarini differs from Wilamowitz-Moellendorff in that she adds a question mark, turning the sentence introduced by *tís* (line 1) into a direct question. But given the response forthcoming in lines 3 and 4, with the phrase "if you ask me to tell" or, better still, "if you order me to tell" (*eí me keleúeis exeipeîn*), the question mark is not at all necessary. The author of the epigram did not write, "If you ask

34. Russo, "The Persistence of Oral Culture in Classical Greece."
35. It dates from the "first quarter of the fifth century," according to Lazzarini, p. 273.
36. U. von Wilamowitz-Moellendorff and G. Karo, "Aus Halikarnassos," *Mitteilungen des deutschen archäologischen Instituts. Athenische Abteilung,* 45 (1920), pp. 157–162; H. J. Rose, "The Speaking Stone," *Classical Review,* 37 (1923), pp. 162–163; *Supplementum Epigraphicum Graecum,* 1, J. J. E. Hondius, ed. (Leiden, 1923), p. 111, no. 424; Lazzarini, pp. 129–130. In Lazzarini's collection, the inscription is numbered 688.

me the question." The phrase "if you order me to tell" is a response
to the imperative *lége* 'tell!' in line 1, and that imperative can be
followed perfectly well by an indirect question, "Tell who has set
up this *ágalma,*" with no question mark and laying the stress on
"tell." I have gone to such lengths in considering the question of
punctuation because the placing of a question mark reflects an
interpretation that presupposes, in my opinion wrongly, that the
first interlocutor of the epigram is speaking from a position of
ignorance—ignorance the second interlocutor proceeds to do away
with. In my view such a rendering prevents the interpreter from
perceiving the logic of the text, which is not articulated around a
question and a reply (ignorance/knowledge) but around an order
and its execution.

My second comment is a briefer one. Lazzarini quite simply
sidesteps the difficulty raised by the adjective *tekhnéessa* in line 1 by
translating it "issuing from." I will return to this point.

First, here is the text, without a question mark and expressed in
normalized spelling:

αὐδὴ τεχνήεσσα λίθου λέγε τίς τόδ᾽ [ἄγαλμα]
στῆσεν Ἀπόλλωνος βωμὸν ἐπαγλαΐ[ῶν].
Παναμύης υἱὸς Κασβώλλιος, εἴ με κ[ελεύεις]
ἐξειπεῖν, δεκάτην τήνδ᾽ ἀνέθηκε θε[ῷ].

Leaving aside the matter of the translation of *tekhnéessa* for the
moment, I would render the text as follows: "Voice *tekhnéessa* of the
stone, say who has set up this statue to give brilliance to the altar of
Apollo!" "Panamyes, the son of Kasbollis—if you order me to say it
aloud—dedicated this tithe to the god."

The essential information in this dedication, "Panamyes, the son
of Kasbollis . . . dedicated this tithe to the god" (which corresponds
to the formula *ho deîna anéthēke tôi theôi*[37]) is complemented by a
series of elements that turn the four lines into a dialogue between
two interlocutors, whose identities need to be established. The
dedicator, the third person with whom the interlocutors are concerned, was a historical character: Panamyes, the son of Kasbollis,

37. See Lazzarini, p. 58; see above, p. 38.

is one of the *mnḗmones* mentioned in a law of Halikarnassos, dating from 465–450 B.C.[38] In Halikarnassos, an official known as a *mnḗmōn* "one who remembers"—a kind of living human city archive—was, it seems, a person of sufficient substance to offer a bronze statue as a tithe to Apollo.[39]

For Lazzarini, this epigram is a dialogue between the passerby and the inscribed stone, whereas for Wilamowitz it was a dialogue between the passerby and the bronze statue, despite the fact that the passerby addresses the inscribed stone. For Lazzarini, the second line ends with a question mark that places the first interlocutor in a state of ignorance. He asks the stone a question. This interlocutor can only be a passerby. The "voice *tekhnḗessa* of the stone" is considered a metaphorical expression that refers to the inscription, the "skillfully worked voice of the stone" or *kunstvolle Stimme des Steines,* as Wilamowitz rendered it.[40] In support of this rendition, Rose, the other interpreter of this line, cites a metaphor from Sophocles' *Tereus: phōnḕ kerkídos* "the voice of the shuttle".[41] Deprived of her voice, Philomela has woven an account of her rape, to let it be known; Apollodorus goes so far as to speak of woven *grámmata.*[42] The voice she lacks is substituted by the "speaking" shuttle. There are substantial differences, however, between *audḕ tekhnḗessa líthou* and *phōnḕ kerkídos.* We can better understand the metaphor if we contrast the stone, which is the passive basis for writing and is mute, with the shuttle, which is the active instrument for a sort of writing, and is therefore endowed with a voice.[43]

38. G. Dittenberger, *Sylloge Inscriptionum Graecarum,* 3d ed., 1 (Leipzig, 1915), no. 45, pp. 11–13 and 30–31; R. Meiggs and D. Lewis, *A Selection of Greek Historical Inscriptions to the End of the Fifth Century B.C.* (Oxford, 1969), no. 32.

39. Interest in the figure of the *mnḗmōn* and in his relationship to writing has been renewed since the publication of the contract drawn up between the *mnḗmōn* Spensitheos and the Cretan city of Lyttos. The contract dates from about 500 B.C. See, in particular, L. H. Jeffery and A. Morpurgo-Davies, "Ποινικαστάς and ποινικάζειν. BM 1969, 4–2, I, a New Archaic Inscription from Crete," *Kadmos,* 9 (1970), pp. 118–154.

40. Wilamowitz-Moellendorff and Karo, "Aus Halikarnassos," p. 159. See R. Kassel, "Dialoge mit Statuen," *Zeitschrift für Papyrologie und Epigraphik,* no. 51 (1983), p. 11. See also *Greek Anthology* 7.262.

41. Sophocles in Aristotle *Poetics* 16.1454b37 (= Sophocles frag. 538 Nauck²).

42. Apollodorus *Library* 3.14.8.

43. See Euripides frag. 523 Nauck²: *kerkìs aoidós* "singing shuttle". See H. Blümner, *Technologie und Terminologie der Gewerbe und Künste bei den Griechen und Römern,* 1 (Leipzig, 1912), p. 151n.9.

Christos Karousos rejects the Wilamowitz interpretation and proposes an alternative. He suggests that the dialogue takes place between the passerby and the bronze statue, bypassing the stone.[44] But his interpretation comes up against the difficulty raised by the word *líthou:* the voice supposedly does not belong to the bronze but to "the stone." Karousos struggles desperately to get around this impasse, producing three explanations for the presence of *líthou:* (1) It might be a *catachresis,* which he compares to what he believes to be a similar phenomenon in a poem by Simonides, criticizing the epitaph on Midas;[45] (2) it might be an instance of poetic license, explained by metrical constraints (the metrical value of *khalkoû,* ‾ ‾, is different from that of *líthou,* ˘ ‾); and (3) it might be that the author of the epigram is ignorant of the material used by the sculptor. Faced with such a hermeneutical impasse, we must seek another solution and undertake a far more literal reading of the epigram.

Let us start by examining now the meaning of the adjective *tekhnéessa* that qualifies *audé* 'voice'. As normally used, the noun *audé* is not of a human being, which is probably what has persuaded some interpreters of the epigram to consider it as a thing. Something that is *tekhnéessa* is clearly "worked skillfully," such as the *desmoì tekhnéentes* "the chains skillfully wrought," which Hephaistos uses in the *Odyssey.*[46] But the *audé* with which we are concerned is not just a thing. It is personified and addressed as though it were a person; it is ordered to speak (*lége* 'tell!'). That means it is capable of doing something. It is like a person. And a *tekhnéessa* person is not "a person wrought skillfully" (passive), but one who "possesses a *tékhnē*" or "works with skill": in short, one who is "skillful" (active). *Tekhnéeis* is the word that qualifies the "skillful" weavers among the Phaeacians, that defines the manner in which Odysseus handles the rudder, and—significantly enough—that describes Palamedes, the man said to have invented writing.[47] The personified voice is thus a voice "that possesses a *tékhnē,*" namely the skill of a reader. It knows how to read. It is a "reading" voice. By reading

44. Karousos, "Perikalles agalma," pp. 126–127.

45. As if the word *líthos* in Simonides frag. 76.5 Page referred specifically to the "bronze virgin" in the Midas epitaph (Pfohl, no. 24).

46. *Odyssey* 8.296–297.

47. Ibid. 7.110, 5.270: *tekhnééntōs,* and Gorgias frag. B 11a(25) Diels-Kranz. For Palamedes as the inventor of writing see Stesichorus frag. 36 Page.

aloud, *audè tekhnéessa líthou* "reading voice of the stone," the vocative being addressed to itself, it demonstrates the *tékhnē* that it is
thought to possess. The inscription counts on that *tékhnē* of the
reader, which suggests that *lége* should be translated as "read!"
(rather than "tell!" or "say!"[48]). This is the *tékhnē* that the voice puts
at the service of the stone; through that *tékhnē* the voice is distinguished from other, "unskillful," illiterate voices. We are thus led to
the following translation of the first line: "O voice that reads the
stone, read out who set up this statue. . . ." The parallelism between
Mnesitheos' epitaph and Panamyes' dedication is now strikingly
revealed. Both follow the same schema:

1. The reader addressed in the vocative (*deûro ión*/*audè tekhnéessa*
   [synecdoche]).
2. 'Read' imperative (*anáneimai*/*lége*).
3. An indirect question introduced by *tís*.
4. A form of *hóde* in the indirect question (*têide*/*tóde*).
5. The proper name of the individual commemorated (Mnesitheos/
   Panamyes).
6. A form of (*ex-*)*eipeîn* denoting the act of reading (future: *ereî;*
   aorist: *exeipeîn*).[49]

But according to the first line, one may object, the voice is the
voice "of the stone" (*líthou*), not of the reader. And at first sight that
does seem to be the case. The two genitives, however, are not of the
same order. If only one of these genitives is made explicit, it is
because the inscription is being elliptical. In a culture in which
reading was practiced aloud, it could afford to be elliptical, since
everyone knew that stone—*líthos áphthongos* 'voiceless', as Theognis puts it[50]—has only one voice, to wit, that which the reader
lends it. Had the text been explicit, "the voice of the reader" would
have been an ordinary possessive genitive, whereas the "voice of the

48. See above, p. 52.
49. This parallelism should set us on our guard against interpretations that,
following Wilamowitz, assume that the conventions of a much more recent (Hellenistic or Roman) period than that of Panamyes' epigram are involved. To make it a
dialogue between the passerby and the stone (or statue) is to tear the inscription
from its historical context and put it in a class of profoundly different epigrams.
50. Theognis 568–569 (see Aristotle *De Anima* 2.8.420b5–6).

stone" (*audè líthou*) is a special kind of genitive expressing a "relationship of service."[51] "The voice of the stone" is thus "the voice at the service of the stone" (which is what justifies the translation "that reads the stone"). It may be compared to the *anagnóstēs tês póleōs* (or *gerousías*), the "reader at the service of the city" (or "of the council of elders"), or to the *doûloi toû nómou,* the "slaves [at the service] of the law," which is how the archons are described in Plato's *Laws.*[52] Just as those magistrates are at the service of the political institutions, the voice—that is to say the reader's voice—is also there to serve. Reading the inscription, the voice places itself at the service of the stone. Through a synecdoche, the reader finds himself reduced to a voice, in its purely instrumental aspect.

The dialogue, then, does not take place between the passerby and the stone, but between the inscription and the voice of the reader, the voice that receives the command that is essential from the point of view of *kléos:* the command to pronounce the name of the dedicator aloud (*ex-eipeîn* means not just 'tell' or 'say', but "tell/say aloud" or even "read out loud").[53] As I have noted, this dialogue is articulated not around a question and an answer (ignorance/knowledge), but around a command and its execution, a command to pass from the mute sign to its voiced realization, giving it *expression in sound* (from silence to sonority). This articulation is all the more significant in that the inscription was to be read from the plinth of a statue—probably a *koûros*—dedicated to Apollo. Why? Because, as Georges Dumézil has reminded us, Apollo is the god of "sound."[54] He is, as we shall see in Chapters 5 and 6, the god of expression in sound. No other deity could so appropriately preside over the operation that makes the name of Panamyes, son of Kasbollis, resound. And that operation is the very purpose of the inscription, which, without the voice of the reader, would remain

51. The *Dienstverhältnis* referred to by E. Schwyzer and A. Debrunner, *Griechische Grammatik,* 2d ed., vol. 2: *Handbuch der Altertumswissenschaft,* 2.1.2 (Munich, 1959), p. 118, under β. See below, Chapter 10, p. 193 and n. 18.

52. F. Hiller von Gaertringen, *Inschriften von Priene* (Berlin, 1906), nos. 111, 194; W. R. Paton and E. L. Hicks, *The Inscriptions of Cos* (Oxford, 1891), no. 238. Plato *Laws* 4.715d5.

53. See above, p. 53 and n. 28.

54. G. Dumézil, *Apollon sonore et autres essais. Esquisses de mythologie* (Paris, 1982).

incomplete in the eyes of the Greeks, not because it lacks an internal life, as Socrates would say,[55] but because it lacks sound. The inscription is a machine designed to produce *kléos.*

The minute the reader pronounces the word *audé,* at the beginning of the inscription—the *audé* which leads into the reading—the inscription finds, or recovers, the interlocutor that it needs. From that minute on, the "you" of the first line acquires a reality, a sonorous reality. So it could be said that the sound of the voice is indispensable if the inscription is to recover its meaning. The voice of the reader is the eternally renewable referent thanks to which the inscription finds full realization. Without it, the inscription remains incomplete, without sound, without sense: in short, *álogos.*[56] In this way, therefore, the reader who puts his "voice at the service of the stone" helps to produce, or reproduce, its meaning. The writing needs a living voice, not, as in Plato, in order to defend itself, explain itself, reason. Instead, it needs that voice in order to resound.

Now, Panamyes, the *mnémōn* of Halikarnassos and, as such, probably a professional when it came to writing, was a compatriot of Herodotus, a fact that will perhaps justify my concluding with a few remarks on the verb that Herodotus (and no doubt also Panamyes) used for "to read": namely, *epilégesthai.* For in Ionian, "to read" was normally rendered as *epilégesthai,* a verb whose meaning Pierre Chantraine explained on the analogy of the Latin *legere,* mistakenly, in my view.[57]

The fundamental meaning of the verb *epi-légein* is "to speak on the subject of [*epi*-] something." The *légein* or *lógos* (the noun from *légein*) is thus added (*epi*-) to a fact or an action, as a commentary

---

55. Plato *Phaedrus* 275d; see above, Chapter 2, p. 29 and n. 12.

56. See below, Chapter 9, p. 164 and n. 18.

57. P. Chantraine, "Les Verbes grecs signifiant 'lire'," in *Mélanges Grégoire,* 2 (Brussels, 1950), p. 121. It is, however, quite legitimate to believe that it was the Greek *légō,* in the sense of 'to read' (see above, pp. 52 and 60), that, as understood by the Romans when they were learning the Greek alphabet, gave them the idea of using the Latin *lego* as a technical term: see A. Ernout and A. Meillet, *Dictionnaire étymologique de la langue latine,* 4th ed. (Paris), pp. 349–350. The sense of "assembling, gathering" is not in my opinion fundamental for the semantics of the Latin *legere* meaning 'to read', even though it played a role later on (see, for example, Cicero *For King Deiotarus* 7.19, cited by Ernout and Meillet, *Dictionnaire étymologique,* p. 349), once *legere* became the technical term for the activity of reading. See also below, p. 115.

or reflection on it. Understandably, then, the middle *epi-légesthai* comes to mean "to read": the reading is understood as a *lógos* endowed with sound that is added (*epi-*) to a piece of voiceless writing, which is incomplete without it. So it is not the writing here that supplements the voice, but the voice that supplements—in both senses of the word—the writing. The writing *lacks* a voice that is added to it to *supplement* it.[58] Like the middle *ananémesthai* that we have read on Mnesitheos' stele, the middle *epilégesthai* indicates that the reader involves himself in the act he performs.[59] The voice is the instrument that allows the "listeners" to the text (if there are any) as well as the reader himself to become acquainted with the content of what is written. The written word cannot, on its own, communicate that content.[60] By using his own voice, the reader thus adds a *lógos* to what is written, a *lógos* that makes it possible for the writing to become a succession of sounds intelligible to the listener, but a succession of sounds that lacks any internal life, just as the writing does. Panamyes' dedication can be read, therefore, as a presentation of the meaning of the verb *epilégesthai,* one of whose elements it uses when it addresses the reading voice by means of the imperative *lége* 'read!', for *epilégesthai* is the verb that makes reading aloud the "epilogue" that the written speech-act cannot do without.

---

58. The reader will no doubt recognize, in inverse form, the logic of the inscriptional *supplement* analyzed by J. Derrida in *Of Grammatology* (Baltimore, 1976), pp. 144f., and *Writing and Difference* (London, 1978), p. 212.

59. See above, p. 52 and n. 22.

60. We will return to this subject in Chapter 9.

CHAPTER 4

The Child as Signifier:
The "Inscription" of the Proper Name

The first alphabetic writing in ancient Greece was a writing of proper names. Whether using practical or prestige objects, the writer appears to us first and foremost in the role of a name-giver (*onomatothétēs*): he "attaches names," denoting the owners, craftsmen, donors, and addressees. Once committed to writing, those proper names sound forth each time a reader puts his voice at their service. The *kléos* that is silently watched over by one such as Phrasikleia will come to life each time a reader reads the epigram aloud. This reading provides the only posterity that Phrasikleia, who died before marriage, will ever acquire, a posterity that is not biological but acoustic and which the reader is instrumental in creating. In similar fashion, the reader who is set on stage by the inscription from Eretria is nothing but a "vocal distributor" (*ananemómenos*) of the name of the deceased, to wit Mnesitheos; and in the dedication by Panamyes of Halikarnassos, essentially the operation consists in "pronouncing aloud" (*exeipeîn*) the name of the dedicator. From this point of view, the same probably applies to inscriptions such as those that appear on Nestor's cup or Kleimachos' amphora. Objects in daily use and votive or funerary monuments all served as material to support writing, the purpose of which was to prompt the reading aloud of a name, within a suitable framework.

If the Greeks set names in a position of the first importance when they began to write, we can reasonably assume that their particular conception of writing may have had something to do with this set of priorities. The primary interest of writing in an oral culture might boil down to the fact that names could be attached to objects in a material and durable fashion, so that they could then be read aloud. That is an early, still very limited concept of writing, in which it is essentially reduced to the giving of names, in short to an "onomatothesis." Conversely, the Greeks' concept of names must itself have affected their notions of reading and writing. Writing probably appeared to them as a way of allowing a name to sound forth, a new way of producing *kléos*. Long before the arrival of the alphabet in Greece, names were sounded forth with a view to producing *kléos:* onomatothesis had "always" been practiced. It certainly constituted part of the cultural framework into which alphabetic writing burst forth during the first half of the first millennium B.C. As soon as writing arrived in Greece, it was put in the service of names. To that extent, writing was determined by names. But that determination might imply the very finality of the principles that governed the attribution of a name to a newborn child. Our task, then, is to define the precise modalities of that determination. If we seek to discover how it was that the Greeks began to write, we must accept the evidence for and study the specific significance of onomatothesis, or name-giving in Greek culture.

It comes as an agreeable surprise to find that, in this domain, our knowledge leaves little to be desired, even in this period, which is so opaque in many other respects. In epic, the principles of Greek name-giving are clearly discernible. We can study those principles, which are, moreover, confirmed by historical examples, within the context of heroic lineages. A name functions within the framework of 'procreation' (*génesis*). To have descendants is to be able to give names to individuals who will continue to bear them in the future, even after the name-giver has died. With its recognizable semantic elements, a Greek name turns name-giving into a signifying practice. The name-giver must attach to the newborn child a name whose elliptical message will be heard by the generations of the future.

From Homer to Plato, the Greeks believed humans could achieve immortality in two ways: through 'generation' (*génesis*) or through 'renown' (*kléos*). As Gregory Nagy points out, the hero Anchises wins immortality through his line of descent, while a hero such as Achilles wins by himself his own immortal renown.[1] The one will survive in the children of his own child: "You will have a son who will be king among the Trojans, and to his sons, sons shall be born in days to come," Aphrodite tells Anchises.[2] The son of Anchises, Aeneas, is not slain on the field of battle as Achilles is: "It is ordained unto him to escape," Poseidon declares in the *Iliad,* "so that the race [*geneḗ*] of Dardanos perish not, without seed [*áspermos*] and be seen no more."[3] After his union with Aphrodite, Anchises will have not a *geneḕ áspermos,* but a *spérma áphthiton,* an "imperishable seed", to borrow a useful expression from Pindar.[4] He stands in contrast to Achilles, who is to die before the walls of Troy and thereby win *kléos áphthiton* "imperishable renown". *Kléos* is what Homer can confer upon an individual who has accomplished a memorable exploit.[5] Indeed, *kléos áphthiton* is the formula used to refer to the bard's song, regarded as the hero's imperishable renown sounded forth.

On the one hand, the example of Anchises and his son Aeneas, followed by the whole lineage descended from Aeneas, represents immortality through a line of descent that never fails, that is to say, through a *spérma áphthiton.* On the other, the example of Achilles, the hero of the *Iliad,* represents immortality through the voice of the bard, that is to say, through *kléos áphthiton.* In both cases what is involved is what Plato calls "the desire for immortality." Let us listen to the words of the Athenian in the *Laws:*

> The human race, by nature's ordinance, shares in immortality, a thing for which nature has implanted in everyone a keen desire. The desire to win glory [*genésthai kleinón*] instead of lying in a nameless [*anṓnumon*] grave aims at a like object. Thus mankind is by nature

---

1. G. Nagy, *The Best of the Achaeans* (Baltimore, 1979), pp. 119, 267–268.

2. *Homeric Hymn to Aphrodite* 196–197. See *Iliad* 20.307–308, with the same expression *paídōn paîdes* in line 308; see also Virgil *Aeneid* 3.98, *nati natorum* "Aeneas' children's children".

3. *Iliad* 20.302–304.

4. Pindar *Pythian* 4.42 f. For the expression *spérma áphthiton,* used by Pindar to refer to the clod of earth in his account of the origins of Cyrene, see *Olympian* 6.51, and *Nemean* 7.100, 10.17 (analogous expressions referring to human procreation).

5. See above, Chapter 1, p. 12 and n. 19; p. 14 and n. 29. See also Nagy, *The Best of the Achaeans,* p. 135.

coeval with the whole of time, in that it accompanies it continually
both now and in the future; and the means by which it is immortal is
this: by leaving behind it children's children [*paîdas paídōn*] and con-
tinuing ever one and the same, it thus by reproduction [*génesis*] shares
in immortality.[6]

Kléos and *génesis* are thus two facets of the same desire for immortality. Although in Plato *génesis* is valued less highly than *kléos*,[7] the
former clearly makes immortality through *kléos* possible. Without
biological posterity there can be no spiritual posterity. But once
biological posterity is assured (or considered to proceed on its own),
men can give free rein to their boundless desire to win fame. As
Diotima tells us in the *Symposium*, the desire for immortality explains "how singularly they are affected with the love of winning a
name [*onomastoì genésthai*] and laying up fame immortal for all time
to come [*kaì kléos es tòn aeì khrónon athánaton katathésthai*]:[8] for this,
even more than for their children, they are ready to run all risks, to
expend money, perform any kind of task, and sacrifice their lives."[9]
Diotima goes on to explain that Alcestis, Achilles, and Kodros acted
not so much out of love (for Admetus, Patroklos, and Athens
respectively) as out of a desire to ensure for themselves "a deathless
memory for valor" (*athánaton mnémēn aretês péri*).[10] They are "in
love with what is immortal."[11] Seen from this heroic point of
view, people who immortalize themselves through their descendants have a rather mediocre air. But as the following passage
shows, *génesis* is not anonymous. Through one's line of descent,
one is assured of posthumous renown, even if of a different degree
from the heroic type. "Now, those who are teeming in body betake
them rather to women and are amorous on this wise: by getting
children, they acquire an immortality as memorial [*mnémē*] and a

6. Plato *Laws* 4.721b–c. *Paîdas paídōn* is indicative of the Homeric formula. See
also the references provided by E. des Places, in the Collection des Universités de
France edition of the *Laws*.

7. Plato *Symposium* 209e.

8. The expression constitutes a hexameter; not without good reason does
Diotima make use of heroic meter at this precise point.

9. *Symposium* 208c–d.

10. Ibid. 208d6.

11. Ibid. 208e1.

state of bliss that, in their imagining, they for all succeeding time procure."[12]

The works of Marcel Detienne and, more recently, Gregory Nagy have by now made us familiar with the importance of *kléos,* a veritable obsession among the Greeks. But what about the other way of attaining immortality, namely procreation? For those who do not accomplish an exploit so great as to match the heroes of the oral tradition, procreation is the only means of achieving immortality. But for that immortality not to be anonymous, *génesis* needs something else. How is the lasting memory of the one who immortalizes himself through his line of descent transmitted to his "childrens' children"? Let us take a well-known and verifiable example, that of Odysseus, for there is nothing to stop a man whose exploits are sung by the bards from also engendering children. Odysseus "lives on" thanks both to his *kléos* and to a *génesis* that is not at all anonymous. In the first place, he has a son, Telemakhos, left behind in Ithaca when his father set off "to fight far away." Indeed, *Télémakhos* means "who fights far away" (both in Troy, as well as at a distance as an archer).[13] While Odysseus, unlike the suitors, is fighting far away, his son—who is the perfect image of his father—remains, like a memorial, in Ithaca, reminding everybody of what his father is doing.[14] The son must remain alive if he is to fulfill his commemorative function, which is to bear his name. In truth, it is not Telemakhos who is "fighting far away," but his father. In a

12. Ibid. 208e. My discussion here follows closely E. des Places, *Pindare et Platon* (Paris, 1949), pp. 111–112.

13. See Eustathius *Commentarii ad Homeri Odysseam,* 1.1479.56 Stallbaum: "For he [i.e., *Télé-makhos*] has grown while his father has been fighting far away [*têle makhoménou toû patrós*]."

14. *Odyssey* 4.141 f. On the proper name as a *sêma* (= *mnêma:* if the *sêma* 'indicates', then the *mnêma,* for its part, 'recalls'), see D. Sinos, *Achilles, Patroklos, and the Meaning of* Φίλος, Innsbrucker Beiträge zur Sprachwissenschaft, 29 (Innsbruck, 1980), p. 49. See also Prokleidas' *sêma* (G. Pfohl, *Greek Poems on Stones,* vol. 1, *Epitaphs: From the Seventh to the Fifth Centuries B.C.,* Textus Minores, no. 36 [Leiden, 1967], no. 164 [hereafter referred to as "Pfohl"]: "This *sêma* will be called 'Prokleidas' "), analyzed in Chapter 2, and the "*sêma* of Halirrhothios" (*sêma Halirrhothíou*) (*Scholia to Pindar,* 1:331.12 f. Drachmann), considered by the scholiast as a *periphrasis* of the name Halirrhothios (see *hierề ìs Telemákhoio* "the holy strength of Telemakhos"). The *periphrasis* is all the more significant in view of the fact that Halirrhothios is the son of Poseidon (Apollodorus *Library* 3.14.2) and bears one of his epithets as a name (on Poseidon *halirrhóthios,* see *Scholia to Pindar* 1:331.24–25).

culture of mimesis, a Telemakhos who seeks to imitate his father by doing himself what his name announces will be a model son, for the best thing that could be wished for a child is that he should resemble his father.[15] At his birth, however, it is too soon to tell whether that will be the case. All one can do is hope for the best. The primary meaning of the name Telemakhos refers not to the newborn child or the young boy who bears it, but to Odysseus, his father, whose part in the Trojan War constitutes one of his essential exploits.

Now let us consider the name of Odysseus himself. The *Odyssey* tells us that Autolykos, the father-in-law of Laertes, decided on the name for the newborn child. Autolykos tells his son-in-law and his daughter: "Give him whatsoever name I say. Inasmuch as I have come hither as one who has been angered [*odussámenos*] with many, . . . let the name by which the child be named be 'child of wrath' [*Oduseús*]."[16] According to Homer, Odysseus thus received a name that refers not to his own state of mind, but to the sentiments of his maternal grandfather. The linguistic correctness of this explanation for the name Odysseus need not concern us here. What is important is how the author of the *Odyssey* regards it: not as referring to the one who bears it, but to his grandfather. *Oduseús* is the signifier; what is signified is the state of mind of his grandfather. Similarly, Telemakhos is the signifier; what is signified is one of his father's most identifiable essential exploits. In other words, the name of the son is an *epithet* for the father or the grandfather. As we shall soon see, that is a statement that should be taken absolutely literally.

When Odysseus finally escapes with his friends from the cave of Polyphemus the Cyclops, he reveals his true identity to Polyphe-

15. M. Sulzberger, "Ὄνομα ἐπώνυμον. Les noms propres chez Homère et dans la mythologie grecque," *Revue des études grecques,* 39 (1926), p. 406 (hereafter cited as Sulzberger). From the point of view of Nagy's research, in contrast, the name as denoting its bearer is the central point of interest. For example, *Akhi-leús* "whose *laós* has *ákhos*, whose host of fighting men has grief", refers to the figure of Achilles himself (Nagy, *The Best of the Achaeans,* p. 69 f.). All the same, there is no reason why this name should not refer also to the father of Achilles, Peleus, who exiled himself from Aegina in the company of the Myrmidons. See Nagy's own comment, p. 146n.2, where he cites L. Clader, *Helen: The Evolution from Divine to Heroic in Greek Epic Tradition* (Leiden, 1976), pp. 30–31, and M. Van der Valk, "On Apollodori Bibliotheca," *Revue des études grecques,* 71 (1958), p. 147n.164.

16. *Odyssey* 19.406–409.

mus. "Cyclops, if any one of mortal men shall ask you about the shameful blinding of your eye, say that Odysseus, the destroyer of cities [*ptolipórthios*], blinded it: it was the son of Laertes, whose home is in Ithaca."[17] Odysseus thus attributes to himself the epithet *ptolipórthios* "destroyer of cities", which—as Nagy would say—represents his exploits in a compressed form.[18] Any traditional epithet may be developed in a narrative, and the second line of the first book of the *Odyssey* might well be read as an early development of the epithet *ptolipórthios,* preparing for the actual narrative: *Troíēs hieròn ptolíethron éperse* "he destroyed the holy city of Troy". The next development of this epithet comes in Book 8, where Homer summarizes the exploits sung by Demodokos.[19] The destruction of Troy constitutes one of the essential exploits of Odysseus' life, for he played a major part in it. Just as the epithet that refers to it can be expanded in the narrative, the narrative can be compressed or condensed in the epithet.

Odysseus apparently bestowed that very epithet upon a son whom he fathered with Penelope after his return to Ithaca—Ptoliporthes.[20] Odysseus' renown was thus underwritten both as regards *kléos* and as regards *génesis:* the epithet that is attached to him in the epic proclaims the same thing as the name of his son. The exploit of the father is summed up in a name, a name that may, on its own account, be developed in a narrative. In an elliptical fashion, the name Ptoliporthes transmits the memory of that exploit to future generations. But that is not all; according to the *Thesprotis,* an epic poem cited by Pausanias, a daughter of Odysseus also went by the name of Ptoliporthe.[21] The epithet attached to the father could thus also serve as a name for his daughter. And if it was indeed from the "children's children" onward that a line of descent began to interest the Greeks—as Edouard des Places maintains[22]—Odysseus

17. *Odyssey* 9.502–505. See also *Iliad* 2.278, 10.363, and *Odyssey* 8.3, 14.447, 16.442, 18.356, 22.283, 24.119.

18. According to Nagy, the bard could choose between a compression of the heroic narrative or a more or less elaborate expansion of it. This "accordion theory" of his was presented in a series of lectures at the Collège de France in 1978.

19. *Odyssey* 8.492 f.

20. Apollodorus *Epitome* 7.35.

21. Pausanias 8.12.6.

22. E. Des Places, in the Collection des Universités de France edition of Plato *Laws* 4.721c.

again provides a model. By Telemakhos he had a grandson who was named Persepolis,[23] which, although its components (derived from *pérthein* and *pólis*) are switched around, means the same as Ptoliporthes, namely "destroyer of cities", and refers to Odysseus' exploits.

As an historian, Pausanias had occasion to draw upon the principle on which such name-giving is based. In Book 7 he explains that Archandros and his brother came from the Phthiotis to settle in Argos, where they became the sons-in-law of Danaos. Pausanias goes on to say, "A very clear proof that they settled in Argos is the fact that Archandros named his son Metanastes."[24] The meaning of Metanastes is "settler,"[25] an epithet that applies to the father, not to the infant who is Danaos' grandson. The name thus condenses Archandros' past—elliptically, admittedly, but sufficiently clearly for Pausanias to use it as proof. The name of the son summarizes the essential event in the life of his father. It commemorates it just as a memorial would. Metanastes is the living memorial of his father.

Max Sulzberger deserves the credit for having systematically illustrated the logic behind Greek name-giving, a logic that these few examples have already illustrated. Even if Sulzberger's long article, which appeared in 1926, today seems out of date by reason of its evolutionary perspective, the body of documentation the author collected has retained all its interest.[26] Consider some of the most striking examples collected by Sulzberger, starting with the name of Hektor's son, Astyanax (*Astu-ánax*).[27] Literally, it means "lord of the city", and Homer himself explains why this was the name given to Hektor's son: "For only Hektor guarded Ilios [Troy]."[28] Clearly, the name of the son refers to the role played by his father. As Sulzberger points out, "Astyanax is simply an epithet for Hektor, which has become the name of his son."[29] Hektor's own name is glossed by Homer, albeit more discreetly: "You said that you would

23. Hesiod frag. 221 Merkelbach-West.
24. Pausanias 7.1.6.
25. See *Etymologicum Magnum*, 581.44, which glosses the word *metanástēs* by *métoikos* 'metic' and *phugás* 'refugee'.
26. Sulzberger.
27. Ibid., pp. 385–386.
28. *Iliad* 6.403.
29. Sulzberger, p. 386.

hold [*hexémen*] the city alone," Sarpedon says to Hektor.[30] In antiquity, *Héktōr* was simply a variant of *ekhétōr* "he who holds, governs".[31] Hektor's name would thus appear to refer to the one who bears it. But we should also look further afield. Sappho uses the name as an epithet for Zeus, whose son Hektor "claims to be."[32] Hektor is descended from Zeus and bears his epithet as his name. So much the better if he bears that name also in his own right as the "holder" of the city of Troy. That is not its primary meaning, however. In all probability, the names of his father and his grandfather obey the same principle, even if they too appear to apply to those who bear them. In the Aeolic dialect, Priam was called *Pérramos,* a synonym for *basileús* 'king'.[33] Although *pérramos* certainly suits Priam himself as an epithet, the word in the first instance applies to his father, King Laomedon. *Lao-médōn* means "who governs the people",[34] an epithet that of course suits Laomedon himself, but in the first instance and above all applies to his father, King Ilos. In a lineage in which the function (or profession) is handed on from father to son, the epithet that applies to the father can easily appear to describe the function of the son, once he succeeds his father. But here the name Astyanax, borne by one whom the force of circumstances will prevent from succeeding his father, may serve as a corrective. The name originally is not a functional description of the person to whom it is given but an epithet that applies to his father or grandfather—whom he must, if possible, resemble.

Three of Nestor's sons, mentioned in the *Odyssey,* bear the names *Ekhé-phrōn* "who possesses intelligence", *Thrasu-médēs* "with ambitious plans", and *Peisí-stratos* "who persuades the army". One is bound to agree with Eustathius when he declares, "The names of Nestor's sons are derived from the qualities [*aretaí*] of the father."[35] All three could have served as the traditional epithets of the father. The same is true of the names *Eú-mēlos* "rich in sheep" and *Peri-mḗlē*

30. *Iliad* 5.473; Sulzberger, p. 398.
31. *Cratylus* 393a; *Suda* s.v. *Héktōr; Etymologicum Magnum* 324.25.
32. Sappho frag. 180 Lobel-Page; the quotation is from *Iliad* 13.54.
33. Hesychios, s.v. *Pérramos;* Sulzberger, p. 398.
34. Sulzberger, ibid.
35. Sulzberger, pp. 391 and 430, citing the *Odyssey* 3.413–415, and Eustathius *Commentarii ad Homeri Odysseam* 1.1474.29 f. Stallbaum.

"very rich in sheep", borne by the children of Admetus, famed for his flocks, whose home receives the epithet *polu-mēlótatos,* the superlative of *polú-mēlos* "with innumerable sheep", in Euripides.[36] Similarly, the children of Bellerophon bear the names *Lao-dámeia* "who governs the people" and *Ís-andros* "the equal man". The king of Lycia had given half his kingdom, along with the hand of his daughter, to Bellerophon, who thus acceded to the "government of the people" as the king's "equal partner".[37] *Toxeús* 'archer' is the name of a son of Eurytos, the redoubtable bowman whose bow eventually came into the hands of Odysseus.[38] *Peri-phḗtēs* "who spreads the message" is the name of the son of the herald Kopreus.[39] *Euru-sákēs* "with the wide shield" is the son of Ajax, whose *sákos* 'shield' is his traditional attribute.[40]

Among the daughters of Nereus cited in the *Iliad* and in Hesiod's *Theogony,* it is worth noting *Nēmertḗs, Apseudḗs,* and *Themistṓ,*[41] names that are actually epithets for their father. "And Sea begat Nereus . . . who is true [*apseudḗs*] and lies not; and men call him the Old Man because he is trusty [*nēmertḗs*] and gentle and does not forget the laws of righteousness [*thémistes*]."[42] The names of the three daughters thus correspond to the fundamental characteristics of their father, as he is described by Hesiod; here the epithets and the names are identical. Similarly, Okeanos has a daughter whose name is the epithet applied to her father: she is called Kallirhoe. In the *Orphic Hymns,* Okeanos receives the epithet *kallí-rhoos* "which flows pleasantly".[43] Many other Nereids and Oceanids also bear names that might well have been epithets applied to their respective fathers, and the same goes for countless other Greek children. For the moment, let us limit ourselves to a few examples in the poetic

36. Sulzberger, p. 392, citing *Iliad* 2.764 and Hesiod frag. 256 Merkelbach-West; Euripides *Alcestis* 588–589.

37. Sulzberger, pp. 392–393; *Iliad* 6.191–193.

38. Sulzberger, p. 394; Hesiod frag. 26.30 Merkelbach-West; *Odyssey* 21.31–35 (see also 8.223–225).

39. Sulzberger, p. 396; *Iliad* 15.638–640.

40. Sulzberger, p. 433, citing Sophocles *Ajax* 574–576; see *Iliad* 7.219.

41. *Iliad* 18.46; Hesiod *Theogony* 261–262; see Sulzberger, p. 392.

42. Hesiod *Theogony* 233–235. *Themistes* (approximately) 'laws'.

43. Sulzberger, p. 393; Hesiod *Theogony* 288, 351, 981. Sulzberger, p. 393n.1: *Orphicorum fragmenta,* 15.1 and 115.1 Kern.

tradition, in which the name of the child is to be found as an epithet for the father.

Let us begin with the epithet *tīsamenós* (= *teisámenos*) "who has avenged", attributed to Orestes, who avenged his murdered father.[44] We know that Orestes married Hermione, the only daughter of Helen and Menelaos, whose successor on the throne of Sparta was Orestes. By Hermione Orestes had a son who received the name *Tisamenós,* and in his turn he also became king of Sparta.[45] The epithet that was applied to the father and the name of the son are identical: both commemorate an essential exploit in the life of Orestes. That is the opinion of many ancient authors cited by Sulzberger.[46] But if we consider the case of a figure to some extent parallel to Orestes, namely Telemakhos, whose son, Persepolis, recalls the exploit of the grandfather Odysseus, we cannot rule out the possibility that the name Tisamenos is also a reference to what, after all, became the greatest exploit in the life of his grandfather, Menelaos: vengeance for the abduction of Helen (the Trojan War).[47] Tisamenos is the grandson of Menelaos, who produced no legitimate son. On that account, Tisamenos is closer to his maternal grandfather than an "ordinary" grandson would have been. His biological father Orestes, the cousin of his mother Hermione, put himself at the service of the house of Menelaos so that a legitimate son should be born, a son who could become his grandfather's successor. In this virtually *epíklēros* 'heiress' situation, it seems perfectly normal that Tisamenos' name should refer to the exploit of Menelaos rather than that of Orestes.[48]

Nómios 'pastoral' is the epithet applied to Apollo; *aristaîos* 'the best' applies to Zeus. Apollo is the father, Zeus the grandfather of the son to whom the nymph Cyrene gives birth, who is known as both *Nómios* and *Aristaîos*.[49] The hero Hippotes is described as *alétēs*

44. *Anecdota Graeca (Oxon.)* 2.321.1 Cramer.
45. Sophocles, *Hermione, TGF,* p. 176 Nauck²; Pausanias 2.18.6.
46. See Sulzberger, pp. 438–439, who cites *Anecdota Graeca* 2.868.27–28 Bekker; *Etymologicum Magnum* 760.1; and Eustathius *Commentarii ad Homeri Odysseam* 1479.14 f.
47. The parallelism is explicit in Homer: see *Odyssey* 1.293–302.
48. On the *epíklēros* status, see above, Chapter 1, p. 22 and n. 64.
49. Sulzberger, pp. 439–440, citing Pindar *Pythian* 9.62–65 (together with *Scholia to Pindar* 2.231.10–12 Drachmann). On *nómios* as an epithet for Apollo, see

'wandering', which becomes the name of his son, *Alétēs*.[50] *Halir-rhóthios* "breaker of the waves" is both the epithet applied to Poseidon and the name of one of his sons.[51] Perseus, the *gorgo-phónos* "slayer of the Gorgon", had a daughter named *Gorgo-phónē* and a grandson named *Gorgo-phónos*.[52] The epithet *aníkētos* 'invincible' is attached to Herakles, one of whose sons is named *Aníkētos*.[53] One of the epithets applied to the Sun, *pasi-phaés* "which shines for all", became the name of his daughter *Pasi-pháē*.[54] Pasiphae is also an ancient name of the Moon, one of whose epithets, *phaîdra* 'shining', became the name of Pasiphae's daughter, *Phaîdra*.[55]

These examples show clearly how the Greek practice of name-giving is put in the service of the cause of renown. The child bears a name that is (or could be) an epithet applied to one of his or her parents or grandparents. Usually, the name of the son redounds to the fame of his father. Alongside this method of sounding forth renown through the name given to a son, we find another method of name-giving. It is relatively rare in Homer but became more common in post-Homeric Greece. This was isonymy, *isōnumía*, to borrow Pindar's term, namely the custom of giving the newborn child the same name as a parent or an ancestor.[56] Thus, in the *Iliad* Orsilokhos is the grandson of Ortilokhos; Glaukos is the great-grandson of Glaukos, the son of Sisyphus.[57] In these two cases, the name of the newborn child is really the re-naming of his (great)

Callimachus *Hymn to Apollo* 47; Theocritus 25.21; Apollonius of Rhodes *Argonautica* 4.1218. On *aristaios* as an epithet for Zeus, see Callimachus *Aetia* 3 frag. 75.33 Pfeiffer.

50. Sulzberger, p. 440, citing Tzetzes *Scholia to Lycophron, Alexandra* 1388; *Etymologicum Magnum* 61.50–53 (s.v. *Alétēs*); Pindar *Olympian* 13.15.

51. Sulzberger, citing *Scholia to Pindar* 1.331.23–24 Drachmann (Poseidon *halirrhóthios*); on Halirrhothios, son of Poseidon, see primarily Apollodorus *Library* 3.14.2.

52. Sulzberger, p. 441, citing Nonnos *Dionysiaca* 18.305, 31.12; Apollodorus *Library* 2.4.5, 1.9.5.

53. Sulzberger, citing Tyrtaeus, frag. 11.1 West; Apollodorus *Library* 2.7.7.

54. Sulzberger, p. 444, citing *Orphic Hymns* 8.12, and Apollonius of Rhodes *Argonautica* 3.999.

55. Sulzberger, citing Pausanias 2.26.1; *Odyssey* 11.321; Aeschylus *Agamemnon* 298.

56. Sulzberger, pp. 419–420, calls this custom "*papponymie.*"

57. For Orsilokhos see *Iliad* 5.541–549. See also Pausanias 4.30.2. For Glaukos see *Iliad* 6.152–155, 196–197, 206.

grandfather, so this type of name-giving is not basically different from the type that we examined earlier. To give the child the name of a grandfather is to make it sound forth once again and thereby to increase the *kléos* of the ancestor who is already, or soon may be, dead.

Pindar says: "The bride of Lokros bore in her womb the seed of Zeus, and the hero rejoiced at seeing the son that had been given him, and called him by the selfsame name as his mother's sire. Wondrous he became in beauty of form and in the works of his hands."[58] The king of Locris, Lokros, was *áteknos* or *ápais* "without descendants" according to the scholia.[59] He married the daughter of Opous, the king of Elis, a princess who was already bearing Zeus' child. When the child was born, he named him after his maternal grandfather, namely Opous. The king of Locris thus came to bear the same name as his maternal grandfather, the king of Elis.

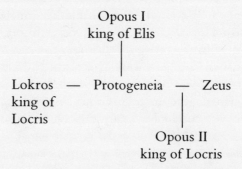

In this way, the king of Locris, through his name, evoked the memory of his maternal grandfather. He was his living 'memorial' (*mnêma*), recalling the name and person of his ancestor, phoneme by phoneme.

This case of *isōnumía* calls to mind another, more famous one, which brings us into the field of historical name-giving. Cleisthenes the Athenian was the isonym of his maternal grandfather, Cleisthenes the Sicyonian.[60] The latter, seeking a husband for his daughter Agariste, allowed the thirteen suitors for his daughter's hand to stay in his house for a year, in order to choose the best one of all.

---

58. Pindar *Olympian* 9.62–66.
59. *Scholia to Pindar* 1.289.25, 290.19 Drachmann.
60. Herodotus 6.126–131.

The name of his daughter, *Ag-arístē* "by far the best", gives us a notion of the value that Cleisthenes placed on, not so much his daughter, but himself. The name could be an epithet for the father. Only the best young man in all Greece could be worthy of that epithet. From the thirteen suitors who had traveled from every corner of Greece in the hope of being chosen by Cleisthenes, only one would be chosen as the very best of the best and, as such, worthy of the tyrant's daughter. The choice eventually fell upon the Alcmaeonid, Megakles of Athens, "and thus," comments Herodotus, "the fame of the *Alkmaionidai* was noised abroad in Greece."[61] The son of Agariste and Megakles was to bear the same name as his maternal grandfather. The name of Cleisthenes the Athenian was at once a *mnêma* and a hope; when spoken aloud, the name evoked the memory of Cleisthenes the Sicyonian, the grandfather whom it was necessary to resemble. And, Herodotus tells us, Cleisthenes "did imitate [*emiméeto*] his maternal grandfather, Cleisthenes" in the realm of political organization.[62] The hope to which the name testified was thus realized.

In the historical period, *isonumía* was common enough. For example, the eldest son of Themistokles was called Neokles, as was his paternal grandfather.[63] But the names of Themistokles' other children are equally instructive: *Arkhé-ptolis* "who governs the city," *Mnēsi-ptoléma* "who remembers the war," *Niko-mákhē* "victorious battle", and *Asía* "Asia" are all names that could well have been epithets for Themistokles himself, charting the various stages of his career, including his exile.[64]

One of Themistokles' rivals, the Corinthian Adeimantos, also had children whose names reflected many elements in the biography of their father. Opposing the "malice" of Herodotus, who gives an unfavorable portrait of Adeimantos, Plutarch cites the fact that the Corinthian general, victor over the Persians at Artemision, called one of his daughters *Nausi-níkē* "naval victory", another *Akrothínion* "the first fruits of war", a third *Alexibía* "who resists force", and his son bore the name *Aristeús* "the bravest one". If Adeimantos had not distinguished himself at Artemision, he would

61. Ibid. 6.131.
62. Ibid. 5.67.
63. Plutarch *Life of Themistokles* 32.1, 1.1.
64. Ibid. 32.1–3.

not have dared to give his children such names, according to Plutarch, who is confident of the message borne by names, as is
Pausanias, who reconstructs Archandros' itinerary on the basis of
the name Metanastes.[65]

Herodotus himself is familiar with the principle of this kind of
name-giving. He recounts that he met the grandson of a Spartan
named Archias; in conformity with the principle of isonumía, this
grandson bore the same name as his grandfather. But that is not all.
The father of Archias the younger was called Samios, a somewhat
surprising name, one would have thought, for the son of a Spartan.
Herodotus tells us that Archias the younger "respected Samians
more than all other foreigners: he said that his father had given him
the name Samios because his father Archias had died so gloriously
in Samos."[66] Far from being an indication of the ethnic origin of its
bearer (as we would probably have assumed were it not for the
information provided by Herodotus), the name Samios here sums
up the most glorious of the exploits of the Spartan Archias, Samios'
father. Each time that Samios is addressed by name, the kléos of his
father resounds.

The point of this digression—which could easily be prolonged—
is to show that the logic behind the name Télé-makhos is by no
means fortuitous, for it conforms to the principle of Greek name-
giving. His name could well have been an epithet for his father,
since we know that Odysseus did indeed go "to fight far away" just
after the birth of his son. In the case of most Greek names we cannot
verify their associations in this way, but in all likelihood many of
them obeyed the same principle. Thus Greeks whose kléos was not
sung by the bards could expect to achieve immortality—through a
theoretically interminable line of descendants, all of whom bore
names that evoked the memory of their ancestors. Génesis 'procreation' was thus a means of transmitting a minimal kléos within a
lineage. Each time that Telemakhos' name was called, the kléos of
Odysseus sounded forth. In the resonance of that kléos, the father
constantly "returned," even after his death. His cunning as a name-
giver consisted in bestowing a name through which he could return.[67] The name of the son was purely and simply renown for his

65. Plutarch, *On the Malice of Herodotus* 871a, criticizing Herodotus 8.5.
66. Herodotus 3.55.
67. I am thinking here of the etymology of *nóos* 'thought' and *nóstos* 'return',

father. And in a similar way the names of Opous the Younger and Cleisthenes of Athens were really renown for their respective maternal grandfathers, whose names were repeated, just as they would be when read from an inscription, each time that their respective grandsons were called by name.

This study of Greek name-giving shows that a name functioned as a memorial to a parent or an ancestor, indeed, as an "inscription," proclaiming the ancestral *kléos,* in particular that of fathers and grandfathers. The newborn child was a blank space "for writing," where the epithet or name of a relative could be engraved. When asked "What is your name?" the child would always produce the same answer; and those who called for him would also always use the same name, as if they were reading it from this child who had become a memorial. Later the dramatic poets were to manipulate that "inscriptional" space for the duration of a performance, wiping out the name of the actor in order to inscribe other (fictitious) names upon his memory.[68] But apart from that kind of manipulation, at which Odysseus already was a past master, a name appears as something stable, unalterable, inscriptional.[69] With its rare stability, a name sounded forth the *kléos* of a father or an ancestor. The one to whom the name referred in this way "survived," just as did the hero whose *kléos* was hymned by the bards. And to a certain degree—unlike the heroes of epic—the name-giver was master of the situation; he had no need of bards or poets to ensure his future *kléos.* Everyone needs a name: the name-giver made the most of that fact and thereby satisfied his "desire for immortality," leaving behind him a name—either an epithet that commemorated him or his own name—borne not by a funerary stone but by a descendant. 'To call' (*kaleîn*) the bearer of that name was thus at the same time "to celebrate in sound" (*kleîn,* from *kléos*) the person commemorated by it.[70]

---

both derived from *néomai* 'to return (home, from darkness)'; see above, Chapter 1, p. 25 and n. 75. Using *nóos,* the name-giver is assured of his *nóstos.*

68. We will return to this subject in Chapter 9 (below, p. 180).

69. Consider, for example, Book 19 of the *Odyssey,* where Odysseus calls himself "Aithon" (verse 183).

70. As I have already pointed out, *kleîn* is sometimes a synonym for *kaleîn* (see above, Chapter 1, p. 18 and n. 48).

CHAPTER 5

The Writer's Daughter:
Kallirhoe and the Thirty Suitors

The relationship between names and commemoration which we studied in Chapter 4 seems fundamental enough to be regarded as one of the models, if not *the* model, through which the Greeks first elaborated the concept of writing. To what use did they put the Phoenician letters if not to that of inscribing a name upon objects more durable than children who might, after all, die before producing children of their own? An archaic inscription we have already cited declares: "This *sêma* will always be called Prokleidas." The name of the deceased is written in the nominative case, not the genitive.[1] The inscribed memorial is not the memorial "of Prokleidas," it simply is "Prokleidas." The memorial will be called Prokleidas; the deceased gives his name to the memorial, which will be his isonym forever. The memorial thus fills the place of an isonymous descendant. The commemorative *sêma* is substituted for the child. The inscriptional space offered by a tombstone has taken the place of the inscriptional space offered by a newborn child. Now a whole new field opens up before the name-giver who has run out of children: the name that he would have liked to leave to a child, so that it should sound forth in the future, may be committed to

---

1. G. Pfohl, *Greek Poems on Stones,* vol. 1, *Epitaphs: From the Seventh to the Fifth Centuries B.C.,* Textus Minores, no. 36 (Leiden, 1967), no. 164: see above, Chapter 2, p. 36 and n. 48. On other nominatives of this type, see the references given above, Chapter 2, p. 31, n. 23.

writing for readers, reading aloud, to make it resound even longer. In this sense, the writing could be said to be the equivalent of a child.

That transference, at any rate, is what seems to be the implication in the story of Aktaion, the royal inventor of the Phoenician letters, as it is told by Skamon of Mytilene (himself the namesake of his maternal grandfather).[2] Let us reread the story, to which we have already referred. "In Book II of the *Inventions*, Skamon says that the letters [*grámmata*] were called 'Phoenician' [*phoinikḗïa*] after Phoinike, the daughter of Aktaion. Aktaion is said to have had no children of the masculine sex, only daughters: Aglauros, Herse, Pandrosos, and Phoinike, who died when still a young girl [*parthénos*]. For that reason Aktaion called the letters 'Phoenician,' wishing to attribute a share of honor [*timḗ*] to his daughter."[3]

For the inventor of what the Greeks called the *phoinikḗïa grámmata* or sometimes simply the *phoinikḗïa,* the adjective *phoinikḗïos,* which reappears in a simplified form in the name of one of his daughters, Phoinike, would thus seem to be a most suitable epithet.[4] But in the story recorded by Skamon, the causal relationship between *phoinikḗïa* and *Phoiníkē* is reversed; according to his account, the *grámmata* received the epithet (or name) *phoinikḗïa* in memory of *Phoiníkē.* The conventional causal relationship has been replaced by another, as if in this particular case it were important to emphasize that the *phoinikḗïa grámmata* came to fill the place left vacant by the deceased princess. The writing is a substitute for *Phoiníkē,* by whose name it is known.

Aktaion was the king of Aktaia (Akte), an ancient name for Attica.[5] As the father of Aglauros, Herse, and Pandrosos, he appears as the double of Kekrops, the autochthonous king of Athens who was the inventor of marriage, funerary practices, and even,

2. *Suda,* s.v. *Hellánikos.*

3. Skamon *FGrH* 476 F 3. According to the scholia to Dionysius Thrax, Andron of Halikarnassos and Menekrates of Olynthus told the same legend (*Anecdota Graeca* 2.782.19–20 Bekker; *FGrH* 10 F 9), which gives us some idea of its diffusion in the fourth century B.C.

4. See Herodotus, 5.58; *Sylloge*[3], no. 38.37–38 Dittenberger.

5. Aktaion (*Aktaíōn*) is called *Aktaîos* in Pausanias 1.2.6. He appears to have been the first king of what later became Attica, but was earlier known as *Aktaía* (or *Aktḗ,* according to Stephanus of Byzantium; see s.v.; see also Euripides *Helen* 1673).

according to one tradition, writing.[6] But that is not what is most important: Aktaion is an Attic version of Kadmos, to the extent that the Boeotian king Kadmos was the inventor (or introducer) of the alphabet and the father of four daughters.[7] In view of the Phoenician genealogy of Kadmos, whose father is sometimes called Phoinix, one of his daughters might well have been called *Phoiníkē* 'Phoenicia',[8] but in fact she had a different name—*Auto-nóē*. Following Gregory Nagy's analysis of *nóos,* this name may be considered as the functional equivalent of *Phoiníkē.*[9] An *autó-noos* Kadmos would be a Kadmos capable "on his own" of "decoding" what he has "encoded" using alphabetical signs. *Auto-nóē* thus becomes a suitable epithet for Kadmos, the inventor of the alphabet. This daughter of Kadmos in her turn had a son who, it would seem from his name, might have been the grandson of Aktaion, the king of Attica, for his name is exactly the same as that king's—Aktaion.[10] These accounts of the invention of writing could thus be said to "inter-think each other."[11]

The purpose of the story of Aktaion and Phoinike seems to be to connect the invention with the origins of Athens, thereby destroying any prior claims by the Boeotians and the Phoenicians in this accomplishment. Nevertheless, it does not efface all signs of the model account; on the contrary, the latter even supports its mean-

6. For Kekrops as the father of Aglauros, Herse, and Pandrosos, see Pausanias 1.2.6; Apollodorus *Library* 3.14.2; as the inventor of marriage, Clearchos in Athenaeus 13.555d (= *FHG* 2.319 Müller); as the inventor of funerary practices, Cicero *Laws* 2.63; as the inventor of writing, Tacitus *Annals* 11.14.

7. On Kadmos, see R. Edwards, *Kadmos the Phoenician* (Amsterdam, 1979). For the historian Ephorus, Kadmos was the inventor [*heurétēs*] of letters (*FGrH* 70 F 105); for Herodotus, the man who introduced them in Greece (5.58). According to Euripides *Bacchae* 1305, Kadmos had no sons (like Aktaion). Elsewhere, he is said to have had one, Polydoros.

8. *Scholia to Apollonius of Rhodes, Argonautica,* 3.1186 (p. 252.12 Wendel). Compare the daughter of Themistokles, called *Asía,* 'Asia' (Plutarch *Life of Themistokles* 32.3) on account of her father's links with Asia Minor.

9. G. Nagy, "*Sêma* and *nóēsis:* Some Illustrations," *Arethusa,* 16 (1983), particularly pp. 38–39. Reworked as chap. 8 in G. Nagy, *Greek Mythology and Poetics* (Ithaca, 1990), pp. 202–222.

10. On this Aktaion see, for example, Ovid *Metamorphoses* 3.138 f.

11. This is, of course, the expression used by C. Lévi-Strauss in *The Raw and the Cooked* (London, 1981), p. 12, where the translation given is "as if the thinking process were taking place in the myths."

ing. For if Aktaion invented writing, it was because he had no male line of descent; unlike Kadmos, he had no grandson, to be named Aktaion. But he found one through this writing that he had fathered. The dead princess merges with the invention that bears her name. She is in a way a dead letter, which may be resuscitated, however, and through which the king will have a male descendant, engendered by the reader who pronounces the king's name aloud. From the mute writing that refers to Aktaion will be born a sonorous *lógos*, "Aktaion" [say it aloud], the namesake of his maternal grandfather. This grandson is the bearer of the re-name and the renown the king thought he would never possess. The king, as father of a daughter named "Phoenician Writing," discovers that she will serve as well as a real princess, provided she meets Reader, who will be son-in-law to Writer, the king. For Reader will be united with Phoenician Writing, whose son will not be the image of Reader, but of his maternal grandfather, Aktaion. Reader thereby finds himself reduced to the instrument of Writer's posterity.

This sonorous "Aktaion," the son of writing, read aloud by the reader, might be compared to an analogous figure evoked by Apollonius of Rhodes in Book 1 of the *Argonautica*. Kyzikos (*Kúzikos*) is the mythical founder of the town of the same name situated on the southern side of the Propontis. The king's wife is *Kleítē* 'Renown' (it is as if *kûdos* 'strength' were united with *kléos* 'renown').[12] She has not yet borne him a child when he is tragically slain by Jason during a nocturnal battle.[13] Childless and despairing of ever conceiving, Kleite kills herself; the tears that nymphs shed over her gather to produce a spring, which is named after the dead queen.[14] The re-name/renown of the hero married to the now unquenchable Renown is ensured by Apollonius' poem, which describes the funeral ceremonies and games held in honor of Kyzikos, on a 'Plain' (*pedíon*) that is probably a metaphorical one: the plain of Poetry,

12. See M. Detienne, *Les Maîtres de vérité dans la Grèce archaïque* (Paris, 1967), p. 20: "Now, in the sphere of combat, the aristocratic warrior appears to be obsessed by two essential values, *kléos* and *kûdos*." The connection between *Kúzikos/kûdos* is all the more striking given that *Kúzikos* was pronounced *Kúdsikos*.

13. Apollonius of Rhodes *Argonautica* 1.1012 f.

14. Ibid. 1063 f. On the nymph-spring-bride association, see Photius, s.v. *númphē* (cited below, p. 96, n. 66); on the spring-*kléos* association, see below, p. 91, n. 45.

"where even now rises this barrow [*tóde sêma*] to be seen by people of a later day."[15] The referent of *tóde sêma* can only be the passage of Kyzikos that is being read. Thus, this passage of Apollonius' poem is Kyzikos' metaphorical *sêma*. Because of this memorial, Kyzikos will finally have a "son" (not by Kleite but by the writing that commemorates him), namely "Kyzikos," his acoustic namesake engendered by the reader.[16] In a sense, the historian Neanthes of the city of Kyzikos seems to confirm that interpretation when he claims, unlike Apollonius, that the hero Kyzikos did have a son, named Kyzikos.[17]

We have already encountered this way of looking at the relations between the Writer, the Writing, and the Reader in Chapter 1, devoted to Phrasikleia. This young Athenian girl, who died unmarried and whose *kléos* is supposed to be revived by a reader reading out the inscription, resembles her compatriot, the princess Phoinike, in a number of respects. Just like the writing of which Aktaion is the father (in the double sense of both inventor and writer), Phrasikleia "shows the *kléos*." Silently, she shows what is destined to be heard by future generations—renown. Without sounding it forth herself, she shows it, indicates it, mimes it. And she will prompt its proclamation. In this way, she merges with her inscription, just as Phoinike merges with the writing invented by her father. These dead daughters both stand for writing. What could be more natural than to think of writing as a girl, if one speaks a language in which writing is a feminine noun, *graphê*?[18] And what could be more natural than to consider *graphè sigôsa* "silent writing" as a daughter, if one is immersed in a culture in which silence is a feminine virtue?[19] The only voice that this writing has is that of the reader. This pattern of thinking also confirms the gender of the

---

15. *Argonautica* 1.1061–1062. This Plain of commemorative poetry should be compared to the "Plain of Aletheia" (Plato *Phaedrus* 248b; Plutarch *On the Disappearance of Oracles*, 422b); see Detienne, *Les Maîtres de vérité dans la Grèce archaïque*, pp. 125–129.

16. See Nagy, "*Sêma and nóēsis*," p. 51n.55.

17. Neanthes of Kyzikos, *FGrH* 84 F 11. Apollonius and Neanthes were contemporaries (third century B.C.).

18. Conversely, it might be thought, what could be more perverse than to consider it as a son? We will return to this point in Chapter 10.

19. Euripides *Iphigenia in Tauris* 762–763. For silence as a feminine virtue, Aristotle *Politics* 1.5.1260a29–31, citing Sophocles *Ajax* 293.

writing. Artemidorus explains that if a Greek dreams of learning the Latin alphabet, it may mean that he will marry a Roman girl; if a Roman dreams of learning the Greek alphabet, that he will marry a Greek girl.[20]

This nubile girl who merges with writing must clearly have had forebears; for the Greeks, the writer was normally seen as a father, which is the case of the very first writers such as Aktaion, the father of Phoinike, and Theuth, whom Plato explicitly calls the "father" of what he writes, and likewise in the case of the writer in general, defined by Plato as the "father" of what he writes.[21] And, in Artemidorus, that is also the case of any man who dreams he is a writer; he will engender children who will be legitimate or bastards, depending on whether he writes from left to right or from right to left.[22] The implication of this father/daughter relationship is that the reader is put in the position of a son-in-law, united with Writing, the daughter of Writer, in order to engender a legitimate, sonorous *lógos*.

Because he is an instrument, the reader does not resemble the man who brings a wife to his own house, there to become the instrument of the posterity of that house.[23] Instead, the reader is a foreigner who, like Odysseus on the island of the Phaeacians or Bellerophon staying with King Iobates in Lycia, is seen as the perfect son-in-law for a king with no male descendants.[24] And the reader is like a man who marries an 'heiress' (*epíklēros*) and who accordingly must efface himself so that his wife can give birth to a son who, for practical purposes, is considered as the son of the maternal grandfather.[25] At any rate, Reader will follow Writing into the house of Writer, where he will put his voice at the service of

20. Artemidorus *The Interpretation of Dreams* 1.53.
21. Plato *Phaedrus* 274e, 275e.
22. Artemidorus *The Interpretation of Dreams* 3.25. Cf. *Greek Anthology*, 9.489: "Having made love, the daughter [*thugátēr*] of the writing master [*grammatikoû*] gave birth to a child who was male, female, and neuter," a riddle for which I would propose the following solution: *Phthóngos, Phthongē̂,* and *Phthégma,* all meaning 'Voice.' See also Artemidorus ibid. 2.49.
23. See, for example, J.-P. Vernant, *Myth and Thought among the Greeks* (London, 1983), p. 132n.23.
24. See Vernant, *Myth and Society in Ancient Greece* (New York, 1988), pp. 71, 72n.58.
25. See above, Chapter 1, p. 20 and n. 56; Chapter 1, p. 22 and n. 64.

the latter's posterity. For what Writing lacks is, precisely, a voice, so he will read her aloud. In this connection it is worth remembering that one of the verbs meaning 'to read', *entunkhánein,* also means "to have sexual relations with".[26] Solon's laws stipulated that a man who took an *epíklēros* girl as a wife should "have sexual relations with her" (*entunkhánein têi epiklḗrōi*) at least three times a month.[27]

The union between Writing and Reader will result in a son, a sonorous *lógos,* in whom the features of the grandfather will be recognizable. If Cleisthenes is the re-name/renown of a flesh and blood maternal grandfather, so too is the "Aktaion" pronounced aloud by Reader. From the point of view of *kléos,* a "Cleisthenes" is as good as an "Aktaion." The difference between them is that the former was produced by a woman, Agariste, the latter by Phoenician writing, which is the double of a princess named Phoinike. In the first case, the re-name/renown is initiated by the man who names his grandson after himself, in the second by the reader who, by coming into contact with the writing, engenders a sonorous *lógos.*

Let us now move on to a story that also seems to present this homology between the daughter of a father and the writing that commemorates that father. It is a Boeotian story, apparently rooted in local traditions, the most complete version of which is given by Plutarch in his *Love Stories*—the story of Phokos and Kallirhoe. The text runs as follows:

> Phokos was by birth a Boeotian, for he was from the town of Glisas, and he was the father of Kallirhoe, who excelled in beauty and modesty. She was wooed by thirty young men, the most highly esteemed in Boeotia; but Phokos found one reason after another for putting off her marriage, for he was afraid that violence would be done to him. At last, however, he yielded to their demands, but asked to leave the choice to the Pythian oracle. The suitors were incensed by the proposal, rushed upon Phokos and killed him. In the confusion the maiden got away and fled through the country [*khóra*], but the young men pursued her. She came upon some farmers making a threshing floor and found safety with them, for the farmers

26. P. Chantraine, "Les Verbes grecs signifiant 'lire'," in *Mélanges Grégoire,* 2 (Brussels, 1950), pp. 122–126.
27. Plutarch *Life of Solon* 20.4.

hid her in the grain, and so her pursuers passed by. But she waited in safety until the festival of the Panboeotia, when she went to Koroneia, took her seat on the altar of Athena Itonia, and told of the lawless acts of the suitors, giving the name and birthplace of each. So the Boeotians pitied the maid and were angry with the young men. When they learned of this they fled for refuge to Orchomenos, and when the Orchomenians refused to receive them, they forced their way into Hippotai, a village lying on the slope of Mount Helikon, between Thebes and Koroneia. There they were received. Then the Thebans sent and demanded the slayers of Phokos, and when the people of Hippotai refused to deliver them, the Thebans, along with the rest of the Boeotians, took the field under the command of Phoïdos, who at that time administered the government of Thebes. They besieged the village, which was well fortified, and when they had overcome the inhabitants by thirst, they took the murderers and stoned them to death and made slaves of the villagers; then they pulled down the walls and the houses and divided the land between the people of Thebes and Koroneia. It is said that in the night before the capture of Hippotai, there was heard many times from Helikon a voice of someone saying "I am here," and that the thirty suitors recognized the voice as that of Phokos. It is said also that on the day when they were stoned to death, the old man's monument [*mnêma*] at Glisas ran with saffron, and that as Phoïdos, the ruler and general of the Thebans, was returning from the battle, he received the news of the birth of a daughter and, thinking it a good omen, he named her Nikostrate.[28]

Let us begin with the myth's ending, its *télos* or "head," as Plato would say.[29] A daughter is born to a victorious general, a daughter who, on account of her father's exploit, is named *Nikostrátē*, literally "victorious army".[30] The father's renown, and his essential epithet,

28. Plutarch *Love Stories* 774d–775b (translation here based on Fowler). For the Greek text, see Appendix at the end of this chapter. In tackling the analysis of this passage, I was aided by the observations of Pierre Ellinger who, in his *Thèse d'Etat* (forthcoming), studies the same story from the point of view of a "war of attrition."

29. On the metaphor of the "head" of the myth, see L. Brisson, *Platon, les mots et les mythes* (Paris 1982), pp. 72–75 (*Gorgias* 505d; *Timaeus* 69b; *Laws* 6.752a; see also *Philebus* 66d). Here, the "head" of the myth means its ending, or its 'end' (*télos*).

30. Here is an analogous case: after his return from Troy, Menelaos had a son whom he named *Nikó-stratos* (*Scholia to Sophocles, Electra* 539; Hesiod frag. 175.2 Merkelbach-West).

might well be thus condensed. The daughter's name certainly commemorates one of her father's important exploits; it is the signifier
of what is signified, namely the exploit. The choice of the name and
the reasons for it are made perfectly explicit here, and the bestowing
of the name Nikostrate upon the general's daughter clearly demonstrates a fundamental law of Greek name-giving. Placed as it is, at
the "head" of the account (to adopt a Greek point of view), this
conclusion prompts us to reflect on the other names that appear in
the story, in particular that of the other 'significant' (sēmaínousa)
daughter, namely Kalli-rhóē, "who flows beautifully".[31] Is it possible that the law that governed the choice of the name Nikostrate
also applies for the name Kallirhoe? I believe it does. Of course, this
Kallirhoe is not the Oceanid mentioned in Chapter 4, nor is she one
of the Kallirhoes who are daughters of river gods,[32] nor yet the
daughter of Hermokrates who vanquished the Athenians in Sicily
(Like Phoïdos, Hermokrates was a general.).[33] This Kallirhoe is the
daughter of a certain Phokos about whom not much is known. For
this Phokos is not the Phokos of Aegina, the uncle of Achilles, nor is
he the eponymous ancestor of the Phocidians. He is simply a Boeotian and the father of an extremely beautiful girl. But, on looking
into the text more closely, we see that Phokos does have one
noteworthy characteristic: he is a man with a remarkable gift of
words. He speaks. He makes his voice heard, even after death. And
for the Greeks, ever since Homer and Hesiod, a voice was envi-
sioned as something that "flowed."[34] The epithet kallírhoos could
thus be suitable for (the voice of) someone who spoke admirably.
Pindar actually uses that adjective to qualify the voice.[35]

Now, if Phokos is kallírhoos in that sense (a man with a voice that
"flows beautifully") and if Kallirhoe bears a name that recalls that
idea, Phokos' mnêma 'memorial' also refers to it in an explicit fash-

31. Plutarch Love Stories 774 f.
32. See M. Sulzberger, "Ὄνομα ἐπώνυμον. Les noms propres chez Homère et
dans la mythologie grecque," Revue des études grecques, 39 (1926), p. 443.
33. The daughter of Hermokrates is the heroine of the novel Khaireas and
Kallirhoe (by Chariton of Aphrodisias).
34. Iliad 1.249; Hesiod Theogony 39, 84, 97.
35. Pindar Olympian 6.83. For the Theban poet, speech is frequently "liquid":
Olympian 6.91, 7.1–10, 10.10 and 98–99; Pythian 4.299, 5.96–101, 8.57, 9.103–104,
10.56; Nemean 3.6–7 and 76–79, 4.4–5, 7.12 and 62–63; Isthmian 6.1–9 and 21, 7.19,
8.64.

ion. As if in an act of mimesis, it begins to "run with saffron" (*krókōi rheûsai*), and "to run with saffron" is assuredly "to flow beautifully". The documentation on saffron is vast.[36] Let us for the moment limit ourselves to two observations. At first sight, the presence of saffron seems to symbolize the triumph of the old man over the suitors, as a citation from Plutarch himself indicates. He tells us that in Artemision, the marble steles commemorating the victory over the Persians—one of which bore an inscription to that effect—took on "the color and smell of saffron" (*khróan kaì osmèn krokízousan*) when they were rubbed by hand.[37] Accordingly, in the story with which we are concerned, the saffron might represent a spectacular manifestation of the sentiments of the deceased. That connotation is not to be dismissed. But there is more to it, of even greater importance from our point of view. In one of his articles, Louis Robert cites a papyrus from Leiden which deals with matters of chemistry and which explains that the saffron of Cilicia was used in the gilding of inscriptions on marble. The saffron was used to produce golden letters without having recourse to real gold.[38] In other words, the saffron on Phokos' memorial is the gilding on its inscription. In this narrative, the verb *gráphein* and its derivatives are strangely absent, but the writing nevertheless shines forth in gilded splendor.[39]

The *krókos* 'saffron', which Sophocles qualifies with *khrusaugés* "with rays of gold",[40] is thus used to paint the letters incised in the marble, to make them easier to read, no doubt, but also to render them symbolically precious.[41] In this connection, it is worth recall-

36. See primarily I. Chirassi, *Elementi di culture precereali nei miti e riti greci* (Rome, 1968), in particular pp. 124–135.

37. Plutarch *Life of Themistokles* 8.4.

38. L. Robert, "Recherches épigraphiques," *Revue des études anciennes*, 62 (1960), p. 334n.3. The subject is the Leiden chemical papyrus, 10.73.

39. Only to the extent that *kléos* can be committed to writing does the story about Phokos and Kallirhoe set out an inscriptional situation, for, as we shall see, it is above all a story about *kléos*. There is nothing surprising about this secondary nature of the written word. For example, for Plato writing has no status at all independent of oral speech; it is simply a *lógos* "committed to writing" (*gegramménos*) (see below, p. 213).

40. Sophocles *Oedipus at Colonus* 685. See *Greek Anthology*, 12.256, *krusanthès krókos* "saffron with flowers of gold."

41. That is what follows from a comparison between the inscription *IG* I^2.761 with Thucydides 6.54.6. See W. Larfeld, *Griechische Epigraphik* (Handbuch der klassischen Altertumswissenschaft, 1:5), 3d ed. (Munich, 1914), p. 131n.1.

ing Pindar's seventh *Olympian,* celebrating Diagoras of Rhodes. According to the historian Gorgo, the poem was inscribed in letters of gold in the temple of Athena at Lindos, possibly within the lifetime of the poet.[42] Now, if "saffron flows" on Phokos' memorial, it means that somehow the inscription was gilded on the day that the suitors were stoned to death. Admittedly, Plutarch's account conveys the impression that the gilding was a supernatural effect, produced without the intervention of any human hand. But one need not necessarily understand it in this way. Plutarch's expression, primarily intended to establish the connection (which is of capital importance in the economy of the narrative) between the name of the girl (*Kalli-rhóē*) and the memorial stone that begins to "flow with saffron" (*krókōi rheûsai*), may equally be understood as an ellipse in which the gilder's handiwork is simply taken for granted.[43]

All this takes place at a precise geographical spot—Glisas, a little northeast of Thebes. But the manuscripts give a different name: *Kleísas.* Glisas is simply a textual conjecture, reasonable enough in itself. If the emendation of our text has restored Plutarch's own reading, a very interesting *lapsus* has occurred at some point in the transmission of the text (and at a very early date, to judge by the unanimity of the manuscripts on this point). I believe that Kleisas is the correct reading, that of the archetypal text, and that Kleisas is not necessarily the name of an historical place any more than is the "town" Hippotai, of which no trace can be found, even though Plutarch gives precise indications as to its location.[44] Phokos' memorial was, in all probability, inscribed with letters of gold at a spot

---

42. Gorgo, *FGrH* 515 F 18 (= *Scholia to Pindar* 1.195.13–14 Drachmann). The Greeks described such an operation as *khrusographía* 'chrysography'.

43. The Loeb translation ("the old man's monument . . . ran with saffron") gives the impression that the stone exuded saffron, but the Greek simply says that "saffron ran on the old man's monument." For the expression *mnêma krókōi rheûsai* see *Iliad* 4.451 (= 8.65), *rhée d'haímati gaîa:* the earth does not exude blood, but blood "runs on the earth" as a result of wounds having been sustained (wounds that the text does not mention but implies in describing a battle in general terms).

44. *Kleí-sas* could have been formed on the model of *Glí-sas,* which would be possible to recognize without feeling the necessity to correct the text. On Hippotai, see P. Roesch, *Thespies et la confédération béotienne* (Paris, 1965), p. 53n.1 (cited by the Collection des Universités de France edition, p. 160).

known as Kleos-town, the town of sonorous renown, particularly the posthumous variety.[45]

In this same town the story begins. We are presented with a father and his daughter, who is seemingly a potential *epíklēros* 'heiress', but whose hand in marriage is sought by thirty suitors. A Greek proverb refers to this demand in marriage: *Phókou éranos* "the *éranos* of Phokos"; the proverb applies to "those who give banquets that lead to their own destruction." The explanation continues: "For once there was a certain Phokos who had a nubile daughter [*epígamon*] and, as she had many suitors, he gave feasts-of-which-the-cost-was-shared [*eránous*]. Entertaining [*hestiôn*] the suitors in this fashion, he tried to put off [*anebálleto*] the wedding. Filled with anger, the suitors killed Phokos during a banquet [*sumposíōi*]."[46]

Another father of a "significant" daughter, namely Oinomaos, also sought to defer his separation from the one who bore his epithet as her own name. This king of Pisa likewise tried to "defer the wedding" (*anabállesthai gámon*); he did not want his daughter to be married.[47] He therefore set a test for the suitors to accomplish; whoever was successful would win his daughter's hand. The test was a horse race in which the suitor had to seize the daughter from the father and carry her off in a chariot, pursued by the father, who would endeavor to catch and slay him. It was a daunting test, for Oinomaos was so skilled in 'horsemanship' that his daughter was called *Hippo-dámeia*. The daughter's name was the epithet attached to her father. To win this daughter as a wife, a suitor had to prove himself better in, precisely, "horsemanship." Thanks to a cunning trick, Pelops, the thirteenth and last of all the suitors, succeeded where those who had gone before had failed.[48]

45. The reading *Kleísas* clearly affects the interpretation I gave above of the name *Kalli-rhóē*, for what "flows beautifully" at a spot called Kleos-town is, of course, *kléos*, one of whose epithets is, precisely, *aénaon* "which always flows, never dries up, is unquenchable", making *kléos* a spring or a flow of water (Simonides frag. 26.9 Page; Heraclitus frag. B 29 Diels-Kranz). See above, p. 83 and n. 14.

46. *Corpus Paroemiographorum Graecorum*, 1:172 Leutsch-Schneidewin.

47. Pindar *Olympian* 1.80; see Plutarch *Love Stories* 774e: *anabolàs poieîsthai* (on the subject of Phokos).

48. The number of suitors killed by Oinomaos was twelve, according to Tzetzes *Scholia to Lycophron, Alexandra* 156, and also according to the *Scholia to Euripides, Orestes* 990 (thirteen according to Pindar *Olympian* 1.79; see *Scholia to*

Phokos' daughter's name is not Hippodameia; it is Kallirhoe. But her father seems every bit as attached to her as the king of Pisa was to the princess Hippodameia. The signified does not wish to be separated from the signifier. Phokos defers the wedding of his daughter, as if not one of the suitors could lay claim to the quality or competence to which the name of the daughter refers. He puts off the marriage in order to avoid his own death (which would leave his daughter alone with her beauty and her *sōphrosúnē*[49])—and also, no doubt, to make the most of the extended feasting for which the suitors themselves help to pay. For this is an *éranos* 'feast-of-which-the-cost-was-shared', unlike the feasting in Sicyon, where Cleisthenes wished to choose a son-in-law worthy of his daughter *Ag-arístē*, after treating all the suitors to his own hospitality over the period of a year. In Sicyon, even the losers were offered generous compensation. In contrast, in Kleisas there is no *gámos*, only a series of *éranoi*.[50] The feast offered by Phokos is a feast for which the guests themselves pay. In a place called Kleisas, Kleos-town, this clearly takes on a particular significance: the *kléos* is a feast paid for by those who make it sound forth instead of by the one who is the subject of that *kléos*. Similarly, I would suggest, the reading of something written is a feast at the expense of the reader. The suitors cannot tolerate the situation: tension mounts to the point of exploding into murderous violence. Phokos is killed during a banquet.

In Plutarch, who mentions no *éranoi*, the reason for murder is explained differently: it is a *lógos* or, to be more precise, the "proposition" put forward by Phokos, who suggests leaving the choice of a husband to the Pythian god.[51] With that *lógos*, the man whose voice "flows beautifully" sings his own death-warrant: he is murdered by the suitors, as if the god—the sonorous god Apollo, the guarantor of *kléos*—wished to indicate the impossibility of any such

---

Pindar 1.45.7–46.6 Drachmann). We may recall that Agariste's suitors also numbered thirteen (Herodotus 6.127).

49. Plutarch *Love Stories* 774d ("of singular beauty and virtue [*sōphrosúnē*]"). Note that the adjective *sōphrōn* is formed from *sôs* 'intact' and *phrḗn* 'thought, attention' (on *phrḗn*, see Chapter 1, nn. 25, 34, 40, and 44).

50. Herodotus 6.130, and see above, pp. 76–77. On the *gámos*/*éranos* opposition, see *Odyssey* 1.226, and Aristotle *Nicomachean Ethics* 4.2.20.1123a23.

51. Plutarch *Love Stories* 774e.

5. The Writer's Daughter   93

choice.[52] In Kleos-town, it is not possible to convert the reading of
the memorial called Kallirhoe into a personal asset. And as if to
underline that impossibility, the daughter—now since her father's
death fully *epíklēros* and accordingly more bound than ever to the
center, or hearth, of the house—chooses a dramatically centrifugal
course, fleeing the house like a signifier finally freed from what it
used to signify.[53]

Is it really possible for one individual to be the *mnêma* of another?
I claimed in Chapter 4 that it is, but this is perhaps the point at
which to clarify the idea, using in the first instance a passage from
Sophocles' *Antigone*. After the death of Antigone, Haimon has
fallen upon his sword. Kreon enters, carrying his son's corpse or, as
the chorus puts it, "bearing in his arms an inscribed *mnêma,* if one
may put it thus: namely, the disaster for which he alone is responsible."[54] The reason for the chorus's adding "if one may put it thus"
(*ei thémis epeîn*) is probably that the veritable puzzle that he presents
to the audience is considered somewhat tasteless, given the context.
For Kreon's son is compared to a funerary stele, a 'signifying'
(*epísēmon*) memorial, that is to say, one that bears an inscription[55]—
this being nothing less than the wound that the young prince has
inflicted upon himself with his own sword. As we have seen,
gráphein may indeed mean 'to wound, to scratch';[56] consequently,
the blood from the wound, the *haîma,* is an inscription that marks
the end of not only Haimon, the "Bloody One," but Kreon's entire
lineage. Jean-Pierre Vernant's study on the body double or *kolossós*
has apprised us of the analogy that Greek thought perceived between the still corpse and the tombstone.[57] Here the corpse and the

52. See above, Chapter 3, p. 61 and n. 54; and below, p. 106.
53. See above, pp. 19–20, 22.
54. Sophocles *Antigone* 1258–1260.
55. On *epísēmos* in the sense of "bearing an inscription," see Herodotus 1.51.
56. *Iliad* 17.599.
57. J.-P. Vernant, *Myth and Thought,* pp. 305–321 "The Representation of the
Invisible and the Psychological Category of the Double: The Colossos." Two other
references should be added: Pfohl, no. 4, where the marble monument takes the
place of the deceased woman, *antì gunaikòs . . . Paríou líthou . . . mnēmósunon;*
Antoninus Liberalis 33.3–4, where a stone takes the place of Alkmene in her coffin
(see Plutarch *Life of Romulus* 28.7, together with the note by R. Flacelière in the
Collection des Universités de France edition).

stele merge once again, and, furthermore, they bear an "inscription" whose meaning can be only "I am the *mnêma* of the Bloody One." Since the father is himself responsible for the bloody death of his son, the name Haimon could truly now (even if not hitherto) be the most suitable of epithets for his father, just as Phokos' posthumous manifestations eventually make Kallirhoe the most suitable of epithets for *her* father.

In *Antigone,* Haimon dies and Kreon survives, but the reverse seems to happen in Kleisas, where Phokos dies, leaving behind a living daughter, the daughter whose name commemorates the particular skill of her father. A clear contrast seems to exist between Haimon, the stiff, dead memorial, and Kallirhoe, so agile and full of life; it likewise exists between Kreon, who survives, and Phokos, who dies. In Thebes, the child dies before his father; in Kleisas, the father dies before his child. So it is only in Kleisas that commemoration through a name can function normally; in Thebes, the son's name in a sense rebounds against his father. In these circumstances, speaking of Kallirhoe as the living *mnêma* of her father might seem imprudent.

Yet there are a number of reasons why we ought to grant full weight to the homology between the daughter sought in marriage and the *mnêma;* the semantic link between *Kalli-rhóē* on the one hand and the expression *krókōi rheûsai* on the other is but one of them. The Greek word for "suitor" is *mnēstḗr,* a noun derived from the verb *mnáomai.*[58] Now, *mnēstḗr* means not only "suitor" but also, in conformity with the verb from which it is derived, "one who must remember, who does remember."[59] Hesychius glosses the plural of *mnēstêres* as follows: "those who intend to marry someone. Also those who remember [*hoi memnēménoi*]."[60] In the sense of "who must remember," *mnēstḗr* is the epithet Pindar attaches to *nómos*—the musical 'nome'—and it accordingly denotes an agent that is eminently sonorous. The *mnēstḗr* may behave as a reader who

58. P. Chantraine, *Dictionnaire étymologique de la langue grecque* (Paris, 1968–1980), pp. 702–703.

59. See E. Benveniste, *Noms d'agent et noms d'action en indo-européen* (Paris, 1948), p. 47.

60. Hesychius, s.v. *mnēstêres.*

"recalls" by reading aloud.[61] In contrast, the *mnêma* is mute, a mute "reminder," to which reading may supply sound. And, in contrast to the verb *mnáomai* "to ask in marriage, to remember" from which it is derived, the word *mnêma* is not attested in senses other than those relating to commemoration ('memorial', "funerary monument").

Linked with an accusative, *mnáomai* means "to ask in marriage"; with a genitive, it means 'to remember'.[62] Analogously, *ktáomai* with an accusative means 'to acquire'. Now, "what has been acquired" is called *ktêma*. Thus, in formal terms, the equation

$$ktáomai : ktêma :: mnáomai : mnêma$$

suggests as a meaning for *mnêma* "(daughter) sought in marriage." Even if, as the dictionary indicates, the Greek language does not make use of that possibility, it may clearly afford a chance for wordplay that can be understood by all. The context of the narrative we are considering suggests that this is how it is being used here. For the saffron that flows on the *mnêma* on the day that the scheming *mnēstêres* are stoned to death is bound to reactivate the meaning of the name *Kalli-rhóē,* suggesting that the girl is, in a sense, identical to the funerary monument. The *mnêma* that commemorates the man whose voice "flowed beautifully" thus merges with the daughter sought in marriage. In the last analysis, it is on account of her that Phokos pronounces his fatal *lógos:* like the *mnêma,* she signifies his death.

Now, in a way, the marriage the father deferred finally does take place—when the *mnêma,* the "daughter-sought-in-marriage", takes on the color of saffron. That is because it so happens that saffron is associated with marriage: Hymen himself is clad in a saffron-colored cloak.[63] The nubile daughter is thus finally married (we will return to the modalities of that marriage in a moment). But the

61. Pindar *Pythian* 12.24.

62. See E. Benveniste, "Formes et sens de μνάομαι," in *Festschrift Debrunner* (Berne, 1954), pp. 13–18, which demonstrates the unity of the verb *mnáomai* (against those who have postulated the existence of two separate verbs).

63. Ovid *Metamorphoses* 10.1; see also *Iliad* 14.348.

symbolism of the *krókos* 'saffron' is not exhausted yet. The saffron that gilds the letters of the *mnêma* is also the blood of a young hero called *Krókos* who was killed by a discus thrown by Hermes. After his death, he underwent a metamorphosis that turned him into the flower that bears his name—a flower that constitutes a constantly renewable *mnêma* to the young man.[64] As we have seen, the "blood of Krokos" is used for a precise technical purpose: it is used in writing, just as is the blood of Haimon, as represented by Sophocles. The *krókos* has one peculiar property. Pliny the Elder tells us: "The root is fleshy and longer-lived than that of any other plant. Saffron likes to be trodden on and trampled under foot; destroying it makes it grow better. For this reason, it is most luxuriant near footpaths and fountains."[65] To grow better, the *krókos* must die (the verb used by Pliny is *perire*). The naturalist's remarks about saffron, which flourishes close to springs (inevitably, one thinks at this point of *Kalli-rhóē*[66]) are particularly relevant to Phokos of Kleisas, whose renown can only be won at the cost of his life: he must die if his *mnêma* is to triumph.

Behind the story of Krokos' death lies another, better known and much older—the story of Hyakinthos, who was accidentally killed by Apollo when the god's discus struck the young man's temple.[67] Hyakinthos was immediately transformed into a flower. We know that the Greeks saw this flower as a representation of the letters AI AI, a transcription of the grief of Apollo.[68] (After the death of Ajax, this same flower sprang up at Salamis, but in relation to this hero those letters take on a different meaning.) Apollo's grief is no doubt the grief of a pederast, for in Greek pharmacopoeia the hyacinth was used to arrest the development of puberty: to arrest the de-

64. Galen *Medicorum Graecorum Fragmenta* 13.269 Kühn.

65. Pliny *Natural History* 21.18; see Theophrastus *History of Plants* 6.6.10.

66. Particularly in view of a gloss by Photius, s.v. *númphē: pēgḗ.kaì hē neógamos gunḗ* "nymph: spring; also applied to bride."

67. See as early as Hesiod frag. 171 Merkelbach-West; Euripides *Helen* 1471–1473; Philostratus *Imagines* 1.24.

68. Ovid *Metamorphoses* 10.215. For other references, see the commentary to Books 10 and 11 of Ovid's *Metamorphoses* by F. Bömer (Heidelberg, 1980), pp. 70–72. *AI AI* is not Latin but Greek; the same letters are to be found in the first line of the Phrasikleia epigram (see above, p. 17): *keklḗsomAI AIeí,* a cacophony that lends it a plaintive note.

velopment of hair growth in the *erómenos* 'beloved' was the dream of the *erastés* 'lover'.[69] The dead Hyakinthos is, as it were, fixed in a perfect state, as impervious to change as the writing in his flower. For the memory of Hyakinthos blooms anew every spring, when the hyacinth opens up and reveals its inscription. Quite literally— and that is certainly the right word to use here—the *kléos* of Hyakinthos thus becomes 'unwilting' (*áphthiton*), for it lives again, thanks to the flower that bears his name and to an inscription destined to be read time and again for evermore.

Krokos and Hyakinthos, the beardless *erómenoi,* are fixed by death in a state of perfection related to writing. Crushed, the former will flourish all the better, while the latter will enjoy a constantly renewed posterity in that everyone will join in Apollo's lament by reading aloud the letters inscribed and reinscribed within this flower that grows in every corner of Greece. In the Greek tradition, these two heroes accidentally killed by the discus are flanked by others, chief among them Phokos of Aegina, who was slain either deliberately or accidentally by his brother, Peleus.[70] Upon the tomb of this Phokos, whose name rings so familiar to us, there was placed a funerary *mnêma,* the stone discus hurled by Peleus and stained with his brother's blood.[71] For this Phokos, as for his homonym in Kleisas, the *mnêma* truly is the sign of death—in both senses of the expression. The *mnêma* of the former is the fatal discus, now a funerary monument (this kind of funerary discus, bearing an inscription, is archaeologically attested[72]); the *mnêma* of the latter is the "daughter-sought-in-marriage," the reason for his murder.

In the case of the Phokos from Kleisas, it is not as an *erómenos* that he has been fixed forever by death in a state impervious to change, but as the father of an inscribed *mnêma,* in other words as a writer. It is as if Apollo, by failing to come to the aid of the man who asked

69. Dioscorides 4.62; Pliny *Natural History* 21.170. For the pederast, the first beard of his beloved signals the end of their loves: see Theognis 1327–1328, and cf. M. Foucault, *The Use of Pleasure* (New York, 1985), pp. 199–201. The problem of the boy's hirsuteness is a major theme in Book 12 of the *Greek Anthology,* nos. 25– 27, 31, 35, 36, 39.

70. Pausanias 2.26.9; Diodorus Siculus 4.72.6.

71. Pausanias ibid.

72. Pfohl, nos. 40 and 49 (= Peek, nos. 58 and 57): marble discuses.

him for help, was trying to say: if one is to become a writer in the full sense, one cannot keep one's writing at home; to be worthy of commemorative writing, one must first die. For, like the *krókos,* which flourishes anew when crushed, the father of the *mnêma* must die in order for his inscription to flow triumphantly with saffron— for all to behold. To be sure of a posterity at Kleos-town, the last thing one should do is choose a son-in-law from among the possible suitors. One has to die on account of one's *mnêma,* be separated from it, die of it, that is to say, die on account of a "daughter-sought-in-marriage," so that this daughter can become fully inscriptional. She will be present where the writer will be absent, and present for a theoretically infinite number of readers.

Kallirhoe does flee the paternal home. The *mnêma* escapes. In her flight, the daughter "comes upon" some peasants. The verb used here is *entunkhánein,* meaning 'to meet' but also, as I mentioned earlier, "to have sexual relations (as with an *epíklēros* [heiress] wife)" or "to read." Normally, according to Solon's law, recorded by Plutarch himself, the husband of an *epíklēros* wife was expected to 'have sexual relations' (*entunkhánein*) with her at least three times a month. But Kallirhoe is not a wife; by fleeing the paternal home, she even rejects her *epíklēros* status. She does not remain on the inherited property, the *klêros.* It is as if the verb used in the episode describing her flight was designed to lend discreet emphasis to her negation of that status. With her thirty vengeful suitors in pursuit, the "daughter-sought-in-marriage" must not let anybody *entunkhánei.* Instead, it is Kallirhoe herself who *entunkhánei.* Furthermore, I would add that neither is the *mnêma* subject to *entunkhánein,* in the sense of "read," for the moment of maximum publicity has not yet arrived.

All that Kallirhoe needs for the moment is the protection that the threshing floor affords her: her pursuers will charge past it. At first sight, the impression is that she escapes them because, hidden on the threshing floor, she is invisible to them. But, as has been pointed out,[73] the proverb "you are hiding in the threshing floor" (*en hálōi krúptēi*) means "you are hiding in a place where it is impossible to

---

73. See the Collection des Universités de France edition, p. 160n.5.

hide."[74] In other words, Kallirhoe is not hiding at all when she "hides in the threshing floor." In the full public view of the threshing floor, nothing can be hidden. Thanks to the reference to that proverb, we know that the text manages to indicate the opposite of what it seems to be saying. The daughter is in fact protected by the public nature, the openness of the threshing floor.

But as if to provide a somewhat clumsy gloss on this reference to the proverb, Plutarch's text adds a "realistic" detail: the peasants do hide the girl "in the grain" (*en tôi sítōi*).[75] Not only is she "hidden" in the threshing floor (that is to say, protected by its openness), but she is also literally buried "in the grain." We must bear in mind both these aspects of the episode in the threshing floor, without emphasizing either at the expense of the other. I have already commented on the first aspect. Let us now consider the second, which, at a superficial level only, seems to contradict the first.

In a culture in which marriage is perceived as an agricultural activity, as the ploughing of a furrow and the sowing of seed, the association of a nubile girl with wheat grain is bound to be heavily charged. The traditional formula pronounced by the father of the future bride at a betrothal ceremony ran, "I now betroth you to my daughter, young man, with a view to a ploughing (*ep' arótōi*) for legitimate children."[76] The son-in-law is the one who "ploughs" and "sows" a piece of "land"; the seeds that he sows will lead to the birth of legitimate children.[77] Thanks to those seeds, regeneration is assured. The father of an *epíklēros* 'heiress' daughter thus resembles an ear of wheat without grain, cut from its roots in the course of the harvest. He lacks the grain necessary for the regeneration of his house. He has no son. All that he leaves behind him is a piece of "land."

74. *Corpus Paroemiographorum Graecorum* 1:74–75, 360, 2:69, 110, 163, 406 Leutsch-Schneidewin.

75. Plutarch *Love Stories* 774e.

76. Menander *Dyskolos* 842–843 (for other references, see the Collection des Universités de France edition). Cf. Artemidorus *The Interpretation of Dreams* 1.51, 2.24. See Vernant, *Myth and Thought*, pp. 139–140.

77. "For the ploughed earth is none other than the woman," Artemidorus writes (ibid. 1.51), and A. J. Festugière comments that this is an "assimilation that is almost as ancient as the Greek language." See Liddell-Scott-Jones, s.v. *ároura*, 1.5.

While still intact, the grains of wheat represent the possibility of regeneration. But once milled, they represent death. Kallirhoe is not hidden in a heap of flour, but in a pile of unmilled grain. Now, the Greek word for 'flour' is *áleuron,* the word for 'to mill', *kataléō.* In view of the fact that 'to stone' is *kataleúō* and that the fate of Kallirhoe's suitors was, precisely, to be stoned,[78] it seems justifiable to regard the unmilled grains of wheat in which Kallirhoe is buried as standing in opposition to the suitors who are stoned to death. The latter are crushed by stones, the wheat grains are not.

Let us try to substantiate this connection between the unmilled wheat and the crushed suitors. In Book 20 of the *Odyssey,* Odysseus asks Zeus to give him two signs to show that he will be successful in exacting vengeance. Zeus obliges, producing first a flash of lightning. The second favorable sign comes when one of the *aletrídes* "female servants who grind the grain of wheat" stops her milling and observes out loud that she, for her part, hopes for the destruction of the suitors. Homer continues: "So she spoke, and . . . Odysseus was glad at the word of omen and at the thunder of Zeus, for he knew that he would be avenged."[79] It is no mere accident that it is a female servant who grinds the grains of wheat, an *aletrís* in the process of milling, who predicts to Odysseus that he will crush the suitors, thereby confirming the earlier sign vouchsafed by Zeus who, in Lycophron, is described as *Muleús* "of the mill".[80] The fact is that *áleuron* 'flour' is glossed by Hesychius with the word *táphos* 'tomb' (and a scholion to the *Iliad* glosses the word *táphos* with *phónos* 'murder').[81] In comedy, "the daughter [*kórē*] of Demeter"— the very same daughter who becomes the wife of Hades—means, precisely, 'flour'.[82]

In the *Odyssey,* wheat is *muléphatos* 'murdered by the millstone', as Plutarch explains.[83] The epitaph of a miller refers to the millstone as Demeter's *puréphatos* servant (the servant who "murders the

78. Plutarch *Love Stories* 775e: *katéleusan.*

79. *Odyssey* 20.100–121.

80. Lycophron *Alexandra* 435.

81. Hesychius, s.v. *áleuron: táphos. Kúprioi. Scholia T to the Iliad* 23.29: *Kúprioi dè táphon tòn phónon.*

82. Athenaeus 3.108b–c, 10.449c (= Eubulus frag. 75.10 Kock; Antiphanes frag. 52.9 Kock).

83. *Odyssey* 2.355. Plutarch *Roman Questions* 289e–f.

grains of wheat"[84]). In other words, the millstone is to the grains of wheat what the *mákhaira* 'knife' is to sacrificial victims. In the milling, the grain dies; it loses its "power to germinate" (*tèn spérmatos dúnamin*).[85] For grain that is crushed there will be no rebirth, no posterity. Respecting this logic, the compatriots of Kyzikos, who was slain by Jason, as a mark of grief refused to eat any food containing flour. Turning the millstone, "murdering" grains of wheat, would have been an ill-fated way of recalling the fact that Kyzikos died without leaving any biological line of descent.[86] Similarly, during the first days of the Hyakinthia in Sparta, no bread was consumed. Hyakinthos, the boy who was crushed by Apollo's discus, was a descendant of Myles, the king of Sparta who invented milling.[87] The similarity between the shapes of the discus and the millstone is recorded in a passage in Pausanias which explains that Ajax's 'knee-cap' (*múlē*)—literally 'millstone'—was the size of the discus used by the boys who took part in the pentathlon.[88]

The relationship between the uncrushed grains, that are neither milled nor sown, and the suitors, crushed by stones as if in a public process of milling, is thus one of contrast or opposition.[89] But let us proceed step by step. The first thing Kallirhoe does is go to Koroneia for the national festival of the Boeotians, which takes place at the beginning of October, about three months after the completion of the threshing and just before sowing takes place. At the Panboeotian festival she can expect to obtain the widest possible public exposure; her moment has come. She takes refuge at the altar of Athena—the goddess of the *méson,* the goddess of publicity—in order to tell of her father's murder.[90] The *mnêma* called Kallirhoe

---

84. *Greek Anthology,* 7.394.

85. Plutarch *Roman Questions* 289f.

86. See above, p. 83. Apollonius of Rhodes *Argonautica* 1.1070–1077.

87. Athenaeus 4.139d; Pausanias 3.1.1–3; 20.2; 4.1.1.

88. Pausanias 1.35.5

89. See Apollonius of Rhodes *Argonautica* 1.1077. The citizens of Kyzikos used a collective millstone, no doubt to avoid doing their milling individually. The death of Kyzikos was due to a collective, not an individual, mistake.

90. For Athena, the goddess of the *méson,* see J. Svenbro, *La Parole et le marbre. Aux origines de la poétique grecque* (Lund, 1976), p. 89n.73. In the *Iliad* Athena places herself precisely *es mésson.* The verb meaning 'to recount' in Plutarch's text is *diēgeîsthai,* which, as N. Loraux points out (in "Enquête sur la construction d'un meurtre en histoire," *L'Ecrit du temps,* no. 10 [1985], p. 15n.32), belongs to the

begins to 'signify' (sēmaínein). But unlike a normal mnêma, which refers to the deceased one buried beneath it, this mnêma—in a disquieting reversal of the usual schema—refers to the names and homelands of the deceased man's assassins.[91] Those who refused to let the Pythian god, Púthios (that is to say, Apollo), choose her husband take to flight "when they learn" (puthómenoi) that the Boeotians have taken pity on the girl who, like a mnêma, has the power to 'indicate' (sēmaínein) them in the fullest blaze of public view.[92] The suitors try to take refuge at Orchomenos, where they are rejected since they are defiled by their murder. At Hippotai, however, they do find asylum. But the Boeotians, led by Phoïdos, proceed to lay siege to Hippotai. Deprived of water, villagers and suitors alike are forced to surrender. The very men who sought to win the hand of Kalli-rhóē, who "flows beautifully," are thus, through a stroke of irony, deprived of water because of her.

At this point, in the night, the suitors hear the voice of the man whom they have killed. Suffering from extreme thirst, they hear the flowing voice of the one whom they believed, since he was dead, to be powerless over them. Now the 'voice' (phōnê̄) of Phokos tells them: "I am here" (páreimi). The "I" here belongs to the "one who speaks" (légontós tinos); yet that one is not specifically identified with Phokos. All we are told is that the suitors recognize the phṓnēma, the "word pronounced", as coming from Phokos (hóti Phṓkou eíē).[93] The phṓnēma belongs to Phokos, which, however, is

---

vocabulary of legal rhetoric. So the translation here could be, "Kallirhoe expounded the evidence of the crime."

91. Cf. Iliad 7.89–91, where Hektor imagines the sêma raised over his adversary. The passerby will name Hektor, not the deceased whom he has slain. Cited above, pp. 16, 53.

92. On the wordplay, see Scholia to Apollonius of Rhodes, Argonautica 1.209 (p. 25 Wendel): "Pytho [Pūthṓ] is the town in Phokis where the famous oracle is to be found; it is called this either because people go there to ask for oracles [punthánesthai tòn manteiôn] or because the Snake rotted there [sesêphthai, from sēpomai = púthomai 'to rot']." There is thus a definite semantic connection between Pytho's god of oracles, the Púthios, and the verb punthánesthai (aorist pŭthésthai 'to ask successfully, to learn'), a connection that this story exploits with sarcastic intent. Those who were not willing to punthánesthai from the Púthios nevertheless were vouchsafed a kind of (terrible) reply "when they learned" (pŭthómenoi) what had taken place at the Panboeotia, sealing their death warrant.

93. Plutarch Love Stories 775b.

not to say that it is necessarily pronounced by Phokos. In Chapters 2 and 3, I stressed that a *mnêma*'s voice has to be that of the reader who, in reading, lends it to the *mnêma*. Similarly, I would argue now, the "voice of Phokos" is simply the voice that is being lent to Phokos, as one deceased, in order to reactivate his words at one remove. The narrative seems to make that point when it refers to a voice "of someone saying" (*légontós tinos*), especially since *légein* 'to say' can also mean 'to read'.[94] What is important here is not the supernatural nature of the episode but the fact that the voice is believed to belong to Phokos; it is precisely the voice that the recalcitrant "readers" refused to lend to the writer. Thanks to an anonymous entity who "says" or "reads," Phokos returns to life in the middle of the night. The *phónēma* is like a child, a sonorous grandson, born thanks to his *sēmaínousa* 'signifying' daughter and an anonymous *légōn* 'reading' son-in-law. This is *kléos* in its pure state, worthy of a citizen of Kleisas: an incorporeal voice affirms and reaffirms that the deceased is present, mediated by his daughter.

The use of the first person in this story is significant. The man who feared assault and was then assaulted, just as he feared he would be, suddenly assumes the position of the first person and, as such, is recognized by the suitors just before they are themselves wiped out. The suitors meet their deaths in the very place where Kallirhoe's father affirms his presence from beyond the grave. They are wiped out along with the entire village, which, having been razed to the ground, reverts to "open country" (*khóra*). These very men who laid claim to the voice "that flows beautifully," who attempted to gain possession of it by violent means, who thought they could tear the daughter from her home and take possession of her, are now reduced to nothing. They are stoned, put to death by the community, cast out into the most absolute anonymity.

As for Kallirhoe, she "signifies," and thereby merges with the real *mnêma* of her father which, on the very day when the suitors are stoned to death, is inscribed with gilded letters in the city of *kléos*. By stationing herself in a public place, Kallirhoe makes sure of the maximum public exposure for her father's renown. The writing is

94. Plato *Theaetetus* 143c: *allá, paî, labè tò biblíon kaì lége* "Well then, slave, take the book and read" (see above, p. 52).

displayed to the public and will ensure that the *kléos* sounds forth every time that the public undertakes to read it aloud. The public "marries" the writing. And herein lies the real cunning of Phokos, his masterstroke as a writer, the paradoxical triumph that Apollo grants him. By refusing to choose from among the suitors, the potential "readers" of his daughter, and by getting killed before any choice has been made, he forever defers the choice of a reader for his writing, so that each and every reader of his *mnêma* will be able to imagine himself to be the ideal son-in-law, without fear of contradiction—on condition that he himself stands aside to make room for a first person that is not his own.

The story of Phokos and Kallirhoe can thus be read as a representation of a particular way of understanding writing put at the service of posthumous renown and also the relationship established between writer and reader. Once her father has been murdered, the daughter becomes his *mnêma,* through which his posterity must pass. In reaction against the violence of these readers, the suitors, who are unwilling to efface themselves and so become the instrument of a father-in-law's posterity, the father announces another kind of violence, which wipes out the suitors, reduces them to anonymity, ejecting them from a place where it is necessary to lend one's voice to a piece of mute writing that, though mute, makes use of the first-person singular.

In truth, the first type of violence stems from that very use of the first person. The reader who pronounces the inscription written in the first person finds upon his lips an *egó* that is not his own. Inscriptions in the third person ("This is the *mnêma* of so-and-so," not "I am the *mnêma* of so-and-so") defuse the violent relationship between the writer and the reader (for the effect of the use of the third person is that the formula might have been pronounced by anyone who happened to be well enough informed), and, through an apparently levelling operation, they endeavor to mask the violent tension that nevertheless subsists. In contrast, inscriptions that adopt the first-person form accentuate that violence so as to reveal the clash of forces clearly. The violence obliges the reader to efface himself and become the instrument of the *kléos* that he proclaims, and that submission on the part of the reader is analogous to the submission demanded by the deceased father of an *epíklēros* daughter, by an Alkinoos or an Iobates for instance, who regard the foreigner without connections as the ideal son-in-law, since such a foreigner is prepared to integrate himself totally within the father's own house.[95] The ruse of writing that is as *radiant* as the daughter of Phokos—the writing must be beautiful if it is to attract the attention of the readers—holds out the possibility of "returning" to the realm of the living by means of the sonorous *kléos* (as opposed to the mute stone), thanks to the readers of Kleos-town, a city that is not to be found anywhere on the map precisely because it is everywhere.

Following this in-depth examination of the story of Phokos, Kallirhoe, and the thirty suitors, let us now read the text once more, this time as a sequence of episodes, or rather a journey through a symbolic topography. As we do so, we soon realize that the narrative is organized in a perfectly symmetrical fashion, as the diagram below shows.

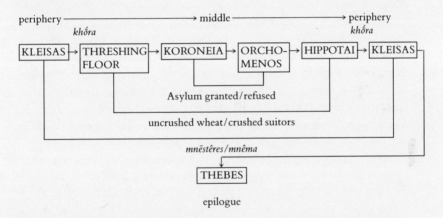

One preliminary point needs to be made. That is, the symmetry depends on setting Thebes to one side, but this is justifiable since General Phoïdos' arrival in Thebes is not part of the main plot. Its relationship to the rest of the narrative is that of an epilogue that provides us with the key to the reading: namely, the principle of Greek name-giving (the daughter of the victorious general is given

95. See above, p. 85.

the name *Niko-stráte*). I will later suggest another reason for considering this episode as an epilogue that is distinct from the rest of the narrative.

Looking at this topography, one is struck by its quadrifunctional character (I use that expression in the sense that Georges Dumézil gave it in his book *Apollon sonore et autres essais*[96]). Kleisas or Kleostown obviously represents the vocal function that characterizes Apollo; the threshing floor represents the function of production and reproduction; Athena's altar, with the protection that it affords, represents the religious function, as does Orchomenos, where the murderers are refused admittance; Hippotai (Knightstown[97]), the fortified village to which Phoïdos lays siege, represents the warrior function.

In this narrative that begins and ends in Kleisas we are presented not with a trifunctional topography but with a quadrifunctional one. *Kléos* is sonorous renown, renown given a vocal form, in short, a voice, which cannot be reduced to the functions of (re)production, religion, and warfare. *Kléos,* par excellence, represents the vocal function, the attribute of sonorous Apollo. This representation confirms the importance that I have ascribed to Apollo in this narrative, even though he only appears for a moment in connection with a *lógos,* namely the fatal proposal that Phokos makes.[98] It also confirms the importance attributed to the voice in Greek reading. In the violent tension set up between the writer and the reader, what is at stake is a voice, the reading voice that the writer considers "his" voice. The reader is nothing but the instrument of the posterity that the writer creates for himself. A terrible fate awaits recalcitrant readers.

Plutarch himself, or, rather, Plutarch as read and reread by Dumézil,[99] provides further confirmation of this quadrifunctional interpretation, and we are indebted to him for the story of Phokos and Kallirhoe. In Rome, Carmenta was the goddess responsible for

96. G. Dumézil, *Apollon sonore et autres essais. Esquisses de mythologie* (Paris, 1982), pp. 9–108.

97. In Boeotian dialect, *toì hippóte* = *hoi hippeîs* 'the knights' (see Liddell-Scott-Jones, s.v. *hippótes,* citing *IG* 7.3087).

98. Consider also the wordplay *Púthios-puthómenoi.*

99. Dumézil, *Apollon sonore et autres essais,* pp. 101–106.

carmen 'song, expression, poem, oracle'. But within that primary vocal function, Carmenta was also a trifunctional goddess. Plutarch writes as follows: "This Carmenta is thought by some to be a Fate presiding over human birth, and for this reason she is honored by mothers. Others, however, say that the wife of Evander the Arcadian, who was a prophetess and inspired to utter prophecies in verse, was therefore surnamed Carmenta, since 'Carmina' is their word for 'verses,' her own proper name being *Niko-státē*."[100] The daughter of the general Phoïdos is thus homonymous with a quadrifunctional goddess, to wit, Carmenta. Not simply at the level of name-giving can the last episode in the narrative be thought to provide the key for the rest of the story. Through this homonymy it also does so at the level of the story's "functional" structure. The Roman character of this same episode is, furthermore, underlined by the name of the Boeotian general. Phoïdos does not appear to be a Greek name, but rather a Greek transcription of the Latin *foedus* 'treaty', which appears in the word *con-foederatio* 'confederation'. The general of the Boeotian confederation, therefore, bears an allegorical name; he is the Graeco-Latin personification of the military unity of the Boeotians. This detail provides added justification for setting aside from the essential plot the last episode in the story. It is simply an epilogue that provides us with the keys for reading the rest of the story, a kind of accretion or graft, a little metanarrative in which the text itself elliptically proposes how it should be used.

APPENDIX. Plutarch *Love Stories* 4 (*Moralia* 774d–775b) from the Collection des Universités de France edition. Greek text (English translation, above, p. 86).

Φῶκος Βοιώτιος μὲν ἦν τῷ γένει, ἦν γὰρ ἐκ Κλείσαντος, πατὴρ δὲ Καλλιρρόης κάλλει τε καὶ σωφροσύνῃ διαφερούσης. Ταύτην ἐμνηστεύοντο νεανίαι τριάκοντα E εὐδοκιμώτατοι ἐν Βοιωτίᾳ· ὁ δὲ Φῶκος ἄλλας ἐξ ἄλλων

---

100. Plutarch *Life of Romulus* 21; Dumézil, *Apollon sonore et autres essais,* pp. 105–106.

ἀναβολὰς τῶν γάμων ἐποιεῖτο, φοβούμενος μὴ βιασ-
θείη, τέλος δὲ λιπαρούντων ἐκείνων, ἠξίου ἐπὶ τῷ Πυθίῳ
ποιήσασθαι τὴν αἵρεσιν. Οἱ δὲ πρὸς τὸν λόγον ἐχαλ-
έπηναν καὶ ὁρμήσαντες ἀπέκτειναν τὸν Φῶκον· ἐν δὲ
τῷ θορύβῳ ἡ κόρη φυγοῦσα ἵετο διὰ τῆς χώρας· ἐδίωκον
δ᾽ αὐτὴν οἱ νεανίαι. Ἡ δ᾽ ἐντυχοῦσα γεωργοῖς ἅλω συν-
τιθεῖσι σωτηρίας ἔτυχε παρ᾽ αὐτῶν· ἀπέκρυψαν γὰρ
αὐτὴν οἱ γεωργοὶ ἐν τῷ σίτῳ. Καὶ οὕτω παρῇξαν μὲν οἱ
διώκοντες· ἡ δὲ διασωθεῖσα ἐφύλαξε τὴν τῶν Παμβοιω-   F
τίων ἑορτήν, καὶ τότε εἰς Κορώνειαν ἐλθοῦσα ἱκέτις
καθέζεται ἐπὶ τῷ βωμῷ τῆς Ἰτωνίας Ἀθηνᾶς καὶ τῶν
μνηστήρων τὴν παρανομίαν διηγεῖτο, τό τε ἑκάστου
ὄνομα καὶ τὴν πατρίδα σημαίνουσα. Ἠλέουν οὖν οἱ
Βοιωτοὶ τὴν παῖδα καὶ τοῖς νεανίαις ἠγανάκτουν· οἱ δὲ
ταῦτα πυθόμενοι εἰς Ὀρχομενὸν καταφεύγουσιν. Οὐ
δεξαμένων δ᾽ αὐτοὺς τῶν Ὀρχομενίων, πρὸς Ἱπ|πότας   775
εἰσώρμησαν· κώμη δ᾽ ἦν παρὰ τῷ Ἑλικῶνι κειμένη
μεταξὺ Θίσβης καὶ Κορωνείας· οἱ δ᾽ ὑποδέχονται αὐ-
τούς. Εἶτα πέμπουσι Θηβαῖοι ἐξαιτοῦντες τοὺς Φώκου
φονεῖς· τῶν δ᾽ οὐ διδόντων, ἐστράτευσαν μὲν μετὰ τῶν
ἄλλων Βοιωτῶν, στρατηγοῦντος Φοίδου, ὃς τότε τὴν
ἀρχὴν τῶν Θηβαίων διεῖπε· πολιορκήσαντες δὲ τὴν
κώμην ὀχυρὰν οὖσαν, δίψει δὲ τῶν ἔνδον κρατηθέντων,
τοὺς μὲν φονεῖς ληφθέντας κατέλευσαν, τοὺς δ᾽ ἐν τῇ
κώμῃ ἐξηνδραποδίσαντο· κατασκάψαντες δὲ τὰ τείχη
καὶ τὰς οἰκίας διένειμαν τὴν χώραν Θισβεῦσί τε καὶ
Κορωνεῦσι. Φασὶ δὲ νυκτός, πρὸ τῆς ἁλώσεως τῶν Ἱπ-   B
ποτῶν, φωνὴν ἐκ τοῦ Ἑλικῶνος πολλάκις ἀκουσθῆναι
λέγοντός τινος «Πάρειμι»· τοὺς δὲ μνηστῆρας τοὺς τριάκοντα τόδε τὸ φώνημα γνωρίζειν ὅτι Φώκου εἴη. Ἧι δ᾽
ἡμέρᾳ κατελεύσθησαν, τὸ ἐν Κλείσαντι μνῆμα τοῦ
γέροντος κρόκῳ φασὶ ῥεῦσαι· Φοίδῳ δὲ τῷ Θηβαίων
ἄρχοντι καὶ στρατηγῷ ἐκ τῆς μάχης ἐπανιόντι ἀγ-
γελθῆναι θυγατέρα γεγενημένην, ⟨ἣν⟩ αἰσιούμενον
προσαγορεῦσαι Νικοστράτην.

CHAPTER 6

Nómos, "Exegesis," Reading:
The Reading Voice and the Law

In his book *La Loi à Rome,* André Magdelain adopted the etymology of the Latin word *lex* proposed by Michel Bréal and Franz Skutsch: *lex* is the noun formed from the verb *legere* in the sense of 'to read'. Law, in Rome, was originally a "reading."[1] At first sight, Roman law thus seems to be a separate concept, without parallel in Greek, where *légein* and *lógos-léxis* do not follow the same semantic path. For although *légein* can mean 'to read', as we have already had occasion to note, *lógos* and *léxis* do not mean "law". In Greek, *nómos* is the word that means "law". No more convincing etymology exists for this word than that which associates it with the practice of 'distributing' (*némein* 'to distribute') land in the colonies, a practice that *nómos* is thought to have been introduced to regulate, in the seventh century B.C.[2] In view of the fact that the meaning of *nómos* extends far beyond the framework of the distribution of land, this etymology owes its success to the absence of any better suggestions.

1. A. Magdelain, *La Loi à Rome* (Paris, 1978), pp. 17f. I am grateful to John Scheid for drawing this book to my attention.
2. See, quite recently, G. Camassa, "Aux Origines de la codification écrite des lois en Grèce," in *Les Savoirs de l'écriture,* ed. M. Detienne (Lille, 1988), p. 137, citing the study by G. P. Shipp, *Νόμος Law,* Australian Academy of the Humanities, Monographs, 4 (Sydney, 1978). As early as Plutarch, *nómos* was explicitly derived from *némein,* in the sense of 'to distribute' (*Table Questions* 644c). See the skepticism of E. Laroche, *Histoire de la racine * nem- en grec ancien* (Paris, 1949), p. 163: "No truly satisfactory etymology has been proposed for the word νόμος."

Now, as soon as one examines the full list of Greek verbs meaning 'to read', one realizes that *nómos* could very well be a noun formed from one of them and might, consequently, represent a case analogous to that of *lex*. For one of those verbs—admittedly not often used with this sense—is in point of fact *némein*. Fragment 144 from Sophocles provides an example. On the eve of their departure for Troy, the Achaean chiefs inspect their troops and give the following order: "You who are seated on the throne and who hold the tablets of writing in your hand, read [*néme*] the list so that we can see if any of those who swore the oath are absent!"[3]

When Tyndaros has to choose a husband for his daughter Helen from the crowd of suitors who have come to Sparta, he makes them all swear to defend the rights of the man upon whom his choice falls.[4] That is how Menelaos is able to count on such a large contingent of heroes when Paris steals Helen from him. In the fragment, the reader holds the list of the names of those who have sworn the oath. Its reading, or—literally—its distribution, will reveal if anyone is absent. This is a reading aloud before an assembly, to which the content of the text is orally "distributed." The reader is the instrument of that distribution, a "living instrument" (*órganon émpsukhon*) or a 'vocal' one (*instrumentum vocale*)[5] at the service of the writing, just as in Plato magistrates are at the service of the *nómoi*.[6]

Némein, then, can mean 'to read.' Hesychius even dwells with a certain insistence upon the point, glossing forms of *némein* with three corresponding forms of *anagignṓskein: némō: anagignṓsko; némeis: anagignṓskeis; némei: anagignṓskei* ("I distribute: I read; you distribute: you read; he distributes: he reads"). As we noted in Chapter 3, in the Dorian dialect, a compound of *némein,* to wit, *ananémein,* was regularly used with the sense of "to read"; and, as

---

3. Sophocles frag. 144 Nauck[2]. As Pierre Vidal-Naquet has pointed out to me, the list in question in this fragment may be compared to the Catalogue of Ships in Book 2 of the *Iliad:* the *néme* 'read!' addressed to the Secretary in Sophocles corresponds to the *éspete* 'say!' addressed to the Muses in Homer (*Iliad* 2.484). You could say that the passage from orality to writing (or from the Muses to the Secretary) might be situated somewhere in between these two points of reference.

4. Apollodorus *Library* 3.10.9.

5. Aristotle *Nicomachean Ethics* 8.11.6.1161b3–5; Varro *Rural Economy* 1.17.1, where the "vocal instrument" is the slave.

6. Plato *Laws* 6.715d.

6. *Nómos,* "Exegesis," Reading   111

we also noted, the middle *ananémesthai* was used in the same sense in
Eretria.[7] According to one scholiast, Pindar in his second *Isthmian*
ode used another compound of *némein* in the sense of 'to read',
namely *aponémein.*[8] Hesychius knows of yet another: *epinémein.*[9]
The documentation is slender but solid enough to establish beyond
doubt that *némein* could be used with the sense of "to read," as could
a number of its compounds.

If *némein* means 'to read', it is perfectly legitimate to wonder
whether *nómos* 'law' might not have possessed the fundamental
sense of "reading." From a formal point of view, there is no reason
why it should not. The trouble is that under the entry *nómos* in our
dictionaries we find nothing to suggest that the word was ever used
in that or any related sense. *Nómos* does not appear to have had any
meaning that even approached that of "distribution by means of the
voice"—except when the word was clearly used in the musical
sense, which at first sight seems very distant from the legal one. The
fact is that from the seventh century on, *nómos* could be used to
mean "melody" and, more particularly, "nome," in the poetic and
musical sense. What birds "dispense" or "diffuse" is their melodious
bird song. Accordingly, Alcman declares: "I know the *nómoi* of all
the birds."[10] A few centuries later, the double meaning of *nómos* is
skillfully exploited in the pseudo-Platonic *Minos:* "And who is a
good apportioner [*nomeús*] of notes struck for a tune, skilled in distributing [*neîmai*] suitable notes, and who is it whose laws [*nómoi*]
are right here? The pipe player and the lyre player. Then he who
conforms most closely to these laws [*ho nomikótatos*] in these matters
is the best pipe player."[11] The musical sense of *nómos* certainly

7. See above, p. 48, and above, p. 51 (G. Pfohl, *Greek Poems on Stones,* vol. 1,
Epitaphs: From the Seventh to the Fifth Centuries B.C., Textus Minores, no. 36
[Leiden, 1967], no. 128.2).
8. Pindar *Isthmian* 2.47; *Scholia to Pindar* 3.222.9–18 Drachmann. Here it is
Nikasippos who has to *aponémein.* See *Olympian* 6.90–91, where Aineias, the chorus
instructor, is responsible for the sonorous realization of the written text.
9. Hesychius, s.v. *epineimátō: epanagnótō.*
10. Athenaeus 9.374d (= Alcman frag. 40 Page). Alcman was a seventh-
century poet: see C. M. Bowra, *Greek Lyric Poetry,* 2d ed. (Oxford, 1963), pp. 16–
17.
11. The whole passage should be read (317a–318d) in order to appreciate the
wordplay fully. See also *Laws* 4.722d–e; Stobaeus 4.2.22; Hermippus in Athenaeus
14.619b (= frag. 88 Wehrli).

suggests that the juridical meaning of the word likewise stems from the fundamental sense of "distribution." As Emmanuel Laroche observes, whatever different translations are sometimes necessary, the verb *némein* always essentially means 'to distribute'.[12]

But that is not all. Consider, in the first place, the *nómos aoidês* of the *Homeric Hymn to Apollo*.[13] Unlike Jean Humbert, the editor of the Collection des Universités de France text, who favors *nómos*, most editors prefer the accentuation of *nomós*, meaning "range [pasturage] of words". Yet most of the manuscripts give *nómos*, and the preferred reading for this passage is the following:

> πάντη γάρ τοι, Φοῖβε, νόμος βέβληται ἀοιδῆς
> ἠμὲν ἀν' ἤπειρον πορτιτρόφον ἠδ' ἀνὰ νήσους.

[Everywhere, o Phoibos, a profusion of song has been distributed for you, across the continent that nurtures heifers and throughout the islands.][14]

In their commentary, Allen, Halliday, and Sikes refer to the *Iliad* 20.249 and Hesiod *Works and Days* 403 to justify their accentuation of *nomós*.[15] In the cases of Homer and Hesiod, the editors do favor *epéōn nomós* "the range of words". The alternative accentuation, *nómos*, however, is attested for both texts, and when we look closely at the passages in question, we realize that *nómos* is far more satisfactory than *nomós*. In Homer, the passage runs as follows:

> στρεπτὴ δὲ γλῶσσ' ἐστὶ βροτῶν, πολέες δ' ἔνι μῦθοι
> παντοῖοι, ἐπέων δὲ πολὺς νόμος ἔνθα καὶ ἔνθα.
> ὁπποῖόν κ' εἴπῃσθα ἔπος, τοῖόν κ' ἐπακούσαις.

---

12. Laroche, *Histoire de la racine * nem- en grec ancien*, p. 16 (and p. 24) cited by B. Borecký, *Survivals of Some Tribal Ideas in Classical Greek: The Use and the Meaning of λαγχάνω, δατέομαι, and the Origin of ἴσον ἔχειν, ἴσον νέμειν, and Related Idioms*, Acta Universitatis Carolinae, Philosophica et Historica, Monographiae, 10 (Prague, 1965), p. 85.

13. *Homeric Hymn to Apollo* 20.

14. Ibid. 20–21. On *bállein* and *aná* see Xenophanes frag. B 8.2 Diels-Kranz (*blēstrízein* is an intensive form of *bállein*), and Theognis 247. See J. Svenbro, *La Parola e il marmo. Alle origini della poetica greca* (Turin, 1984), p. 191n.38.

15. T. W. Allen, W. R. Halliday, and E. E. Sikes, *The Homeric Hymns* (Oxford, 1936), p. 204.

[The tongue of human beings is versatile. In the human mind there
are speeches of all kinds and, running this way and that, great is the
flow of words. You will hear the same kind of things said as you
yourself say.][16]

That is what Aeneas says to Achilles, to make the point that insults
will no longer serve any useful purpose. He sets up an opposition
between the inward thoughts and the words that flow out in a
quarrel, where the transition from the internal to the external is
assured by the "versatile tongue." The expression *éntha kaì éntha*
"this way and that" or "now one way now another" is explained by
the line that follows. The flow of words from one party will be
met by a flow of words from the other. It is hard to see why this presentation of acoustic expression (internal/external)[17] should need to
resort to a pastoral metaphor such as *epéōn nomós* "the range [pas-
turage] of words".[18]

In Hesiod, the situation is very similar. In lines 402–403 of the
Works and Days, some editors favor

$$\sigma\grave{\upsilon} \ \delta' \ \grave{\epsilon}\tau\acute{\omega}\sigma\iota\alpha \ \pi\acute{o}\lambda\lambda' \ \grave{\alpha}\gamma o\rho\epsilon\acute{\upsilon}\epsilon\iota\varsigma,$$
$$\grave{\alpha}\chi\rho\epsilon\hat{\iota}o\varsigma \ \delta' \ \grave{\epsilon}\sigma\tau\alpha\iota \ \grave{\epsilon}\pi\acute{\epsilon}\omega\nu \ \nu o\mu\acute{o}\varsigma.$$

Perses must work, Hesiod declares, in order to avoid the dependent
state of the beggar. And he goes on to say that if you are without
means, "All your words will be in vain and the pasturage of words
will be useless." In my view, the accentuation *nómos,* which is
attested in the manuscripts, makes better sense: "All that you say
will be in vain and the flow of words will be useless." If Perses does
not work, he may speak as much as he likes: his words will be
useless. The two statements express the same idea.

This interpretation is all the more meaningful since Hesiod

16. *Iliad* 20.248–250. See *Scholia T to Homer, Iliad,* 20.249 for the *nómos* accentuation ("some prefer *nómos*").
17. Pindar *Nemean* 4.6–8 for another representation of rendering into sound.
The 'tongue' (*glôssa*) acts as an intermediary between the "deep mind" (*phrèn
batheîa*) and the "sonorous statement" (*rhêma*).
18. Despite Pindar *Olympian* 11.8–9, where the poet says that his 'tongue'
(*glôssa*) likes to allow the themes of athletic victory 'to pasture' (*poimaínein*).

makes *díkē* 'justice' the direct object of *némein*.[19] So in Hesiod's day one "distributed" justice, in exactly the same way as the Homeric hero and Hesiod's own brother "distributed" their words, their *épea*. Given that Hesiod's *díkē* is intended for the ear—*ákoue díkēs* "listen to justice", he tells Perses—its "distribution" is obviously effected by vocal means.[20] In other words, this is *nómos* in its original sense.

What at first appeared to rule against the meaning "vocal distribution" thus itself becomes discountable. The word *nómos* means not only "musical diffusion" or "melody," but also "diffusion of words." One problem remains: how can we explain this transition from "vocal distribution," which is not dependent upon writing (as reading is), to the kind of "distribution" in the sense of "reading" that the verb *némein* suggests?

The vocabulary of reading has a prehistory that antedates the introduction of alphabetical writing in Greece. The same is true of the vocabulary of writing in the strict sense of the term. Before it became the technical term for the act of writing, *gráphein* meant 'to scratch'.[21] The passage from the sense of "to scratch" to that of "to write" is self-explanatory. Let us see whether the vocabulary of reading presents a similar case.

In Herodotus, the verb *ananémesthai* means "to recite from memory" (in connection with the recitation of genealogies) as well as 'to read' (in connection with the stele of Mnesitheos).[22] Bearing in mind the reading envisaged in the case of Mnesitheos' epitaph, where a reader is expected to read aloud to a number of passersby, it is not hard to see how a progression could be made from the meaning "to recite from memory" to that of 'to read'. After all, a "vocal distribution" among listeners can just as well be based upon memory as upon a written text.

That remark applies equally well to the simple verb *némein,*

19. Hesiod *Works and Days* 224. See E. A. Havelock, *The Greek Concept of Justice* (Cambridge, Mass., 1978), p. 216 and n.16, citing *Iliad* 20.249 and *Works and Days* 402–403.

20. *Works and Days* 213.

21. See *Iliad* 17.599.

22. Herodotus 1.173. Pfohl, no. 128.2 (see above, p. 48 f.). I would accordingly postulate that the sense "to recite from memory" is more ancient than that of 'to read', despite the fact that Herodotus' *Histories* are more recent than Mnesitheos' stele.

which can carry not only the above-mentioned meaning of 'to read' but also that of 'to cite'. An example is provided by Simonides' poem to Skopas at the point where the poet declares: "In my opinion, nor is the saying of Pittakos cited in harmony with reality [*emmeléōs*], and yet he was a Wise Man. 'It is hard to be good' is what he used to say."[23] Pittakos' saying—described as a *rhêma* in the *Protagoras*[24]—belongs to the fund of common knowledge that includes sayings and proverbs intended to be distributed whenever the need arises. This collective storehouse also contains genealogies, as in the passage of Herodotus cited above. This knowledge is distributed orally, when needed, but it is not yet "read." Once it has been fixed in writing, however, the use of *némein* in the sense of "to read" presents no problem.

Némein and *nómos* are thus just as possible in an oral situation as in one in which writing is involved. In this, they differ on the one hand from the Latin *legere* and *lex,* which belong to a context in which writing is distributed by being read aloud, and, on the other, from *eírein,* 'to say/tell' and *rhêtra,* which is derived from it and means 'law' in the Laconian dialect. The *rhêtrai* of Lycurgus were not set down in writing—indeed, there was even a *rhêtra* that forbade setting down laws in writing.[25] In Sparta, the law was distributed by being proclaimed aloud, but not on the basis of a written text. It was recited from memory. The situation can be schematically represented as follows:

ORALITY	*eírein* 'to say/tell'	*rhêtra* 'law; treaty'
ORALITY/WRITING	*némein* 'to (re-)cite; to read'	*nómos* 'law; oral diffusion'
WRITING	*legere* 'to read'	*lex* 'law; treaty; reading'

Nómos is thus positioned between two extremes: its meaning is covered neither by that of *rhêtra* nor by that of *lex.* It is doubly open-

---

23. Simonides frag. 37.11–13 Page. In writing "in harmony with reality" I have tried to indicate the musical connotation of *emmeléōs.*

24. Plato *Protagoras* 343b. In the *Protagoras* Plato cites Simonides' poem to Skopas. See Svenbro, *La Parola e il marmo,* Chapter 5, for an analysis.

25. Plutarch *Life of Lycurgus* 13.1–4; cf., however, Pausanias 5.4.5. See T. A. Boring, *Literacy in Ancient Sparta,* Mnemosyne, Supplementa, 54 (Leiden, 1979), pp. 24–31 ("Written Laws in Sparta").

ended. It may be either *ágraphos* 'not written' or *gegramménos* 'written'. All the same, the fact that the Laconian dialect seems to stress the "orality" of its laws by calling them *rhêtrai* suggests that the word *nómos*—in Sparta, at any rate, where the word for 'to read' was *ana-némein*—belonged more to the field of writing (or "reading") than to the field of orality that was peculiar to *rhêtra*. In other words, *nómos* is probably closer to *lex* than to *rhêtra*. For if *nómos* was as ambiguous in its practical application as in its etymology, it could have suited Sparta's requirements as well as it did that of Athens, as a word for "law."

If the word *nómos* has the basic meaning that I suggest, it follows that "reading" came to occupy one of the most—if not *the* most—strategic of positions in the Greek city: a position from which it regulated the behavior of the civic body, through the mouths of the magistrates, who did not just recite but read out the law. Now, those magistrates had a special name in Greece, a name whose fundamental meaning is as misunderstood as that of *nómos* has been. They were known as *exēgētaí,* normally translated in English as "expounders." What did these "expounders" do?

Let us turn first to a passage from Strabo. "The Mazakenoi use the laws [*nómoi*] of Charondas, choosing also a Law-chanter [*nomōidós*] who, like the jurisconsults [*nomikoí*] among the Romans, is the *exēgētḗs* of the laws [*nómoi*]."[26] Thanks to Athenaeus, citing the historian Hermippus, we know that the laws of Charondas were indeed chanted. "At Athens, even the laws [*nómoi*] of Charondas were sung [*ḗidonto*] at symposia."[27] The proem to the laws of Charondas insists upon this chanted recitation: "The law prescribes that all citizens must know the proems and that, during festivals, the one ordered by the *hestiátōr* must recite them after the paeans, so that everybody should be full of their exhortations."[28] If the 'ways' (*trópoi*) of the music changed, the *nómoi* changed too, according to Damon, and this homology between politics and music certainly seems less strange when seen from the point of view of the practices

26. Strabo 12.2.9.
27. Athenaeus 14.619b (= Hermippus frag. 88 Wehrli).
28. For the relation between solemn reading and singing, see the Gothic *siggwan* 'to sing, read'. Stobaeus 4.2.24. See Plutarch *Life of Lycurgus* 18.3.

I have just described.[29] But what is more important is that the practice of singing out the law confirms my earlier hypothesis relating to the etymology of *nómos*. As regards "diffusion," what applied to the *nómoi* of the birds in Alcman applied equally to the laws of the same period, the *nómoi* of Charondas: they were sung.

Let us return to the passage from Strabo. The text states that the *nomōidós* must be the *exēgētḗs* of the law, in the same way as the Roman *nomikós*. The Loeb Classical Library translation by H. L. Jones runs as follows: "(They choose) also a Law-chanter who, like the jurisconsults among the Romans, is the expounder of the laws." Stobaeus, citing a Stoic source, also identifies the *nomikós* with the *exēgētikós toû nómou*.[30] But it seems strange that the only task allotted to the "Law-*chanter*" should be to *explain* them. One would expect him to have sung them out or recited the laws with particular skill. So it is perhaps legitimate to ask what exactly *exēgētḗs* means here.

In Euripides' *Medea* Aegeus offers to swear an oath to Medea. His words are *exēgoû theoús,* which Louis Méridier translates into French as "Explique-moi les dieux à invoquer" (Explain to me which gods to invoke).[31] Medea replies, "Swear by the plain of Earth, and Helios, father of my father, and name together all the gods."[32] That is not an "explanation" or "exegesis" in the modern sense. Aegeus is not requesting an interpretation. He just wants Medea to tell him which gods to invoke; and she provides him with the names that he must repeat. The Latin *praeire in verbis* and the German *vorsprechen* are good translations of what *exēgeîsthai* means here. *Praeire* is, at the most, a metaphor similar to that implied by *exēgeîsthai*. Medea needs to plot out the path that Aegeus must follow, she must go before him as his *hēgemṓn* or 'guide'. So we ought to translate *exēgoû theoús* as "dictate to me the gods to invoke." Here *exēgoû* is the equivalent of the *éxarkhe* in Euripides' *Iphigenia in Tauris,* where the sense is "dictate (the oath)."[33] And this equivalence is all the more telling in

29. Damon frag. 10 Diels-Kranz.
30. Stobaeus 4.2.1.
31. Euripides *Medea* 745. (Méridier is the translator of the Collection des Universités de France *Medea*).
32. Ibid. 746–747.
33. Euripides *Iphigenia in Tauris* 743. It is worth noting that *Medea* 748 is

that, as George Thomson has perceptively pointed out, the *exēgētēs* is a figure that is analogous to the *exárkhōn,* that is to say, the *Vor-sänger* of the Dionysiac chorus, or indeed Apollo, with his hand on the lyre, who 'guides' (the verb is *hēgeîsthai*) the "various songs" (*pantoíōn nómon*) of the Muses.[34]

In Demosthenes *exēgeîsthai* is used in a revealing manner: "This imprecation, men of Athens, is pronounced, as the law directs, by the herald on your behalf at every meeting of the Assembly, and again before the Council at all their sessions. The defendant [Aeschines] cannot say that he is not familiar with it, for when acting as clerk [*hupogrammateúōn*] to the Assembly and as an officer [*hupēretôn*] of the Council, he used to *exēgeîsthai* the statute to the herald."[35] We cannot translate *exēgeîsthai* as 'explain', since the herald clearly has no need for "explanations." What he needs are exact formulas that an individual who is "an officer of the Council" (*hupēretôn tēi boulêi*[36])—Aeschines, in this instance—is in a position to give him. Here, to provide an "exegesis" means to dictate the precise formulas to the herald, so that he can proclaim them.[37] In other words, it means to read out the *nómos* to the herald, who will then proceed to proclaim it aloud.

Andocides provides us with yet more information about the exegesis. Callias had accused Andocides of having placed a suppliant's branch on the altar of the Eleusinium, and he claimed that this action was by law punishable by death, in accordance, Callias claimed, with the way in which his father had 'interpreted' (*exēgēsaito*) it to the Athenians in the past.[38] According to Andocides, Kephalos then spoke as follows: "Callias, you impious scoundrel, first you are giving interpretations of the law [*exēgeî nómon*] when

---

identical to *Iphigenia in Tauris* 738: *tí . . . drásein . . . lége* "What must I do . . .? Tell me!" A comparison of these two passages (745–753 and 735–749, respectively) is instructive.

34. G. Thomson, *Aeschylus and Athens,* 2d ed. (London, 1950), pp. 182–183. For the *exēgētēs/exárkhōn* analogy, see Aristotle *Poetics* 4.1449a11; Archilochus frag. 120 and 121 West; *Iliad* 18.606. For Apollo as the *Vorsänger,* see Pindar *Nemean* 5.22–25.

35. Demosthenes 19 *On the Embassy* 70.

36. On *hupērétēs,* see Plato *Laws* 4.715c; Aristotle *Politics* 3.11.3.1287a20.

37. See Magdelain, *La Loi à Rome,* p. 19, where it is a matter of the "herald to whom a scribe whispers the words."

38. Andocides *On the Mysteries* 1.115. 'Interpreted' (*interprétée*) is the translation given in the Collection des Universités de France edition.

you have no right to do such a thing as a member of the Kerykes. Then you talk of an 'ancient law' [*nómon pátrion*] when the stone at your side lays down that the penalty for placing a bough in the Eleusinium shall be a fine of a thousand drachmas."[39] Upon reading the passage in which Callias "produces an exegesis of the law," one realizes that the exegesis in question amounts to no more than pronouncing a formula using an infinitive: "Callias rose once more and said that under an ancient law the penalty for placing a bough in the Eleusinium during the Mysteries was to be instantly put to death [*eí tis hiketērían theíē . . . , ákriton apothaneîn*]."[40]

This conclusion, namely that an exegesis consists in pronouncing a formula cast in the infinitive (preceded by a condition), is confirmed by a passage from pseudo-Demosthenes, *Against Euergos and Mnesiboulos.*

> Well then, after her death [the death of an old freed slavewoman caused by Euergos and Mnesiboulos], I went to the *exēgētaí* in order to learn what I ought to do in the matter, and I related to them all that had taken place. . . . When the *exēgētaí* had heard all this from me, they asked me whether they should make an exegesis of the law for me and nothing more [*póteron exēgésōntaí moi mónon*] or should also advise me [*è kaì sumbouleúsōsin*]. On my answering them, "Both," they said to me, "Very well, we will tell you the rites to perform [*tà mèn nómina exēgēsómetha*] and also advise you as to how to behave [*tà dè súmphora parainésomen*]. In the first place, if there be anyone related to the woman, let him carry a spear when she is borne forth to the tomb and make solemn proclamation at the tomb, and thereafter let him guard the tomb for the space of three days [*prôton mèn epenenkeîn dóru . . . kaì proagoreúein . . . , épeita . . . phuláttein*]. And now comes the advice that we give you. . . ."[41]

This shows clearly that, strictly speaking, an exegesis consisted quite simply in pronouncing the appropriate formulas—neither more nor less.

That interpretation is confirmed by the fragments of the *Ex-*

39. Ibid. 116.
40. Ibid. 115.
41. Pseudo-Demosthenes 47 *Against Euergos and Mnesiboulos,* 68–69. A passage like this shows how "exegesis" came to mean "interpretation."

egetika of Kleidemos and the *Exegetikon* of Antikleides.[42] Both consist of formulas cast in the infinitive and the imperative, prescribing in detail what procedure should be followed in certain rites. These fragments contain nothing worthy of the name "exegesis" in the modern sense of the term. They are simply collections of formulas, initially no doubt committed to the memory of the *exēgētēs*, but later set down in writing.

We have already encountered the opposition between "memorized formulas" and "written law" in the passage from Andocides: "You talk of 'an ancient law,' when the stone at your side lays down that the penalty for placing a bough in the Eleusinium shall be a fine of a thousand drachmas."[43] The "ancient law" means unwritten law as opposed to the written law inscribed on the stele.[44] The same opposition is to be found in Lysias: "Yet Pericles, they say, advised you once that in dealing with impious persons you should enforce against them not only the written [*gegramménoi*] but the unwritten laws [*nómoi ágraphoi*] also, which the Eumolpidai follow in their exegesis [*exēgoûntai*], and which no one has yet had the authority to abolish or the audacity to gainsay—laws whose very author is unknown."[45] The Eumolpidai were indeed a family of *exēgētaí*, but rather unusual ones, who concerned themselves with the rites of Eleusis, whereas official *exēgētaí*, for their part, concerned themselves with purifications and nuptial and funerary rites.[46] The ancestor of this family was Eumolpos, which means "the-one-who-sings-right." "Rightness of voice" is a very appropriate quality for a family whose members are responsible for the exact vocalization of traditional formulas they have committed to memory and no doubt passed down from one generation to the next. The Eumolpidai were exclusively responsible for that initial vocalization. We have

42. Athenaeus 9.409f–410a; Athenaeus 9.473b–c.

43. Andocides *On the Mysteries* 1.116.

44. See pseudo-Demosthenes ibid. 71: "Having listened to the *exēgētaí*, I consulted the Draconian law on the stele."

45. Lysias *Against Andocides* 6.10.

46. P. Foucart, *Les Mystères d'Eleusis* (Paris, 1914); F. Jacoby, *Atthis: The Local Chronicles of Ancient Athens* (Oxford, 1949), pp. 8–70; J. H. Oliver, *The Athenian Expounders of the Sacred and Ancestral Law* (Baltimore, 1950). A succinct collection of the evidence is provided in J. Defradas, *Les Thèmes de la propagande delphique*, 2d ed. (Paris, 1972), pp. 205–207.

noted the following declaration in Andocides: "Callias, . . . you are giving an exegesis of the law when you have no right to do such a thing as a member of the Kerykes."[47] Callias has no right to cite a *nómos pátrios* relating to the mysteries of Eleusis. His is not the "right voice" for that. It is worth remembering the passage in Strabo where the 'Law-chanter', the *nomōidós*, is described as an *exēgētēs*. The *nomōidós* is responsible for the initial expression of the laws in vocal form, as a kind of *Vorsänger* of the citizens. The analogy between the *exēgētēs*, singing out the law for the benefit of others, and the *exárkhōn*, who leads the Dionysiac chorus, is not just formal (*hegeîsthai* = *árkhein*); it is essential, affecting—as it does— the functioning of the "oral" memory and its later written modalities.

Now, the god of both law and music is Apollo, and one of the epithets applied to him is, precisely, *Exēgētēs*.[48] Jean Defradas cites a number of lines from Aeschylus' *Eumenides* which make that very point. The chorus-leader asks Orestes, "The Prophet guided [*exēgeîto*] you into this matricide?"[49] And a little later, Orestes addresses this *exēgētēs* god directly, "Yours to bear witness now, Apollo, and expound the case for me [*exēgoû dé moi*], if I acted with justice [*sùn díkēi*] when I cut her down."[50] The god's answer is succinct: "with justice [*dikaíōs*]."[51] The god pronounces the word, the one word, that Orestes needs. He is the "sonorous" god, as Georges Dumézil has reminded us, in that he ensures that what is mute, either in the mind or in writing, be sounded forth.[52] His voice, with unequalled authority, makes the *nómos* sound forth, that *nómos* that, as Pindar says, "with a supreme hand, guides and justifies the most violent of actions."[53]

Not only does the complementarity between *nómos* and *exēgētēs*

47. Foucart, *Les Mystères d'Eleusis*, pp. 149–150.
48. *IG* I².78, 77; Plato *Republic* 4.427c.
49. Aeschylus *Eumenides* 595, cited by Defradas, *Les Thèmes de la propagande delphique*, p. 201.
50. Aeschylus ibid. 609–610.
51. Ibid. 615.
52. G. Dumézil, *Apollon sonore et autres essais. Esquisses de mythologie* (Paris, 1982). Thanks to the 'voice' (*ómphē*) of Apollo, the 'will' (*boulē*) of Zeus is communicated sonorously among men (pp. 25 f).
53. Pindar frag. 152.3–4 Bowra.

thus result from the practical coincidence that associated the law with the figure of the *exēgētēs* on a regular basis; it is also an integral part of the terms themselves, lying at the very heart of the words. The notion of an "oral distribution," which is the fundamental meaning of *nómos,* corresponds to that of the "oral distributor" that is implied by *exēgētēs.* The *exēgētēs,* in the sense of a "reader," complements the *nómos,* in the sense of a "reading." That profound complementarity, which is anything but gratuitous, is symptomatic of the way in which Greek culture developed a conception of law inseparable from its conception of reading, both of which set the very highest value upon the word spoken aloud.

CHAPTER 7

True Metempsychosis:
Lycurgus, Numa, and the
Tattooed Corpse of Epimenides

The *nómos* has a voice; in fact it merges with that voice. Of course, the voice of the *nómos* is that which the city magistrate lends it when he recites or reads it, but it does not *belong* to this "slave of the *nómos*," which is what the magistrate is.[1] In the logic of servitude, that voice belongs to the master, that is to say, to the *nómos* itself, the master with which it is practically identified. The *nómos* is a voice that in a way is autonomous (*auto-nómos*); in the absence of its mortal author, this immortal voice needs no body of its own, since through a kind of metensomatosis (rather than a metempsychosis), it can sound forth within the city walls so that the citizens listen to it.[2] The voice of the *nómos* is thus a nonmetaphorical voice even if it has no body of its own; it is a voice in the strict sense of the word, a voice destined for the ear. For the Greeks, 'to listen' was also 'to obey': *akoúein* carried both meanings at once, just as *audire* does in Latin (as we saw in Chapter 6, *lex* meant "ritual reading aloud" before it came to mean 'law'). You could say, then, that this external voice is the voice of the city's Super-Ego.[3] It is the audible "authoritative voice" of the *nómos basileús*.

1. Plato *Laws* 4.715d; see above, pp. 44–48, 60–61.
2. See J. Burnet's commentary to Plato's *Phaedo* 70c8 (*Plato's "Phaedo,"* J. Burnet, ed. [Oxford, 1911], p. 48) for the terms *metempsúkhōsis/metensōmátōsis*. Only the latter corresponds to the notion of reincarnation. Burnet's distinction may be considered too trenchant, but I will respect it here. We will return to this subject later in this chapter.
3. My use of this metaphor drawn from Freudian terminology will be justified in Chapter 9.

The idea of a *nómos* that can take the place of a mortal sovereign, a *basileús, despótēs, túrannos, hēgemón,* or *árkhōn,* begins to appear from 500 B.C. on. Heraclitus, who was himself a king before handing over that function to his brother, declares, "The *nómos* is also to submit to the will of a single individual."[4] Admittedly, that fragment of Heraclitus' is not easy to interpret[5]; but Pindar's formula, *nómos ho pántōn basileús*—which provides the starting point for Marcello Gigante's work, *Nomos Basileus*[6]—unambiguously presents the idea of a *nómos* that takes the place of the king: *nómos* reigns as a king over all of us. According to Pindar, "*nómos,* reigning as a king over all—mortals and immortals alike—with a supreme hand guides and justifies the most violent of actions."[7] *Nómos* takes the place of the king. Demaratos tells Xerxes that among the Spartans *nómos* rules like a *despótēs:* the Spartans fear their law far more than Xerxes' subjects fear their king. The law of the Spartans commands them not to flee, but to fight on to victory or to death.[8] The famous epitaph for the Spartans who fell at Thermopylae refers to that law: Leonidas and his men fell *rhḗmasi peithómenoi,* "through obedience to the laws."[9]

We cannot examine examples of this theme in detail here; we can do no more than note them, in order to assess its importance "from afar," so to speak. What interests me is not the many possible meanings of the phrase *nómos basileús*—upon which Gigante's book sheds light—but the fundamental significance of the operation of turning *nómos* into a metaphorical king.

Many of our examples of the expression *nómos basileús* are quotations or interpretations of that fragment of Pindar's. That is certainly the case of the examples to be found in Herodotus and in Plato's *Gorgias.*[10] Lysias also alludes to the formula in his *Epitaphios,*

4. Diogenes Laertius 9.6; Heraclitus frag. B 33 Diels-Kranz.

5. As I understand it, the people are not willing to obey a single individual; they prefer laws. But "the law is also to submit to the will of a single individual" (see Heraclitus frags. B 44, 114, and 121 Diels-Kranz).

6. M. Gigante, *Nomos Basileus* (Naples, 1956).

7. Pindar frag. 152 Bowra.

8. Herodotus 7.104.4–5.

9. Ibid. 228.2; *rhêma* here is probably synonymous with *rhḗtra,* which is the Laconian word for "law" (see Chapter 6).

10. Herodotus 3.38, and Plato *Gorgias* 484b. See also *Laws* 3.690b–c, 4.715a; *Letters* 8.354b–c.

without, however, mentioning Pindar by name.[11] The name of Pindar is also conspicuous by its absence where the anonymous fifth-century author cited by Iamblichus (the "Anonymus Iamblichi") makes use of his terms; and further on in this same author's text we find the slightly nuanced formula, *nómos hēgemṓn*.[12] Plutarch, on the other hand, does cite Pindar's name when he addresses the "prince without education" in order to explain the meaning of *nómos basileús* to him.[13] It is also in Plutarch that one of the Seven Sages, namely Bias, defines the best democracy as the one "in which the people stood in as much fear of the law as of a despot."[14] This *nómos túrannos* is familiar to us from Plato's *Protagoras*, and Plato's uncle, Critias, speaks in his *Sisyphus* of a *díkē túrannos*, a "justice which reigns as a tyrant".[15] The idea turns up again in Euripides' *Hecuba*, which contains a reference to *kratôn nómos*, the "law which reigns", in this case over the gods.[16] The orator Alcidamas, cited by both Plato and Aristotle, uses the plural: *hoi tôn póleōn basileîs nómoi* "the *nómoi* that reign as kings over the cities".[17]

Alcidamas brings us into the same century as Plato and Aristotle, who between them testify the most eloquently to the idea of *nómos basileús*. In Plato's *Laws* the Athenian says, "Wherever in a State the law [*nómos*] is subservient and impotent, over that State I see ruin impending; but wherever the law is lord [*despótēs*] over the magistrates, and the magistrates are slaves [*doûloi*] to the law [*nómos*], there I discern salvation and all the blessings that the gods bestow on States."[18] It is interesting to compare this passage with a few pages from the *Crito*, where the *nómoi* themselves are made to speak, and they describe Socrates himself as their 'slave' (*doûlos*).[19] Subjection to *nómos* must thus be absolute: it is like a "despotic prescription" (*epítagma turannikón*), in a medical metaphor, which is

11. Lysias *Epitaphios* 19.
12. Anonymus Iamblichi frag. 6(1) Diels-Kranz. See also Gigante *Nomos Basileus*, p. 185.
13. Plutarch *To an Ill-Educated Leader* 780c.
14. Plutarch *Banquet of the Seven Sages* 154e.
15. Plato *Protagoras* 337d, and Critias frag. B 25 Diels-Kranz.
16. Euripides *Hecuba* 799–800.
17. Plato *Symposium* 196c, and Aristotle *Rhetoric* 3.1406a22–23.
18. Plato *Laws* 4.715d.
19. Plato *Crito* 50e.

why, according to the Athenian, it must be sweetened by a 'prelude' (*prooímion*) that will bring persuasion to bear.[20]

In the *Politics* Aristotle also places *nómos* in a position of authority. His starting point is the question of whether it is better to be governed by "an excellent man" (*hupò toû arístou andrós*) or by "excellent laws" (*hupò tôn arístōn nómōn*).[21] In general, he says, whatever contains no "emotional element" (*pathētikón*) is stronger than whatever does. *Nómos* contains no emotional element, whereas the human *psukhḗ* 'spirit' inevitably does.[22] Among equals, it is not 'just' (*díkaion*) that any one person should govern or be governed rather than any other. What is just is government by "each in turn" (*anà méros*): "and this constitutes law [*nómos*]; for regulation [*táxis*] is law [*nómos*]. Therefore it is preferable for the law to rule [*nómon árkhein*] rather than any one of the citizens."[23] Where government is entrusted to a group of men, these must be no more than the "guardians and servants of the laws" (*nomophúlakas kaì hupērétas*).[24] Aristotle continues: "He therefore that recommends that the law shall govern [*nómon árkhein*] seems to recommend that the god and reason alone [*tòn theòn kaì tòn noûn mónous*] shall govern, but he that would have man govern adds a wild animal also; for appetite [*epithumía*] is like a wild animal, and also passion [*thumós*] warps the rule of even the best man. Therefore the law [*nómos*] is mind [*noûs*] without desire [*áneu oréxeōs*]."[25] The *nómos árkhōn* has no personal preferences or interests; it is impartial. And "when men seek for what is just [*tò díkaion*]," says Aristotle, "they seek for what is impartial [*tò méson*]. For law is that which is impartial."[26] Where is this impartial justice to be found? One may at least hope to encounter a judge who does his best, for, writes Aristotle in the *Nicomachean Ethics,* "to go to a judge [*dikastḗs*] is to go to justice [*tò díkaion*], for the ideal judge

20. Plato *Laws* 4.722e; cf. 720a–e; *prooímion:* ibid. 723a.
21. Aristotle *Politics* 3.1286a8–10.
22. Ibid. 1286a19–20.
23. Ibid. 1287a17–20.
24. Ibid. 1287a23; see Plato *Laws* 4.715c: *hupērétas.*
25. Aristotle *Politics* 1287a28–33. See the "Cratylizing" formula used in *Laws* 4.714a: *tḕn toû noû dianomḕn eponomázontas nómon* "giving to this distribution of reason the name *nómos*". See also 12.957c; *Philebus* 28c and 30d; Heraclitus frag. B 114 Diels-Kranz.
26. Aristotle *Politics* 1287b4.

is, so to speak, justice personified [*hoîon díkaion émpsukhon*]."²⁷ A judge can do no more than strive to be the incarnation of justice, for his *psukhê*, with its desires, inevitably renders him weaker than the *nómos* that, for its part, is entirely without emotional content.

The *díkaion émpsukhon* thus appears to be the reverse of the notion of the *nómos basileús*. Philo of Alexandria says as much: "The king is a *nómos émpsukhos*, whereas the *nómos* is a just king."²⁸ On the one hand, the metaphor of the law is used to refer to a living man who reigns; on the other, the metaphor of the king is used to refer to the functioning of the laws, which have no life in the physiological sense. The theme of the *nómos émpsukhos*, complementing that of the *nómos basileús*, is also quite widespread. Besides the passages from Aristotle and Philo cited above, it is worth noting the following remark by Clement of Alexandria: "The Eleatic Stranger declares that a royal and political man is a *nómos émpsukhos*."²⁹ It is a reference to Plato's *Statesman* and to a passage that is of the greatest interest to us, since it contains a discussion of writing. First, the Eleatic Stranger suggests an analogy:

> Let us suppose that a physician or a gymnastic trainer is going away and expects to be a long time absent from his patients or pupils. If he thinks that they will not remember his instructions, he would want to write them down as notes [*hupomnémata*], would he not? . . . What if he should come back after a briefer absence than expected? Would he not venture to substitute other rules for those instructive writings [*grámmata*] if others happened to be better for his patients, because the winds or something else had, by act of god, changed unexpectedly from their usual course? Would he persist in the opinion that no one must transgress the old laws, neither he himself by enacting new ones, nor his patient by venturing to do anything contrary to the written rules [*tà graphthénta*], under the conviction that these laws were medicinal and healthful and anything else was unhealthful and unscientific?³⁰

The Eleatic Stranger declares that such pigheadedness would be

27. Aristotle *Nicomachean Ethics* 5.4.7.1132a21.
28. Philo of Alexandria *Life of Moses* 2.4 (135).
29. Clement of Alexandria *Stromateis* 2.18.4.
30. Plato *Statesman* 295b–d.

most absurd. Similarly, he goes on to say, the lawgiver must be able
to alter the laws that he himself has written down, so as to adjust
them to new situations.[31]

Clearly the point here is not to become a slave to the written
nómos. As the incarnation of *nómos*, the king is even in duty bound
to place himself above the dead letter of the written *nómos*. He is a
living *nómos* endowed with a soul. In his treatise *On Royalty*, the
Pythagorean Diotogenes writes, "The king is either a *nómos émpsukhos* or a magistrate who observes the law [*nómimos árkhōn*]."[32] He
must either be the *nómos* incarnate or he must observe the *nómos*.
The theme here is similar to that of the *Statesman*, although we are
not told whether, as Diotogenes sees it, the *nómos* that the king must
observe is a written *nómos*. But a fragment from pseudo-Archytas,
which belongs to the same philosophical tradition as the Diotogenes fragment, does make this clear: "Of the two *nómoi* that exist,
one is *émpsukhos*, namely the king, while the other is *ápsukhos*,
namely the written word [*grámma*]."[33] What is not clear here is
whether the *nómos émpsukhos* is confused with the *nómos basileús*, as
it is on one occasion in Plutarch,[34] but in any case these three
concepts of *nómos basileús*, *nómos émpsukhos*, and *nómos ápsukhos* are
the three ideas that will direct my inquiry into a number of significant figures in the history of the Greek *nómos*.

To the extent that recitation and reading out the law both employ
the voice, the *nómos* is a voice, a compelling voice that demands to
be heard and obeyed, a voice that remains even when the king is no
longer there. Although it has no individual body, it is nevertheless a
real voice, not a metaphorical one, which makes use of city magistrates, or even its "slaves," the citizens as a whole, in order to sound
forth. For whether the voice depends on memory or on writing, the
nómos is their master, their *despótēs*. Their vocal apparatus is entirely
at its service. They serve as the means of its "exegesis," its vocal
expression, either by recalling its exact formulas, which are lodged

31. Ibid. 295d–296a ff.
32. Cited by Stobaeus, 4.7.61. On other instances of the expression *nómos
émpsukhos*, see Themistius *Orations* 1.93.20, 304.3; 2.220.12 Downey-Norman.
33. Cited by Stobaeus 4.1.135.
34. Plutarch *To an Ill-Educated Leader* 780c.

in their memories, or by reactivating a *nómos ápsukhos,* an inanimate *nómos* that is written and therefore only potential, for it has no voice of its own. The *nómos ápsukhos* is a *nómos* in a state of waiting. It is like a lasting vestige of an ephemeral king, a vestige that, once reanimated by the *exēgētēs,* will fulfill the function of the *nómos basileús.* The *nómos basileús* is just as opposed to the *nómos émpsukhos* as the *nómos ápsukhos* is; if the *nómos basileús* is the *nómos* that takes the place of the king, the *nómos émpsukhos* takes the place of the law, just as a king fills the place of the law. The king embodies it, he is the law in flesh and blood, breathing by himself, whereas an individual body is precisely what the *nómos basileús* lacks.

To seize upon the interaction of these three ideas gravitating around the *nómos,* I examine the traditions of two lawgivers, Lycurgus and Numa, and a figure who might be described as an arch-*exēgētēs,* namely Epimenides. Taking my inspiration from an idea produced by Andrew Szegedy-Maszak,[35] I examine these traditions in order to see whether they give a representation of the ideas mentioned above and, if they do, whether they can tell us any more about the relations between the *nómos,* the *psukhḗ,* and the body, between the voice and breathing, and between reading and writing. Szegedy-Maszak writes:

> Indeed, it might even be said that the hidden hero of the legends is codified law itself; once the code is self-sustaining, the legislator becomes superfluous. It is in this context that all of the details of the legends acquire their significance. They do not represent careless error or simple hagiography. Rather, they are consistent and unified in that they contribute to the idea of the excellence of the laws.[36]

Let us start with the legends on Lycurgus, the lawgiver of Sparta. Could we say that Plutarch's *Life of Lycurgus* stages an identifiable idea of the law? Should Lycurgus be seen as a "generic lawgiver" (using that word in the same sense as in the expressions "generic

35. A. Szegedy-Maszak, "Legends of the Greek Lawgivers," *Greek, Roman, and Byzantine Studies* 19 (1978), pp. 199–209. See also G. Nagy, "Theognis and Megara: A Poet's Vision of His City," in *Theognis of Megara: Poetry and the Polis,* ed. T. J. Figueira and G. Nagy (Baltimore, 1985), pp. 22–81, esp. pp. 36–41 and 78 on Lycurgus and Solon.

36. Szegedy-Maszak, "Legends of the Greek Lawgivers," p. 208.

poet" or "generic philosopher"[37])? Does the *Life of Lycurgus* set on stage a *nómos basileús* or a *nómos émpsukhos?*

Lycurgus was the brother of Polydektes, king of Sparta. Plutarch tells us that when the latter died, "as was generally thought, the kingdom devolved upon Lycurgus; and until his brother's wife was known to be with child, he was king. But as soon as he learned of this, he declared that the kingdom should belong to her offspring, if it should be male, and himself administered the government only as guardian."[38] His sister-in-law, Polydektes' widow, told him that she was willing to do away with the child before it was born so that Lycurgus could become king again, providing he would agree to marry her. Lycurgus pretended to agree, but persuaded her that she should not risk her own health by undergoing an abortion. He told her that he would himself take care of the child. When the child was born, Lycurgus made him king.

Conspiracies developed and Lycurgus decided to leave the country. He went to Crete, where he made a collection of laws, with a view to using them back in Sparta.[39] In Crete he met an important figure, the poet Thaletas or Thales, whose poetic activities masked another of his skills. He was also a lawgiver and one of the best.[40] Lycurgus persuaded him to visit Sparta, "for those who listened (to his song) were insensibly softened in their dispositions, insomuch that they renounced the mutual hatreds that were so rife at the time, and dwelt together in a common pursuit of what was high and noble. Thaletas, therefore, after a fashion, cleared the way [*pro-odopoieîn*] in Sparta for Lycurgus and his discipline."[41]

Meanwhile, the Spartans were beginning to regret the absence of Lycurgus and he allowed himself to be persuaded to return. He assumed authority and began to implement his reforms. "None of his laws were put into writing by Lycurgus, indeed one of the so-

37. For "generic poet," G. Nagy, *The Best of the Achaeans* (Baltimore, 1979), pp. 295 ff. For "generic philosopher," N. Loraux, "Therefore, Socrates Is Immortal," in *Fragments for a History of the Human Body,* pt. 2 (New York, 1989), chap. 1, n. 19.
38. Plutarch *Life of Lycurgus* 3.1–2.
39. See Herodotus 1.65.
40. See Aristotle *Politics* 2.1274a29 ff.
41. Plutarch *Life of Lycurgus* 4.3.

called *rhêtrai* forbids it." In place of written laws, he introduced a *paideía* "system of education" which replaced constraints by good will, inculcated into the young through education.[42] In this education, "of reading and writing [*grámmata*] they learned only enough to serve their turn,"[43] probably just enough to read such things as the funerary steles that stood in the city as *paradeígmata* 'models' for the young (only men who fell in battle and women who died in childbirth had the right to an inscribed stele).[44]

Once he was satisfied with his legislation, Lycurgus was anxious to render it immutable. He called a meeting of the citizens and told them that the constitution was a good one, but there was still one thing of the first importance that he needed to tell them; he could not do so, however, until he had consulted the god. "They must therefore abide by the established laws and make no change nor alteration in them until he came back from Delphi in person."[45] Everyone agreed. They all swore to keep and observe the laws until he returned, and Lycurgus set off for Delphi. Apollo told him that his laws were good and Lycurgus set down the oracle in writing and sent it to Sparta. He then decided that he "would not release the citizens from their oath and would put an end to his own life, there, in Delphi." He starved himself to death.[46]

Plutarch records a number of variants on the death of Lycurgus. According to one tradition, the remains of the lawgiver were brought back to Sparta, but then his tomb was struck by lightning. Others say that he died at Kirrha. Another tradition suggests that his death took place in Elis; others that it was in Crete, where his tomb used to be pointed out. Aristocrates of Sparta, the author of the *Lakonika* (between the second and first centuries B.C.), is quoted by Plutarch as follows: "The friends of Lycurgus, after his death in Crete, burned his body and scattered the ashes into the sea; and this was done at his request and because he wished to prevent his remains from ever being carried to Sparta, lest the people there

---

42. Ibid. 13.1–3.
43. Ibid. 16.10 (see also Plutarch *Lacedaemonian Institutions* 237a).
44. Ibid. 27.3.
45. Ibid. 29.3.
46. Ibid. 29.6–8. See Ephorus *FGrH* 70 F 175.

should change his laws, on the plea that he had come back, and that they were therefore released from their oaths." With these words, Plutarch brings his *Life of Lycurgus* to a close.

The notion of *nómos* as *basileús* 'king' is clearly at work in this biography. Plato confirms this in the following remarks on the legislation of Lycurgus: "It was the *nómos* that ruled as *basileús* over men, not men who made themselves tyrants over the laws."[47] In the first place, Lycurgus truly was a king (as Heraclitus was[48]), but, moved by a "sense of justice" (*dikaiosúnē*), which brought joy to his compatriots, he abdicated in order to devote himself to his work of legislation, which Thaletas' "prelude" introduced in a doubly symbolic fashion, for the effectiveness of this Cretan prelude depended upon its musicality. Once his constitution is completed, Lycurgus makes his co-citizens swear not to change it before his return (the constitution as a whole thus takes the form of a *rhḗtra,* in the sense of an "oral treaty" concluded between the lawgiver and the people). Thereupon he departs for Delphi, where he receives a favorable oracle from the god, which he communicates in writing to his fellow citizens. Although founded upon an oral agreement, the constitution is confirmed in a written text, for the lawgiver is no longer present to do it himself. For the laws to be effective, their author must absent himself, even do away with himself physically. If the king-lawgiver's *nómos* is to be enthroned in his place, it is not enough for him to abdicate. His very corpse, if taken back to Sparta, might release the citizens from their oaths, which is why Lycurgus has himself cremated and orders his friends to scatter his ashes abroad so as to make any return impossible. The effective presence of the law requires the absence of the lawgiver, the king who begins by abdicating and ends up by exiling himself forever. The *nómos* proclaimed aloud now takes the place of the *basileús* who will be mute forevermore. The *nómos* takes the place that used to be filled by the *basileús;* it is in fact a *despótēs* more perfect than any mortal master, for it has no personal interests or emotions, no "bestial" side. Lycurgus' legislation truly is a *noûs* 'mind', which knows nothing of desires, a mind freed from appetite [*órexis*]. The expression comes from Aristotle,[49] who according to Plutarch, declared of Lycurgus that "the honors paid him in Sparta were less than he deserved, although he enjoys the highest honors there."[50]

Plutarch's *Lives* are "parallel lives." Paired with Lycurgus is Numa. What should be said about him, the man whom Plutarch himself describes as a "lawgiver far more Greek than Lycurgus"?[51] What does "far more Greek" mean? This is assuredly a pertinent question, for the present study is not concerned with Rome. On one level (although this is not the one Plutarch had in mind), the answer might be that "far more Greek" is at least almost as Greek as Lycurgus. For the fact is that Numa's origins were Sabine and the origins of the Sabines were supposedly Spartan.[52]

The first difference between Lycurgus and Numa—as Plutarch himself points out—is that Lycurgus divested himself of his royal status in order to become a lawgiver, whereas Numa was elected king so that he could become a lawgiver.[53] Opposite procedures were thus adopted in these two cases, a fact that produced significant repercussions in their respective legislative endeavors.

The second difference concerns their relation to writing. One of Lycurgus' *rhêtrai* 'laws' forbade the use of writing in legislation.[54] Numa, on the other hand, although mistrustful of alphabetical signs, did have his legislation set down in writing. Plutarch tells us that, when he died, "they made two stone coffins and buried them under the Janiculum. One of these held his body, and the other the sacred books that he had written out with his own hand, as the Greek lawgivers their tablets [*kúrbeis*]."[55] Once buried—not cremated as Lycurgus was—Numa lay at rest alongside his written laws, his *grámmata,* which were as 'dead' (*ápsukha*), as the lawgiver

49. See above, p. 126 and n. 25.
50. Aristotle cited by Plutarch *Life of Lycurgus* 31.4.
51. Plutarch *Life of Numa* 23.10.
52. Ibid. 3.6, 1.5. See also *Life of Romulus* 16.1; Dionysius of Halikarnassos 2.49.4–5.
53. Plutarch *Life of Numa* 23.3–5.
54. Plutarch *Life of Lycurgus* 13.1–4, but cf. ibid. 29.6 on the written ratification sent from Delphi by Lycurgus.
55. *Life of Numa* 22.2, which is clearly a reference to Solon's *kúrbeis,* that is to say, the wooden tablets on which he had his laws inscribed. See N. Loraux, "Solon et la voix de l'écrit," in *Les Savoirs de l'écriture,* ed. M. Detienne (Lille, 1988), pp. 95–129.

himself.[56] In this case, the man and his work certainly did not merge into one; but neither were they widely separated.

This difference between Lycurgus and Numa leads to another, which concerns the duration of their respective constitutions. Lycurgus took care to organize a *paideía* "system of education" rather than fix his laws in writing, and this strategy turned out to be successful, since Lycurgus' constitution lasted for over five hundred years.[57] Numa, in contrast, founded a constitution whose aim was peace and friendship, but after his death it did not endure, precisely because it was not based upon a *paideía*.[58]

These differences are those between a *nómos basileús* and a *nómos émpsukhos* (which, suddenly, became irremediably *ápsukhos*). Whereas in Sparta Lycurgus the king made room for a *nómos* that was to outlive him for half a millennium, Numa, an elected king, is seen as the very incarnation of the *nómos*. In fact he is anyway a "living *nómos*" by virtue of the fact that his name is *Numa*, derived— according to Servius—from *nómoi: apò tôn nómōn*.[59] Once that "living *nómos*" was dead, he became as *ápsukhos* as the body of written letters buried at his side, just like a second corpse (or corpus).[60] The *nómos émpsukhos,* a nonmetaphorical king, thus left behind a *nómos ápsukhos*. He consequently lost all power over people's minds, and before long his constitution was replaced by a new one.

If the origin of the concept of *nómos émpsukhos* was Pythagorean—as the fragments of Diotogenes, the Pythagorean, and pseudo-Archytas, cited above, would suggest—the strong link between Numa and Pythagoras seems to be confirmed here.[61] Plutarch tells us that Numa perfected his wisdom by studying philosophy: "He had thus put away from himself not only the infamous passions [*páthē*] of the spirit, but also that violence and rapacity that are in such high repute among Barbarians, believing that true brav-

56. Plutarch *Life of Numa*. The term *ápsukhon* 'inanimate' is that employed by pseudo-Archytas, cited above, p. 128 and n. 33.

57. *Life of Lycurgus* 29.10; *Life of Numa* 26.9.

58. *Life of Numa* 26.10–14.

59. Servius *Commentary to the Aeneid* 6.808.

60. Plutarch *Life of Numa* 22.2: *ápsukha grámmata*.

61. See Ovid *Metamorphoses* 15.1 f., 15.60 f.; Plutarch *Life of Numa* 1.3, 22.5 ff. See P. M. Martin, *L'Idée de royauté à Rome* (Clermont-Ferrand, 1982), pp. 242–245.

ery consisted in the subjugation of one's passions [*epithumíai*] by reason [*lógos*]."[62] In other words, he tried to eliminate everything that, according to Aristotle, prevents man from being as impartial as the *nómos* in its pure state, which is stronger than man. Numa tried to shed precisely that *pathētikón* to which Aristotle referred.[63]

The Greek lawgivers chose a different course. By literally suppressing themselves, they established *nómos* as master in the city. Lycurgus deliberately starved himself to death so that his law would be sole ruler. Zaleukos died in battle and his death is in conformity with his own *nómos*.[64] Most striking of all is the case of Charondas. He had passed a law that forbade the introduction of weapons into the Assembly. One day he entered the Assembly inadvertently carrying a knife on his person, and when it was pointed out to him that he was disobeying his own law, Charondas committed suicide right there, in the Assembly, thereby providing the ultimate demonstration of the superiority of the impartiality of the *nómos* he had created.[65] Once independent from the lawgiver, the *nómos* assumes an auto-nomous existence, reigning over all "with a supreme hand."

These stories about lawgivers set on stage the fundamental notions of *nómos basileús* and *nómos émpsukhos*. For the notion of *nómos ápsukhos* and that of *exēgētés,* which is complementary to it, we must turn to the stories surrounding another figure. He may not be a lawgiver in the strict sense of the term,[66] but he is associated with the laws of Solon in the same way that Thaletas, the Cretan creator of laws, is associated with the legislation of Lycurgus.[67] This figure is Epimenides of Crete, who is known to have purged Athens from

62. Plutarch *Life of Numa* 3.7.

63. See above, p. 126 and n. 22.

64. *Suda* s.v. *Záleukos*. See Herodotus 7.104.4–5; Stobaeus 4.2.24 (p. 153, 5–7 Hense); see also Szegedy-Maszak, "Legends of the Greek Lawgivers," p. 206, on Aelian *Varia Historia* 13.24.

65. Diodorus Siculus 12.19.1–2; see Szegedy-Maszak, "Legends of the Greek Lawgivers," p. 206.

66. But see Diogenes Laertius 1.40, citing Dicaearchus on the Seven Sages, among whom Epimenides is sometimes numbered.

67. Plutarch *Life of Solon* 12.8–9; *On Music* 1146c; *Life of Lycurgus* 4.2–3. See Pausanias 1.14.4.

the defilement caused by the Alcmaeonids and who "cleared the way" (*proōdopoíēsen*) for Solon just as Thaletas, the healer of Sparta, had done for Lycurgus.[68]

By virtue of his activities as a purifier, Epimenides was the precursor of the purifiers-*exēgētaí* of Athens, as James H. Oliver has correctly pointed out in his book on the Athenian *exēgētaí*.[69] Epimenides possessed knowledge that could guide people safely through a crisis. He knew the appropriate *nómos*. He knew the answer to the question the *exēgētés* was always asked: *tí drásō?* (what must I do?). He knew the *drṓmena,* the "things that are done", that is to say, the "rites."[70] When his knowledge was sought, Epimenides went to Athens, where he prepared the way for Solon's legislation (a written legislation); reformed the funerary rites, another area in which the *exēgētaí* played a special role; and purified the city.[71] He then returned to Crete, an olive branch in his hand.

For our present purposes, it is Epimenides' relations with Sparta that make him a particularly significant figure. According to the historian Sosibios of Sparta, "the Lacedaemonians guard his body, in their own keeping, in obedience to a certain oracle."[72] When in Sparta, Epimenides had predicted the victory of the Arcadians over the Spartans (just as he had predicted the occupation of Mounychia in Athens),[73] and it was probably for reasons connected with his activities as a prophet that his corpse was preserved in Sparta.

68. *Life of Solon* 12.8: *proōdopoíēsen* (Epimenides); *Life of Lycurgus* 4.3: *proodopoieîn* (Thaletas), cited above, p. 130. Notice the wordplay here on *hodós/ōidḗ* ('way'/'song'). The verb *proodopoieîn* means "to prepare the way for" but also suggests the musical sense of "serve as a prelude for", on account of the existence of words such as *ōidopoiós* "composer of odes" (Theocritus *Epigrams* 17.4) and *proōidós* 'prelude' (*Scholia to Aristophanes, Birds* 1142; *Etymologicum Magnum* 691.48). The background to this wordplay is clearly provided by *prooímion* 'prelude, proem', formed from *pro*- and *oîmos* 'way, way of song'.

69. J. H. Oliver, *The Athenian Expounders of the Sacred and Ancestral Law* (Baltimore, 1950), pp. 25–26.

70. On *tí drásō* see above, Chapter 6, p. 118, n. 33, and also J. Defradas, *Les Thèmes de la propagande delphique,* 2d ed. (Paris, 1972), p. 200. On *drṓmena* see Plutarch *Life of Numa* 9.8.

71. See Plato *Laws* 12.958d; pseudo-Demosthenes, 47 *Against Euergos and Mnesiboulos* 69; Athenaeus 9.409f–410a. See also above, Chapter 6, p. 120 and n. 46.

72. Sosibius of Sparta, cited by Diogenes Laertius 1.115 (= *FHG* 2.628 Müller).

73. Plutarch *Life of Solon* 12.10.

Epimenides' prophetic knowledge, however, was usually directed toward the past, not the future; it was "retrospective."[74] It related to "faults committed in ancient times that had remained unknown. These it revealed, washing away the defilement by the appropriate rites of purification."[75]

At any rate, his corpse was kept in Sparta, far from Crete. Unlike the bodies of both Lycurgus and Numa, it was neither cremated nor buried. The *Suda* tells us, "When Epimenides finally died, his skin [*dérma*] was found to be tattooed with letters [*grámmasi katástikton*]."[76] Tattooing was not normally practiced among the Greeks, except for marking slaves.[77] For the Greeks, a man who was tattooed was either a slave or a Barbarian. But Epimenides was neither. So what had induced him to be tattooed? An ancient proverb alludes to his tattooed skin; according to the *Suda, tò Epimenídeion dérma* "Epimenidean skin" was an expression used "for secret things" (*epì tôn apothétōn*).[78] What kind of secrets? In Plato's *Phaedrus,* Socrates cites two curious hexameters, saying that they come *ek tôn apothétōn,* from "the reserves" of the *Homeridai.*[79] So it is perfectly possible that Epimenides' *apótheta* are of a poetic nature, especially since this Cretan was himself a hexametric poet in the Hesiodic tradition.[80] Such was the tattooing on this free Greek, and it caused him to become proverbial. In contrast to the withered corpse of Lycurgus, the ashes of which were eventually dispersed, and also to the corpse of Numa, whose mortal remains disappeared in their coffin (alongside which was placed another filled with his secret writings[81]), Epimenides' corpse seems to have been installed

74. Aristotle *Rhetoric* 3.1418a21 f. (= Epimenides frag. B 4 Diels-Kranz).

75. J.-P. Vernant, *Myth and Thought among the Greeks* (London, 1983), p. 87.

76. *Suda,* s.v. *Epimenídēs* (= Epimenides frag. A 2 Diels-Kranz). Epimenides' *sôma* would hardly have been *stripped* of its skin and thereby separated from it. The *Suda* text uses *dérma* rather than *sôma,* for *sôma* occurs immediately before: "It is said of him that his *psukhḗ* came out whenever it wished to and later returned into the *sôma;* when he finally died, his *dérma* was found to be tattooed by letters."

77. See U. Fantasia, "'Ἀστικτὸν χωρίον," *Annali della Scuola Normale di Pisa. Classe di lettere e filosofia,* 6 (1976), p. 1169n.11.

78. *Suda,* s.v. *Epimenídēs* (= Epimenides, frag. A2 Diels-Kranz).

79. Plato *Phaedrus* 252b.

80. See J. Svenbro, *La Parole et le marbre. Aux origines de la poétique grecque* (Lund, 1976), pp. 57–58.

81. Plutarch *Life of Numa* 22.7–8.

in perpetuity in Sparta, inseparable from its *grámmata*. There is no separation between the body and the writing, as there is in the case of Numa, who ensured that his human body and his body of writing were laid alongside each other. Epimenides refused any such separation, as if he wished to rectify the situation envisaged by Plato in the *Phaedrus,* in which writing is separated from its "father" and goes off "rolling to the right and to the left."[82] By having himself tattooed, Epimenides avoids the separation that for Plato constitutes one of the strongest of arguments against the use of writing.

Now, Epimenides' body was not just any body. It was the body of a "shaman," or at least the body of a man skilled in shamanistic techniques. According to a tradition recorded in the *Suda,* "the *psukhē* of Epimenides could leave the body whenever it wished to, and could later return to it."[83] By means of a physical respiratory technique in which the 'diaphragm' (*prapídes*) played a principal role, the *psukhē* of Epimenides was able to concentrate itself in such a way as to leave its body in a state resembling sleep or death.[84] The *psukhē* freed itself from the body.

What is the *psukhē*? To that huge question, I will venture at least a minimal reply, on the basis of the etymology of the word. Etymologically, *psukhē* is connected with *psúkhein* 'to breathe' and it is "definitely perceived as a breath."[85] For an entire philosophical tradition stretching from Anaximander to Diogenes of Apollonia, the *psukhē* was composed of air and was virtually synonymous with respiration.[86] When one breathed one's last, what departed was the

82. Plato *Phaedrus* 275e. Whereas Epimenides writes on his body, Plato wants to write in the *psukhē* (*Phaedrus* 275d–276a; *Philebus* 38e–39a).

83. *Suda,* s.v. *Epimenídēs;* see also s.v. *Aristéas.* On Greek shamanism see, for example, E. R. Dodds, *The Greeks and the Irrational* (Berkeley, Calif., 1951), chap. 5, inspired by K. Meuli, "Scythica," *Hermes,* 70 (1935), pp. 121–177.

84. See L. Gernet, *The Anthropology of Ancient Greece* (Baltimore, 1981), pp. 360–361; Vernant, *Myth and Thought,* pp. 85–86.

85. *Iliad* 20.440. On *psukhē*, see E. Rohde, *Psyche* (New York, 1925); D. B. Claus, *Toward the Soul: An Inquiry into the Meaning of Soul before Plato* (New Haven, 1981); J. Bremmer, *The Early Greek Concept of the Soul* (Princeton, 1983); G. Nagy, *Greek Mythology and Poetics* (Ithaca, 1990), pp. 88–93, 115–116, 142. P. Chantraine, *Dictionnaire étymologique de la langue grecque,* Paris (1968–1980), p. 1294.

86. See Orpheus frag. B 11; Anaximander frag. A 29 (includes evidence for Anaximenes); Xenophanes frag. A 1 (19); "Pythagorean School" frag. 58 B 1a (28

psukhḗ. That had already been Homer's visualization, and Plato's contemporaries continued to share it.[87] It thus seems perfectly logical to suppose, as Diogenes of Apollonia did, that children are born *ápsukha;* the *psukhḗ* enters into them as they draw their first breath of air.[88]

For the Pythagorean tradition, "the *psukhḗ* is nourished by blood, whereas words are breaths of the *psukhḗ* that, like the words, is invisible, since air, precisely, is invisible."[89] The links between the *psukhḗ* and vocal sound are explained in exemplary fashion by Aristotle: "Voice [*phōnḗ*] is the sound produced by a creature possessing a soul [*empsúkhou*], for an inanimate thing [*ápsukhon*] never has a voice."[90] He goes on to say, "The voice [*phōnḗ*] consists in the impact of the inspired air upon what is called the windpipe under the agency of the spirit [*psukhḗ*] in those parts." The voice is a "sound that means something" (*psóphos sēmantikós*) as distinct from, for example, a cough.[91] It is thus "by the body that the spirit [*psukhḗ*] signifies what it signifies [*sēmaínei hà àn sēmaínēi*]," as Plato expresses it in the *Cratylus*. "And for this reason it is justly called *sêma*."[92] The body is not only the 'tomb' (*sêma*) of the *psukhḗ,* but also the 'sign' or the 'signifier' (*sêma*) that the *psukhḗ* uses.[93] Thus in Democritus the tongue is called the "messenger of the *psukhḗ*."[94] Into this framework we should set an analogy that became current in late rhetoric, namely the analogy "body : spirit :: sign : meaning." The scholia to Hermogenes state, "For the Ancients, the *lógos* was called a living being [*zôion*] and, just as a living being consists of a *psukhḗ* and a body, so the *lógos* consists of a *psukhḗ,* namely the

---

and 30); Anaxagoras frag. A 93 (includes evidence for Archelaos); Diogenes of Apollonia frag. A 20 Diels-Kranz.

87. *Iliad* 16.453; Plato *Phaedo* 70a5.

88. Diogenes of Apollonia frag. A 28 Diels-Kranz; see Orpheus frag. B 11 Diels-Kranz.

89. Ibid. 1.450.20–22.

90. Aristotle *De Anima* 2.8.420b5–6. An *instrumentum vocale* is thus necessarily *émpsukhon* (see above, Chapter 6, p. 110 and n. 5).

91. Ibid. 420b27–29. See also Diogenes of Apollonia frag. A 21 Diels-Kranz; ibid., 32–33.

92. Plato *Cratylus* 400b–c.

93. Philolaos frag. B 14 Diels-Kranz; see Plato *Phaedrus* 250c, and *Gorgias* 493a. See also Dodds, *The Greeks and the Irrational*, chap. 5, n.109.

94. Democritus frag. C 6 (5) Diels-Kranz.

meaning [*enthumémata*] and a body, namely the linguistic form [*phrásis*]."⁹⁵

I discuss Epimenides' tattooed body in this context. First, we should consider the nature of the *grámmata* tattooed on Epimenides' body. The *Suda* has nothing to say on the matter, which is to be expected, given that the *dérma Epimenídeion* is synonymous with "secret things" (*apótheta*). I have already put forward a hypothesis regarding the form that these *apótheta* took; that is, they were probably cast in hexameters. For the rest, when one tries to imagine the content of those hexameters, the sacred books of Numa come to mind, the books whose *grámmata* became *ápsukha* the moment their author died, for those books contained the *apórrhēta* of Numa, his "secret teaching."⁹⁶ The *apórrhēta* of Numa and the *apótheta* of Epimenides seem to be analogous, even in respect of their being more or less inseparable from the bodies of their respective authors. But where Numa was only partially successful—it was on his own orders that his books were buried alongside him—Epimenides achieved total success; he was absolutely inseparable from his *grámmata,* just as an inscribed stele is inseparable from its inscription. So long as his corpse existed, its writing would belong to it. For the stele, to be inseparable from its inscription is to be entitled, par excellence, to refer to itself as *egṓ;* it is to be there, present before every reader who passes, present in the absence of the writer who, in the case of the inscriptions, is always a "third person," *ekeî-nos,* and is accordingly always absent.⁹⁷ The fact that Epimenides is inseparable from his own *grámmata* means that he too can claim to refer to himself as *egṓ,* which indicates presence even after death.⁹⁸ *Egṓ* cannot be refused him, at least until such time as his corpse disappears, and the inscription along with it. The absence of the writer, which is the rule in funerary and votive inscriptions and other kinds too, is here replaced by a real presence, in the fusion of writer with inscription, a fusion that seems designed to push the

95. *Scholia to Hermogenes, Perì staséōn,* in *Rhetores Graeci* 14.204.25–205, 4 Rabe.

96. Plutarch *Life of Numa* 22.2–3.

97. See above, Chapter 2.

98. Epimenides (frag. B 1 Diels-Kranz) is an imitator of Hesiod *Theogony* 24 f. (see Svenbro, *La Parole et le marbre,* chap. 2), in which the first person plays an important role. In Epimenides, it is not the Muses who address the *egṓ,* but apparently Justice and Truth, *Díkē* and *Alḗtheia.*

possibilities of writing to their furthest point, so as to produce an *egô* that, albeit transcribed, is not separated.

The idea of this extremist writing would certainly be no more than a fragile hypothesis were it not for a number of fundamental characteristics peculiar to the figure of Epimenides. Epimenides is master of his *psukhế* and his *sôma* to the point of being able to separate them, spatially, at will. Leaving its *sôma,* the 'tomb' of the spirit, the *psukhế* of Epimenides can travel freely for as long as it likes and then return to the body when it wishes to do so.[99] His *psukhế* goes off, as does Sarpedon's in the *Iliad,* when the hero faints but does not die; later, his "breath" returns.[100] The difference between the two is that Sarpedon's *psukhế* leaves him against his will (he is wounded and loses consciousness), whereas when Epimenides' *psukhế* goes off, the departure is willed and perfectly controlled.

When Epimenides finally dies at the age of 157, having spent fifty-seven years in uninterrupted sleep[101]—while his *psukhế* was absent from his body—the status of his body changes. It is a change for which the shaman has cleverly prepared, for his tattoos change his *sôma* into a *sêma,* in both senses of the latter word. Thanks to a study of the first importance by J.-P. Vernant, we are conscious of the affinity that the Greeks saw between the stiff corpse and the funerary stele.[102] This affinity is in play here, in the transition from

99. The *sôma* is to the *psukhế* what the shell is to the oyster, according to the analogy in the *Phaedrus* 250c; and, one might add, the shell speaks "thanks to its living mouth [*zôôi . . . stómati*]" after the death of the mollusk, in Theognis 1229–1230. See also Sappho frag. 118 Lobel-Page (*khélus* with the triple meaning of 'tortoise', "tortoise's carapace", and 'lyre', qualified by *phōnáessa* 'vocal') and G. Pfohl, *Greek Poems on Stones,* vol. 1, *Epitaphs: From the Seventh to the Fifth Centuries B.C.,* Textus Minores, no. 36 (Leiden, 1967), no. 138 (*zôòn . . . kléos* "living *kléos*"). Similarly, the consonants (*súmphōna*) are to the vowels (*phōnéenta*) what the body is to the soul (*Anecdota Graeca* 2.796.18–22 Bekker). This analogy is particularly suggestive in view of the modification that the Greeks introduced into the Semitic alphabet—a modification that made it an alphabet of signs not only for consonants (*áphōna* 'mute', like writing itself) but also for vowels (*phōnéenta* 'vocal', unlike writing).

100. *Iliad* 5.696: *tòn dè lípe psukhế* "his *psukhế* left him".

101. Diogenes Laertius, 1.109 and 111 (traditions on the age at which Epimenides passed away vary considerably).

102. See Vernant, *Myth and Thought among the Greeks,* pp. 305–321, "The Representation of the Invisible and the Psychological Category of the Double: The Colossos." See also Loraux, "Therefore, Socrates Is Immortal," p. 44.

sôma to *sêma.* Epimenides' tomb is constituted by his own body. His tattooed body is an inscribed *sêma,* all ready for reading. But as the inscription relates to *apótheta* "secret teaching"—presumably his *Oracles* (a hexametric poem)[103]—this writing is intended not for the general public, but only for qualified readers, such as *exēgētaí,* who can make the written message sound forth in an appropriate fashion.

What is reading? From the Greeks' point of view, it is the act in which the reader's vocal apparatus is controlled not by his own *psukhḗ* (except in an intermediary fashion) but by the written inscription that he sees before him, so as to produce a particular sequence of sounds that will be intelligible to the ear. To be read is to take control of somebody else's vocal apparatus, to exercise power over the body of the reader, even from a distance, possibly a great distance both in space and in time. The writer who is successful in getting himself read makes use of the internal organs of someone else, even from beyond the grave, making them serve him as an *órganon émpsukhon* or an *instrumentum vocale,* so as to broadcast his own name and his own words. The reader is, as it were, tele-programmed: his breath is programmed when he makes the mute *grámmata* sound forth. He puts his vocal apparatus into action as he is programmed to do by the writer. He is the servant of the writing just as Plato's magistrates are "the slaves of the law."

Now, when the reader puts his own breath at the service of Epimenides' corpse by reading his *grámmata* aloud, the programmed sound returns, and along with the sound of the words that are invisible as air itself (for, as Sappho puts it, words are "made of air," they are *ēéria épea*[104]), comes the meaning of the words, or, if you like, the *psukhḗ* of the words. The reader's voice, this purely instrumental voice that the writing appropriates, takes its orders from Epimenides. So is not the *psukhḗ* that vibrates in it his rather than the reader's? The same *psukhḗ* that in Epimenides' lifetime used to leave his body to return there sometime later now performs a different, yet analogous, movement, made possible by the reading of the *grámmata.* The air the reader sets in movement is the very same air

103. Epimenides frag. 1f. Diels-Kranz.
104. *Poetae Melici Graeci* frag. 938d Page.

from which the writer's *psukhḗ* is composed (as are his words when they are sounded aloud). Through his vocal apparatus, the reader activates the *psukhḗ* of this extraordinary *sêma* in which the writer and the inscription have fused together. The reading of the tattooed body thus represents a triple return, the return of the *psukhḗ* to the body, of the sound to the letters, and of the meaning to the sign.

The place of Epimenides' *psukhḗ,* which has flown off for good, is thus replaced by a succession of *psukhaí,* those of the readers of his tattooed corpse. For the duration of the reading, they belong to that corpse. They come to live in it and reanimate it. Probably the best term to convey that reanimation that the reader's voice achieves is "metempsychosis," a term usually, though somewhat inadequately, used to denote 'reincarnation' (*palingenesía*) in Greek.[105] Reading is a metempsychosis in the most precise sense: not a reincarnation, but a reanimation. Not that the two phenomena (metensomatosis, or reincarnation, and metempsychosis, or reanimation) are unrelated; in fact they come together in the figure of Epimenides, who claimed to be the reincarnation of Aiakos of Aegina, one of the judges in Hades.[106] In reanimation through reading, this Epimenidean metempsychosis, we can recognize the converse of the phenomenon of reincarnation. In reincarnation, a single *psukhḗ* inhabits a succession of different bodies, whereas in metempsychosis a succession of *psukhaí* inhabit a single body. That logical inversion of the terms of reincarnation could well have been invented by Epimenides as he meditated upon the reading of his own corpse.

If the desiccated corpse of Lycurgus, who died of starvation, resembled an uninscribed stele, the corpse of Epimenides resembles a stele that is inscribed, to which the reader imparts life through his voice, which the corpse can claim as "its own." Lycurgus is everywhere and nowhere, just like his unwritten *paideía,* which as we know remained alive for over five hundred years. In contrast,

105. See above, p. 123 and n. 2.
106. Diogenes Laertius, 1.114. On Aiakos, see Plato *Apology* 41a and *Gorgias* 523e. To claim to be a reincarnation of Aiakos was to attribute to oneself a remarkable skill where *nómos* was concerned, a skill that was very appropriate for an "arch-expounder" such as Epimenides. See also Proclus *Commentary on the Republic* 3.58.25–26 Festugière, according to whom Epimenides reappeared among the living after his death.

Epimenides, like Numa, can be traced to a particular spot in space. The *grámmata* tattooed on his body are clearly just as "dead" as those in Numa's sacred books: they are *ápsukha*. But they are not buried; they are available to a small circle of readers. They are like newborn children who have not yet drawn the breath that their "father" was so good at holding.[107] They await the "shock of inhaled air" (Aristotle) that will (re)animate and bring them (back) to a living, sonorous state.[108] And in contrast to Numa, Epimenides is not displaced by his *grámmata*. His voice is not transcribed on an object that will go off "to roll to the right and to the left." It is inscribed, in the very strongest sense of the word, on the surface of his own body, engraved on his skin. It is through his concern over the positioning of his writing that Epimenides makes the programmed return of his *psukhé* possible. It passes through the mouths of others to transform the dead letters into a living voice at the very spot where the mortal remains of Epimenides of Crete are preserved.

107. Lycurgus and Solon are the "fathers" of their *nómoi,* which are called their 'children' *(paîdes)* by Diotima in Plato *Symposium* 209d.

108. Aristotle *On the Soul* 2.8.420b27–29.

CHAPTER 8

Death by Writing:
Sappho, the Poem, and the Reader

In Sparta Epimenides is placed in a hall of reanimation; when the inscription on his body is read aloud, it allows him to return among the living. From beyond death "his voice"—the voice the reader gives up to him—will sound forth at every exegesis, every reading, restoring meaning to the sign. The breath that the Cretan shaman, thanks to his *prapídes* 'intelligence', controlled so perfectly that he could "expire" at will, is now imparted to him whenever a reader sets his vocal apparatus at the service of the writing. And it is imparted at the spot of Epimenides' choice: for this "master of the truth,"[1] who unlike Pythagoras chooses to write (in other words, do away with the *émpsukha* "animate things" by rendering them *ápsukha* 'inanimate'[2]), refuses to be separated from his written statements. Unlike the case of a lawgiver such as Charondas who at the cost of his own life accepts the absolute reign of his own *nómos,* the truth that Epimenides masters is totally inseparable from him. Truth cannot establish itself in any kind of autonomy in relation to

1. See M. Detienne, *Les Maîtres de vérité dans la Grèce archaïque* (Paris, 1967).
2. The Pythagorean precept that bids the faithful "to abstain from living creatures" (*empsúkhōn apékhesthai*) implies first and foremost that they should not kill such creatures, for all the *émpsukha* belong to one and the same 'family' (*homogenê*): "Pythagorean School" frag. 100.40 Diels-Kranz. If the spoken *lógos* is *émpsukhos* 'animate', what is written or *grámma* is, as we have seen, *ápsukhon* 'inanimate'. To fix speech in writing, consequently, would be to kill it; accordingly, the Master does not write. I will return to the refusal to write on the part of Pythagoras (but not all Pythagoreans) and Socrates (but not Plato).

its author. Although *"transcribed,"* Epimenides' truth is not separated from him.[3] Despite his use of writing, Epimenides remains a "master of truth" in the real sense of the expression.[4]

To assess this model of reanimation through reading against another, I have chosen a text by someone who presents enough distinctive features to make a comparison profitable and who may, moreover, have lived at the same time as the historical Epimenides, if it is true that he came into contact with Solon. I refer to Sappho. Solon is known to have been a fervent admirer of Sapphic poetry and, though separated from her by space, lived at the same time. A fragment of Aelian runs: "When Solon the Athenian, son of Exekestides, heard a poem by Sappho sung to him at a banquet by his nephew, he liked it so much that he ordered the young man to teach it to him. And when someone asked him why he was so eager to do this, he replied, 'So as not to die before having learned it.' "[5]

A Greek living around 600 B.C., if reflecting upon the matter of setting down a poem in writing, would probably consider the question in terms of a *transcription* of something that already had a socially recognized existence and that had been technically mastered in an oral or memorized state. Considering the transcription as the operation that rendered the poem lasting or famous would not be necessary; the oral tradition was quite capable of doing that, without the assistance of writing. It relied on *mnēmosúnē* and men's *tónos,* their 'memory' and their 'voice', to borrow the terms that the philosopher Xenophanes used in a poem composed in the second half of the sixth century.[6] It was perfectly self-sufficient, autonomous.

Sappho's poems were sung, and were composed to be sung. They are marked by formal, grammatical features that characterize them as oral and traditional, to use the terms of Milman Parry, who

3. See above, p. 28.

4. Epimenides frag. B 1 Diels-Kranz: Epimenides' knowledge comes from Truth itself, *Alétheia* personified.

5. Aelian cited by Stobaeus, 3.29.58. On Epimenides' dates see Aristotle *Constitution of Athens* 1; Plutarch *Life of Solon* 12; Neanthes in Athenaeus, 602c (= *FGrH* 84 F 16). Plato's chronology in *Laws* 1.642d–e is fantasy.

6. Xenophanes frag. B 1.20 Diels-Kranz. Here *tónos* probably has its vocal meaning ("tone of voice"), although translators of Xenophanes tend to understand the word in the sense of 'effort' (see primarily Liddell-Scott-Jones, s.v. *tónos*).

devoted a study to them.[7] We know them, however, in their written form. And that may even then have been the case for Solon's nephew, although it is equally possible that he had learned the *mélos* 'song' in question through oral transmission. However that may be, we can be relatively sure that Sappho's work was already set down in writing during the lifetime of the poetess, and it seems reasonable to think that she had a hand in that writing, herself wielding the stylus.

As soon as her poems were fixed in writing, that very fact had the effect of noticeably distancing them from their author, as the anecdote about Solon perhaps suggests. Once they became written objects, they could circulate "to the right and to the left," separated from their "mother." I have elsewhere tried to show how the consciousness of such a separation is reflected in the corpus of the works of Theognis, whose correct presentation—that is, presentation in conformity with the author's own wishes—depends on the presence of a "worthy man" (*ho esthlós*) at the moment of the performance.[8] I believe that such a consciousness, which was so important for Plato and the Pythagoreans, who made use of writing but did not make it available to the public,[9] must be taken into account when considering a poetess like Sappho, who lived at a time when lyric poetry was massively, and for the first time, com-

7. M. Parry, *The Making of Homeric Verse: The Collected Papers of Milman Parry*, ed. A. Parry (Oxford, 1971), pp. 347–350 ("The Language of Lesbian Lyric Poetry" [1932]). The small corpus of writings that has come down to us from the Lesbian poets contains a number of formulas such as those noted by Parry. Thus, Sappho frag. 1.17 may be compared with frag. 5.3; similarly, frag. 5.5 with frag. 15.5; frag. 31.6 with Alcaeus frag. 283.3; Sappho frag. 1.10 with frag. 16.2 and 20.6 Lobel-Page.

8. I have translated Theognis 21 *tousthloû pareóntos* as "in the presence of a worthy man" (genitive absolute; on *ho esthlós* "the worthy man", see Theognis 1368: *ho pareón* "the man [who is] present"). See J. Svenbro, *La Parole et le marbre. Aux origines de la poétique grecque* (Lund, 1976), pp. 84–86.

9. Plato *Phaedrus* 275d–e; "Pythagorean School" frag. 58 D 4 Diels-Kranz; G. S. Kirk, J. E. Raven, and M. Schofield, *The Presocratic Philosophers* (Cambridge, 1983), p. 216; Porphyry *Life of Pythagoras* 18. Compare the *apórrhēta* of Numa, which were burned when rediscovered, being judged unsuitable for general circulation (Plutarch *Life of Numa* 22.2–8); also the *apótheta* of Epimenides (see above, pp. 137, 140, 142) and Heraclitus' famous book, deposited in the temple of Artemis and written in an obscure style so that the common people would not be able to understand it (Diogenes Laertius 9.6).

mitted to writing. Although her work stemmed from an oral tradition and she composed her poems for the ear, Sappho was no doubt conscious of the written dimension of her poems once they began to be set down in writing.

Now, in Sappho's day, the "order" of written discourse did not emerge clearly in the field of poetry, either lyric or epic. The reason for this, as I have suggested, is that the oral poem was more important than the written one, in the sense that the latter was a transcription of the living voice of the poet or bard speaking in the first person singular, a transliteration of something that already had a fully recognized existence but was to be fixed in writing—possibly to produce an *ágalma* 'artwork' dedicated to a deity, or a *hupómnēma* 'memorandum' for the use of a group, or perhaps in order to render a particularly successful work immutable forever.[10] The speech-act markers ("I," "here," "now," for example) in the poetry of this period are consequently always those of oral poetry. To that extent, poetry is decidedly not an ideal case in point for those wishing to study the effects of writing upon speech-acts.

But there is another domain where the speech-act is deeply marked by writing, in this case from the very outset. In funerary and votive inscriptions of the archaic period (as in contemporary graffiti), the order of discourse is quite particular and furthermore

10. Thus, Diogenes Laertius (ibid.) says that Heraclitus 'dedicated' (*anéthēke*) his book in the temple of Artemis. As we learned in Chapter 2 (p. 38), this verb has the precise technical sense of 'to dedicate [an *ágalma* to a deity]'.

Consider the "chosen passages" (*léxeis exeilegménai:* "Pythagorean School" frag. 58 D 1 (164) Diels-Kranz)—from Homer or Hesiod—to which the Pythagoreans gave allegorical interpretations. See M. Detienne, *Homère, Hésiode et Pythagore,* "Latomus" collection, 57 (Brussels, 1962), pp. 27, 36.

By contrast, since Thucydides describes his written work as a *ktêma es aieí* an "asset for all time to come" (1.22.4), as opposed to exhibition pieces designed to give pleasure to the audience of the moment, his point of view is already that of a "written culture"; for an oral culture, tradition needs nothing more than memory and human voices to guarantee its lasting permanence. What seems to us the most "natural" reason (one fixes an oral poem in writing so that posterity will come to know it) was probably not one from the point of view of authors such as Hesiod and Sappho. On Thucydides, see G. Cerri and B. Gentili, *Le Teorie del discorso storico nel pensiero greco e la storiografia romana arcaica* (Rome, 1975), pp. 17–45; Cerri and Gentili, "Written and Oral Communication in Greek Historical Thought," in *Communication Arts in the Ancient World,* ed. E. A. Havelock and J. B. Hershbell (New York, 1978), pp. 137–155.

carries the force of an established notion shared by the culture as a whole. The inscribed object refers to itself in the first person, whereas the writer refers to himself in the third person. (Only from 550 B.C. on, as we have seen, does one begin to come across objects that refer to themselves in the third person.[11]) An amphora from the sixth century provides an example: "Kleimachos made me and I am his [*ekeínou eimí*]."[12] When the inscription is read out loud, Kleimachos will no longer be there. He will be absent, as the demonstrative *ekeînos* makes clear. (*Ekeî-nos* is the demonstrative of the third person, indicating that the person is not "here," but "far away," or even "in the beyond": *ekeî*.) The amphora, on the other hand, *is* there: no entity has a better right to lay claim to the *egó* in the inscription. Kleimachos certainly cannot. He writes on the amphora precisely because he foresees his own absence in the future (were that not the case, there would be no point in writing at all). He refers to himself as 'absent' (*ekeînos*), since it is he who will have written the inscription. Everything else will take place between the inscription and the reader, now in a one-to-one situation of "I"/"you," which may be reversed into "you"/"I." The amphora refers to itself as "I" because the reader is its "you," at whom the inscription is aimed. For the reader, who naturally refers to himself as "I," the other party necessarily becomes "you." We came across this kind of reversibility when studying Panamyes' inscription.[13]

Such was the order of written discourse in Sappho's day. The question is, did Sappho simply transcribe poems conceived orally or are we to suppose that she might have come up against the problem of the written "I"? Whatever the answer in Sappho's case, that problem is certainly a real one. Consider the way that Hecataeus, Herodotus, and Thucydides all start off by referring to themselves in the third person, but then immediately slip into the first person. First Hecataeus, who begins, "Hecataeus of Miletus recounts as follows [*hôde mutheîtai*]," and goes on, "I write this [*taûta gráphō*]."[14] Then Herodotus: "What Herodotus of Thurii has

11. See above, Chapter 2.

12. M. Guarducci, *Epigrafia greca,* 3 (Rome, 1975), p. 482. See above, pp. 31 and 42–43.

13. See above, p. 57.

14. Hecataeus *FGrH* 1 F 1a.

learned by inquiry is here set forth [*Hērodótou Thouríou historíēs apódexis hḗde*]," followed by, "As for me [*egò dé*] . . . ,"[15] referring to himself. Finally Thucydides: "Thucydides of Athens has written the history of the war [*sunégrapse tòn pólemon*] between the Peloponnesians and the Athenians," followed by, "But, following the indications that, in the course of the most far-reaching research, have enabled me to arrive at a conviction [*skopoûntí moi pisteûsai xumbaínei*]. . . ."[16] The works of all these historians thus bear monumental inscriptions in the sense that, seen "from outside" (this is the first phrase that permits the reader to enter into the work), they refer to their authors in the third person, as if they are absent.[17] The authors are no longer there. Only through a fiction—a fiction that for us has become a rule—do they refer to themselves in the first person inside their works, just as if they were present in the text. After the introductory sentence, their works thus assume the form of a transcription of a living voice, as if they had first existed orally and only later were faithfully transcribed. In contrast, where Hesiod uses the form of a transcription, referring to himself as *egố,* or even *hóde egố,* thereby setting himself up as an interlocutor who is present, it probably was a real transcription, whether made by Hesiod himself or by someone else.[18] For Epimenides, of a later generation than Hesiod,[19] it is precisely that oral *egố,* transcribed later, that presents a problem. In order not to become detached from it, as he writes, he tattooes it onto his body—a logical enough solution within the Greek context (if an extreme one) since in ancient Greece men who were free were not expected to be tattooed.

Is Sappho's "I" simply an oral "I," mechanically transcribed and

15. Herodotus 1.1.0, 5.3.

16. Thucydides 1.1.1, 2. My observations on the three historians were produced independently from Nicole Loraux ("Thucydide a écrit la guerre de Péloponnèse," *Mètis,* 1 [1986], pp. 131–161). See also Bacchylides 5.11: *pémpei* "he sends", which at the beginning of this epistolary poem introduces the poet as a third person, wishing to sing the praises of the tyrant Hieron, who is the addressee; in line 31, Bacchylides has already become a first person (*emoí* 'for me').

17. If Thucydides describes his work as a *ktêma es aieí,* as I described above (n. 10), the idea of a *mnêma* '(funerary) monument' is not far off (see also above, p. 95). Thucydides is mortal, but his work will endure forever.

18. Hesiod *Theogony* 24, cited above, Chapter 2, p. 33 and n. 30.

19. See Svenbro, *La Parole et la marbre,* pp. 57–58.

implying no more than Hesiod's? Let us take a look at fragment 31 in Lobel and Page, in which "I" appears in the very first line:

φαίνεταί μοι κῆνος ἴσος θέοισιν
ἔμμεν' ὤνηρ, ὄττις ἐνάντιός τοι
ἰσδάνει καὶ πλάσιον ἆδυ φωνεί-
σας ὑπακούει

καὶ γελαίσας ἰμέροεν, τό μ' ἦ μὰν
καρδίαν ἐν στήθεσιν ἐπτόαισεν·
ὡς γὰρ ἔς σ' ἴδω βρόχε', ὥς με φώναι-
σ' οὐδ' ἒν ἔτ' εἴκει,

ἀλλὰ κὰμ μὲν γλῶσσά ⟨μ'⟩ ἔαγε, λέπτον
δ' αὔτικα χρῷ πῦρ ὑπαδεδρόμηκεν,
ὀππάτεσσι δ' οὐδ' ἒν ὄρημμ', ἐπιρρόμ-
βεισι δ' ἄκουαι,

κὰδ δέ μ' ἴδρως κακχέεται, τρόμος δὲ
παῖσαν ἄγρει, χλωρότερα δὲ ποίας
ἔμμι, τεθνάκην δ' ὀλίγω 'πιδεύης
φαίνομ' ἔμ' αὔτ[α.

[He seems to me the equal of the gods, the man who, seated before you, close to you, listens to your gentle voice / and your beguiling laugh—truly, it makes my heart leap in my breast; for as soon as I behold you for a moment, I can no longer say a single word. / My voice breaks and a slight fever immediately spreads beneath my skin, my eyes see nothing, my ears hum, / the sweat pours from my body, a shudder runs right through me; I become more palely green than grass, and seem to myself to be more dead than alive.]

Three people seem to be involved here, an "I" (Sappho), a "you" (defined in the Greek text as being of the feminine gender), and a *kênos* (= *ekeînos:* "that one," the man seated before the "you"). Seen in the perspective of inscriptions, where the writer does not refer to himself as an "I," Sappho's poem, like so many other lyric and epic poems, is an anomaly. For Sappho should have defined herself as 'absent', or even 'dead', using the demonstrative *kếnē* (= *ekeínē*) "that one". Now, while retaining the form of a transcription, like a writer setting down his own epitaph ("I lie dead, below" is what we read on Mnesitheos' stele[20]), Sappho understands that, as a consequence of writing, she will be absent, even dead. For although her poem takes the form of a transcription of a living voice, that voice "breaks" (line 9) even as she transcribes it. She loses her voice as she writes the poem. Her breath is literally suspended; she cannot speak (lines 7–8).[21] She displays the symptoms of a Homeric warrior seriously wounded and terrified at the prospect of death.[22] Like Patroklos or Sarpedon, she *expires,* in the last line of the poem.[23] Just a few syllables before the end of the poem, she says that she is not "far short" (*olígō*) of death. By the time the poem is over, she will be dead.

The order of written discourse requires the writer to define himself as absent, as dead. That is the established notion that informs Greek inscriptions until well after the archaic period. Sappho must have been familiar with that established notion; she certainly shared it. But coming as she did from the oral tradition, she set up the disappearance of the writer in a new way—not by using the third person for herself, but by giving an allegorical description of her own death by writing.

So what becomes of the "he" and the "you" in the poem? The demonstrative *kênos* (= *ekeînos*), which refers to the absent third person, is the polar opposite of the "I" who writes and who dies as a consequence of doing so. Just as, from the point of view of the addresser, *hoi ekeî* "those there" can refer to the addressees of a letter, that is to say its readers,[24] so too it seems justifiable to suppose that *kênos* "that one" can refer to the reader of the poem, absent for the one who is writing "I," that is to say Sappho, who is

20. G. Pfohl, *Greek Poems on Stones,* vol. 1, *Epitaphs: From the Seventh to the Fifth Centuries B.C.,* Textus Minores, no. 36 (Leiden, 1967), no. 128 (= Peek, no. 1210), analyzed above, p. 48.

21. See the Homeric formula *thalerè dé hoi éskheto phōnḗ* "his blooming voice was held back," cited above, p. 24.

22. See L. Rissman, *Love as War: Homeric Allusion in the Poetry of Sappho,* Beiträge zur klassischen Philologie, 157 (Königstein, 1983), pp. 66–118; J. Svenbro, "La Stratégie de l'amour. Modèle de la guerre et théorie de l'amour dans la poésie de Sappho," *Quaderni di storia,* no. 19 (1984), pp. 68–69.

23. *Iliad* 16.856, 5.696: *tòn dè lípe psukhḗ* "his *psukhḗ* left him" (cf. 16.453).

24. Euripides *Iphigenia in Tauris* 771.

present in the written speech-act (although soon to be separated from what she has written).

Sappho does not have her poem tattooed on her. She writes it down and puts it into circulation. Whereas in Sparta Epimenides is forever present together with his secret teaching, Sappho will be absent where her poem is read. Wherever Sappho's poem will be infused with the *psukhê* that she herself breathed out in its last line, she will be absent. That is why she is jealous of the reader who will espouse her own *graphê, her* writing. *Ísos théoisin* "the equal of the gods" is a formula taken from the rites of marriage, in which it is used to denote the young husband.[25] The reader will celebrate his or her marriage with the poem, in the absence of the one who is its "mother." This word "mother" is not used lightly. According to an epigram by Dioscorides which is full of allusions to Sappho's poetry, Sappho's 'odes' (*aoidaí*) are, precisely, her 'daughters' (*thugatéres*).[26] A male writer is the "father" of his writing;[27] likewise, a female one is its "mother."

In this connection, we should remember that Sappho's real daughter bore a significant name: she was called *Kléïs,* a name derived from *kléos* "sonorous renown".[28] Every time the daughter

25. See Sappho frag. 111.5; cf. frag. 44.34, 105b Lobel-Page. See also T. Mc-Evilley, "Sappho Fragment Thirty-One: The Face Behind the Mask," *Phoenix,* 32 (1978), pp. 1–18.

26. *Greek Anthology,* 7.407.9–10: "We still possess your immortal daughters [*athanátas . . . thugatéras*], to wit your songs [*sàs . . . aoidás*]." According to Himerius, Sappho "wrote young girls" *gráphei parthénous* (Himerius *Orations* 1.4 [= Sappho frag. 194 Lobel-Page]). Unfortunately, the text, which is a paraphrase of one or more of Sappho's poems, does not make it possible to determine the nature of this "writing" precisely. But we should certainly not replace the word *gráphei,* which the manuscript tradition gives, by *ageírei* "she gathers", as some scholars have suggested doing. See also Plato *Symposium* 209d, in which Diotima says that good poets leave behind them 'descendants' (*ékgona*) who, "being themselves immortal, are able to confer upon them an immortal *kléos.*" The poems are the immortal children of the poet.

27. See above, p. 85.

28. Sappho test. 1 and 2 Campbell; frag. 98b and 132 Lobel-Page. The name *Kléïs* has nothing to do with the Attic *kleís* 'key', which was pronounced *klâis* in the Aeolic dialect used by Sappho (see Liddell-Scott-Jones, s.v. *kleís*). Besides, the testimonia state that Sappho's daughter was called Kleis after the poetess's mother. It seems very likely that Sappho did belong to a family in which *kléos,* in the sense of 'poetry', was considered particularly important; see above, pp. 13 and 66. The name Kleis could well be a reference to that technical sense of *kléos,* particularly as

was called by her name, the renown of her mother sounded forth, according to the logic studied in Chapter 4. Now, in one poem, Aphrodite seems to promise Sappho *kléos* in a future time when the poetess will be dead.[29] For Sappho, there will be no 'oblivion' (*léthē*), even when she has disappeared physically, for, another fragment runs, "People will remember [*mnásesthai*] us, I declare."[30] Sappho was honored by the gift of the Muses; not for her the fate of the woman "with no share in the roses of Pieria," destined to become an invisible, forgotten shade in the House of Hades.[31] Thanks to her spiritual daughters, her poems, Sappho will enjoy sonorous, posthumous *kléos*.[32]

She will do so, that is, provided that they find a reader prepared to put his or her voice at their service. Thus, "like a god" (*ísos théoisin*) the reader of fragment 31 will put his voice into the material *graphḗ* of the poem—a situation not unlike that in which Hermes infuses a voice into Pandora, according to Hesiod's *Works and Days* (Sappho treated the very same subject in a poem now lost).[33] The poem is a *kórē* 'girl' with the power to set off the voice of a reader, a voice instantly appropriated by the *kórē* herself, who now "speaks" and "laughs." The fact is that the poem occupies the place of the

---

Sappho was concerned with the *kléos áphthiton,* the "unquenchable renown" of the heroes (Sappho frag. 44.4 Lobel-Page). On the mother as a name-giver, see Euripides *Phoenician Women* 58, in which Jocasta names Antigone ('Renée', meaning 're-born').

29. Sappho frag. 65 Lobel-Page.

30. Ibid. frag. 143 Lobel-Page; frag. 147 Lobel-Page.

31. Ibid. frag. 32 Lobel-Page; frag. 55 Lobel-Page.

32. Conversely, if the Arignota (given that that was indeed her real name) of frag. 96 Lobel-Page was a "former disciple" of Sappho's (see frag. 214 B.1 Campbell) and the wife of a citizen of Sardis, she received Sappho's teaching as a kind of writing in her *psukhḗ*, ready to be 'read' or heard by her husband (I am here anticipating a theme to which I will return in Chapter 9). In addition to Sappho's biological daughter, Kleis (a *mnêma* recalling the existence of her mother), and the spiritual daughters represented by Sappho's poems, the poetess's "daughters" also included the young girls who received a "writing" upon their *psukhḗ* before they were married. The resemblances between Sappho's circle and that of Socrates were thus by no means superficial (already noted in the ancient world: see Sappho test. 20 Campbell).

33. Hesiod *Works and Days* 79–80; Sappho frag. 207 Lobel-Page. See also *Rhetores Graeci* 14.398–399 Rabe for the idea of speech as a "young girl" (*kórē*) (*Scholia to Hermogenes, Perì ideōn*).

"you," from the point of view of the one who writes it, as well as from that of the one who reads it. The "you" in the poem is the poem itself, which in an inscription would be qualified as "I" (which, of course, can revert to "you," as we saw in the case of the Panamyes inscription). Here, "the poem is you," an apparently paradoxical proposition (I have borrowed it from John Ashbery[34]) that conforms, however, with the conventions of archaic poetry, as is demonstrated by a few lines from Pindar. Having stressed the superiority of his odes over immobile statues, the poet addresses the ode itself, "O, my sweet song, depart from Aegina [*glukeî' aoidá, steîkh' ap' Aigínas*]."[35] The ode becomes "you" at the moment when it must be separated from the poet.

Instead of writing, as in inscriptions, "I am Sappho's poem; you will read me," Sappho writes, "You are my poem; he will read you." The reader will breathe into the poem the *psukhḗ* that Sappho breathed out there. In short, the reader will restore life, voice, sound, and meaning to the *graphḗ* by making it "speak" and "laugh" each time that he reads it, since the present tense that is used, *upakoúei* "he listens" will always refer to the reading of the poem, at which the reader is the foremost listener. The present tense creates the possibility of an eternally renewable reference.[36] In this perspective, not surprisingly does the reader take on the character of a god: although readers are mortal, the Reader is eternal. Sappho is jealous of that Reader, living in a future in which she will be dead. Another of Sappho's fragments runs: "To die is an evil; thus have the gods decided it. For if it was fine to die, the gods too would die."[37] As presented by the poem, the Reader appears as "the equal of the

34. J. Ashbery, "Paradoxes and Oxymorons," *Shadow Train* (New York, 1981), p. 3, where the expression has another meaning.

35. Pindar *Nemean* 5.5–6. See also *Olympian* 2.1; and the personification of the *aoidaí* in *Isthmian* 2.7–8. The poems of the professional poet, who writes for money, become "girls," in the sense of prostitutes, "with soothing voices" (*malthakóphōnoi*).

36. See above, p. 62. In this context the observations made by L. Rydbeck on the force of *óttis* (followed by the indicative) in line 2 become particularly suggestive ("Sappho's Φαίνεταί μοι κῆνος. ὅττις [line 2]: A Clue to the Understanding of the Poem," *Hermes*, 97 [1969], pp. 161–166). The relative *óttis*, which here virtually equals *ós*, refers to the reader who, seated before the poem, is truly hearing it as he reads it. This is a specific reader to the extent that each reading is a unique event, albeit one that may be repeated.

37. Sappho frag. 201 Lobel-Page.

gods," but the one who writes it appears to be dying. To write is thus to demonstrate one's mortality, one's humanity (the Greek gods do not write, nor do they invent writing; they appear to have no use for it at all).[38] The abstract Reader of the poem, however, is immortal, eternally renewable and, as such, stands as the polar opposite of the one who presents the proposition: "I write, so I shall die." In truth, that is exactly what the majority of archaic inscriptions say, although they do it in a less spectacular fashion—by turning the writer into the third person, that is to say, someone who has already disappeared.

This allegorical reading of Sappho's fragment 31, in which the poem itself is the "you" and the reader is the "he"—"seated before" (enántios) the poem—may seem somewhat extravagant in view of what we believe about the nature of Sappho's poetry, at first sight so remote from learned, allegorical, and enigmatic poetry. But is her poetry really a spontaneous and naive effusion of a woman ruled by her passions? Some poems would appear to prove the contrary. In the Lobel and Page fragment 1, when she uses, not without irony, the Homeric model of war to define her own model of love, we are already a long way from the Sappho who encounters Aphrodite in a "religious vision" and proceeds to describe this encounter in her poem.[39] After all, was not her contemporary, Alcaeus, an allegorical poet? One of his poems gives a detailed description of a ship in distress, a description that is really an allegory of the City, although we might not have suspected that, had it not been for the commentary provided by Heraclitus the Allegorist. He points out that

38. See M. Detienne, *Les Dieux de l'écriture,* forthcoming. And, one might add, if Pythagoras does not write, it is because he wishes to live like a god, as his eating habits also suggest, for the rejection of meat betrays a desire to live in the same manner as the Immortals (see M. Detienne, *The Gardens of Adonis* [Hassocks, 1977], pp. 37–58). See also above, n. 2. Socrates' refusal to write, however, is a complex gesture that, from one point of view, expresses his faith in the immortality of the *psukhē*. If the *psukhē* is eternal, why commit one's thoughts to writing? I will return to another aspect of his rejection of writing in Chapter 10.

39. See Svenbro, "La Stratégie de l'amour," pp. 57–63; Rissman, *Love as War,* especially pp. 18–19. See A. Cameron, "Sappho's Prayer to Aphrodite," *Harvard Theological Review,* 32 (1939), pp. 13–14, which cites a number of naively literal interpretations of the poem, in particular that of C. M. Bowra, *Greek Lyric Poetry* (Oxford, 1936), pp. 193–194. Bowra maintains his interpretation, in a slightly different form, in the second edition of *Greek Lyric Poetry* (Oxford, 1961), pp. 202–203.

Alcaeus used allegory "at a fair number of places", (*en hikanoîs*) and then proceeds to cite the remarkable poem about the Ship of State.[40] The thrust of it is: "I understand nothing about these winds that are rising; the waves crash down now here, now there. And we, in the middle, are borne away on our black ship, / rudely buffetted by the great storm; now the water covers the foot of the mast; all the sails are in shreds, gashed by great rents. / And the anchors are giving way. . . ."[41] Heraclitus comments: "At first sight, this picture, which carries us out to sea, suggests that it concerns sailors frightened by a storm. But no: the poet's intention is to refer to Myrsilos and the conspiracy that he fomented to impose his tyranny upon Mytilene."[42]

If Alcaeus was capable of composing poems that satisfied the demands of the enthusiasts of poetry about the sea at the same time as those of theorists of the city, with no suggestion of a clash, we may reasonably suppose that Sappho could also have composed allegorical poems. I am not sure, however, that if taken as an allegory on writing, fragment 31 really leaves room for the customary interpretation of those who read it as an expression of the love that Sappho feels for the "you" of the poem.

The lover who succumbs, wounded by love, is a traditional figure used before Sappho by Archilochus.[43] But upon looking more closely into the poem, one realizes that if that figure is at all relevant here, Sappho has certainly manipulated it for her own purposes. In truth, nothing in the poem, strictly speaking, suggests the slightest "eroticism" in the relationship between Sappho's "I" and the "you" she is addressing. The "you" of the poem does not refer to some girl with whom Sappho is in love, as has sometimes been thought.[44] The jealousy felt by Sappho is prompted by the imminent separation from her poem, while the Reader will continue to possess it. Her poem is her daughter, a metaphorical Kleïs whom Sappho cannot hope to survive.

40. Heraclitus *Homeric Allegories* 5.5.
41. Alcaeus frag. 326 Lobel-Page.
42. Heraclitus *Homeric Allegories* 5.7.
43. Archilochus frag. 193 West. For other traditional elements, see Pindar frag. 108 Bowra. In frag. 1.3 Lobel-Page, Sappho uses the military sense of *dámnami* in an erotic context: see Svenbro, "La Stratégie de l'amour," pp. 61–62.
44. Myself included: see "La Stratégie de l'amour," p. 67 f.

The whole poem unfolds between two instances of a word signifying 'seeming', the *phaínetai* of line 1 and the *phaínomai* of line 16. The man is not the equal of the gods; he only seems to be. And Sappho is not really at the point of death; she only seems to be. So this is a figurative discourse: it is allegorical, even "phainomenological."

So there is reason to believe that Sappho wrote allegorical poems, even allegories on writing. We possess a fragment of a comedy by Antiphanes (fourth century) titled *Sappho,* in the course of which the heroine sets out the following riddle:

> ἔστι φύσις θήλεια βρέφη σῴζουσ᾿ ὑπὸ κόλποις
> αὐτῆς, ὄντα δ᾿ ἄφωνα βοὴν ἵστησι γεγωνὸν
> καὶ διὰ πόντιον οἶδμα καὶ ἠπείρου διὰ πάσης
> οἷς ἐθέλει θνητῶν, τοῖς δ᾿ οὐδὲ παροῦσιν ἀκούειν
> ἔξεστιν κωφὴν δ᾿ ἀκοῆς αἴσθησιν ἔχουσιν.

[There is a feminine being who, within the folds of her dress, keeps her babies who, although without voices, emit a cry that resounds across the waves of the sea and over the whole of the solid earth, reaching as many mortals as they wish to; those who are not present (the addressees) and those who are hard of hearing (those who are deaf) are all able to hear them.][45]

When her father guesses that she is referring to the city—which puts one in mind of Alcaeus' allegory, cited above—Sappho replies, "You always talk such nonsense!" and proceeds to explain her riddle as follows:

> θήλεια μέν νύν ἐστι φύσις ἐπιστολή,
> βρέφη δ᾿ ἐν αὐτῇ περιφέρει τὰ γράμματα·
> ἄφωνα δ᾿ ὄντα ⟨ταῦτα⟩ τοῖς πόρρω λαλεῖ
> οἷς βούλεθ᾿· ἕτερος δ᾿ ἂν τύχῃ τις πλησίον
> ἑστὼς ἀναγιγνώσκοντος οὐκ ἀκούσεται.

[The feminine being is a letter; the babies that she carries with her everywhere are the *grámmata:* although they have no voice, they can,

45. Antiphanes cited by Athenaeus 10.450e–f (= Antiphanes *Sappho* frag. 196 Kock).

if they wish, speak to those who are far away; and if anyone happens to find himself close to a man who is reading, he will not hear them [for the *grámmata*, although voiceless, "speak" in perfect silence to the deaf.]⁴⁶

Although the text of this fragment from Antiphanes' *Sappho* presents certain problems, at least we can recognize in it the allegory we studied in fragment 31, with which the speech pronounced by Antiphanes' character "Sappho" presents a number of affinities on the level of vocabulary. *Akoúein* 'hear', *akoé* 'hearing', and *plēsíon* 'nearby' all have their equivalents in Sappho's poem.⁴⁷ Like the word *graphḗ* 'writing', the word *epistolḗ* 'letter' is feminine. The letter is a woman; and the idea that the alphabetical signs are her squalling babies is probably a comic version of the basic idea that poems are the offspring of their author.⁴⁸ If there were nothing in Sappho's own works to suggest this remarkable riddle, it is hard to see why Antiphanes would have used it.⁴⁹ I conclude, therefore, that fragment 31—which I believe is not a fragment but a complete poem⁵⁰—is equated with the young woman who "speaks" and "laughs," a young woman whom the reader will espouse at the moment when, seated before her, he breathes into her his reading voice.

46. Ibid. 451a–b. Note the parallelism between the riddle (in hexameters) and its explanation (in trimeters), which complement each other term for term. As for the reader's silence in the last line of "Sappho's" response, Aristotle *Historia Animalium* 4.9.536b3–4 may be cited: "Those born deaf are also dumb." That is why anyone who is "hard of hearing" reads silently. We will return to the subject of silent reading in Chapter 9.

47. Also worth noting: the *bréphē áphōna* "babies without voices", which call to mind the *bréphē ápsukha* of Diogenes (see above, Chapter 7, p. 139 and n. 88). "Before it emerges, the child emits no sound," writes Aristotle *Historia Animalium* 7.10.587a33–34. The "vocal" being is necessarily an "animated" one (see above, Chapter 7, p. 139 and n. 90).

48. See Artemidorus *Interpretation of Dreams* 2.45. On the "writing tablet" (*pinakís*), the *túpoi* 'imprints' of the *grámmata* are the children that it "welcomes," for children are the *túpoi* of their parents (see Liddell-Scott-Jones, s.v. *túpos*).

49. See also pseudo-Julian *Letters to Iamblichus* no. 77.446c–448c (pp. 578–581 Hertlein), in which Sappho is once again associated with writing, albeit less precisely.

50. Svenbro, "La Stratégie de l'amour," pp. 66–67.

CHAPTER 9

The Inner Voice:
On the Invention of Silent Reading

As I showed in Chapter 6, *nómos* 'law' is the noun from the verb *némein* in its sense of 'to recite' and 'to read aloud'. Originally, it meant "oral distribution" ('recitation' or "reading aloud"). As early as Hesiod, kings "distribute" justice in this way; that is to say, they do so orally.[1] And when kings were definitively overthrown in Greece, it was precisely *nómos* that filled the place left vacant by the dethroned king. In the city, the only king would be a sonorous, vocal *nómos*. Through metensomatosis, this *nómos* would become embodied in the persons of the city magistrates, its "slaves," or even in the citizens in general. That is, *nómos* would inhabit them, choosing now one, now another as its vocal instrument, for even if *nómos* did not have a body of its own, its voice had to manifest itself as a real, sonorous, audible voice, not a metaphorical one. Nothing testifies better to the importance that the Greeks attributed to the spoken word than the fact that they installed *nómos* as the king of the city, a vocal *nómos*, a *nómos* that in fact was also a *lógos*. The parallelism between the two pairs of words, *némein/nómos* and *légein/lógos,* is impossible to miss, and the intimate association that has been noticed between *nómos* and *lógos,* in Plato's work for instance, is by no means purely formal.[2] It is deeply rooted in Greek culture,

1. Hesiod *Works and Days* 224, 213.
2. The verb *analégesthai* 'to read' may look like a cross between *anagignôskein* and *epilégesthai* (see P. Chantraine, "Les Verbes signifiant 'lire,'" in *Mélanges Grégoire,* 2 [Brussels, 1950], p. 126), but it is probably simpler to understand it as a

which transforms *nómos* into a *basileús* just as it transforms *lógos* into a *dunástēs*.[3] In a culture that sets *lógos* in power, the law is quite naturally a voice.

This association between *nómos* and *lógos* is so strong that, in an extremely theatrical scene in Plato's *Crito,* the personified *Nómoi*—calling to mind Alcidamas' *nómoi basileîs*[4]—take over to have their own say, in the middle of the dialogue, and continue to hold the floor until almost the very end. Taking their place alongside Socrates and Crito, these *Nómoi* explain at great length why Socrates must not escape from his prison. Whereupon Socrates, who has staged this speech within the dialogue, has this to say: "Be well assured, my dear friend Crito, that this is what I seem to hear, as the frenzied devotees of Cybele seem to hear the pipe; and the sound of these words re-echoes within me and prevents my hearing any other words. And be assured that, so far as I now believe, if you argue against these words, you will speak in vain!"[5]

As the reader will have recognized, the *Nómoi*'s voice, despite the sound that they make, is not a real, external voice. Normally Socrates' internal dialogues—"the soul's dialogues with itself"—do without *phōnḗ* 'sound', as we are told in the *Sophist* and the *Theaetetus*. Socrates' thoughts are produced in silence.[6] But here, that is not the case. The voices of the *Nómoi* are so loud that Socrates cannot "hear any other words" (*tôn állōn akoúein*)—which also means "obey any others". He will obey the *Nómoi,* which are "scolding" away within him, but not his old friend Crito. External voices no longer count. All Socrates can hear is this internal voice telling him what he must not do.

synonym for *ananémesthai,* in which the *-némesthai* element expresses exactly the same as *-légesthai*. This interpretation is confirmed by the active form *analégein* in the sense of 'to read' (Teos, 470–460 B.C.: see P. Herrmann, "Teos und Abdera im 5 Jahrhundert v. Chr.," *Chiron,* 11 [1981], pp. 8 and 11), which is clearly a synonym for *ananémein*. Later we will encounter *astronomía* (below, n. 54), which in ancient Greek is synonymous with *astrología*. Here, *-nomía* means exactly the same thing as *-logía*. See J. Derrida, *Dissemination* (London, 1981), p. 146, for the association in Plato.

3. Gorgias frag. B 11 (8) Diels-Kranz.
4. See above, Chapter 7, p. 125 and n. 17.
5. Plato *Crito* 54d.
6. Plato *Sophist* 263e–264a; *Theaetetus* 189e–190a. See above, Chapter 1, p. 15 and n. 34; below, n. 84.

This internal voice is strongly reminiscent of the "daemonic" voice mentioned in the *Theages,* the *Phaedrus,* and, above all, the *Apology,* in which Socrates says, "I have had this from my childhood; it is a sort of voice that comes to me and when it comes it always holds me back from what I am thinking of doing, but never urges me forward."[7] In the same passage, we learn that Socrates was in the habit of speaking of this internal voice to his fellow citizens; and Meletus seems to allude to it in his accusation.[8] What we would call "the voice of conscience" is presented here as something new, even something shocking. For most of Socrates' contemporaries, the voice of *nómos* was no doubt always an external voice, not an internal, individual one. For them, the *nómos* was distributed in a public fashion—as indeed its etymology suggests. They had very little idea of what the Socratic *daimónion* might be, this "little distributor" that made its speech—for purely personal use—inside an individual, unheard by anyone else.[9]

The *nómos* is thus a "vocal distribution," a "recitation" or a "reading aloud." The "distribution of justice" [*díkē*] is an external operation in which the instrument used is a voice. *Díkē* itself is consequently an external justice that is publicly diffused. As Eric Havelock has shown, not until the time of Herodotus and Protagoras did *díkē* become something internal and the word *dikaiosúnē,* meaning "sense of justice", make its appearance.[10] The point at which this internalization took place can thus be traced at a lexical level, and it confirms the internalization of *nómos,* which, as Plato's work attests, became "the voice of conscience." In truth, it was all part and parcel of the same movement of internalization, the internalization of the "City's Super-ego,"[11] which took place in the course of the fifth century—the century that also provides us with

7. Plato *Theages* 128d; *Phaedrus* 242b–c; *Apology* 31d.
8. That is how I understand 31c7–d2, despite the commentary of J. Burnet, in *Plato's Euthyphro, Apology of Socrates, and Crito,* ed. J. Burnet (Oxford, 1924), p. 128.
9. If *nómos* means 'distribution', *daímōn* means 'distributor' (for it is the noun denoting the agent of *daíesthai* 'to distribute': see P. Chantraine, *Dictionnaire étymologique de la langue grecque* [Paris, 1968–1980], p. 247); *daimónion* is the diminutive.
10. E. A. Havelock, "*Dikaiosúnē:* An Essay in Greek Intellectual History," *Phoenix,* 23 (1969), pp. 49–70, and *The Greek Concept of Justice* (Cambridge, Mass., 1978), pp. 296–307.
11. See above, p. 123.

the first irrefutable evidence of silent reading, that is, the internalization of the voice of the reader, who was now able to "read in his head."

In his article "Silent Reading in Antiquity," Bernard Knox quotes two texts from the fifth century B.C. which seem to show that the Greeks—or rather certain Greeks—practiced silent reading and that, at the time of the Peloponnesian War, the dramatic poets could count on their audience's familiarity with it.[12] The first of these texts is a passage from the *Hippolytus* by Euripides, performed in 428 B.C.[13] Theseus notices a writing tablet hanging from the dead Phaedra's hand and wonders what it may tell him. He breaks the seal. The chorus intervenes, to express its distress, until it is interrupted by Theseus. "Alas! Here is endless sorrow upon sorrow. It passes speech, passes endurance!" he exclaims. At the request of the chorus, he then reveals the contents of the tablet—not by reading it aloud, but by summing it up. He has clearly read it *silently* while the chorus was singing.[14]

The second text quoted by Knox is a passage from the *Knights* by Aristophanes, dating from 424.[15] The scene presents the reading of a written oracle, which a certain Nicias has managed to steal from Paphlagon. "Give it to me, so that I may read it [*hin' anagnô*]," says Demosthenes to Nicias (line 118), who pours him a first cup of wine and asks, "What does the oracle say?" Absorbed in his reading, Demosthenes answers, "Fill me another cup" (line 121). "Does it really say 'Fill me another cup'?" asks Nicias in astonishment, believing that his companion is reading aloud. The joke is repeated and developed in the following lines, until Demosthenes finally explains to Nicias, "Herein, it is said how himself [i.e., Paphlagon] shall perish" (line 127). Whereupon he summarizes the oracle. He does not read it; he already has, in silence. This passage, then, shows us a reader accustomed to reading silently (he is even capable

12. B. M. W. Knox, "Silent Reading in Antiquity," *Greek, Roman, and Byzantine Studies,* 9 (1968), pp. 421–435. Knox's article is a critique of J. Balogh, "Voces Paginarum," *Philologus,* 82 (1927), pp. 84–109 and 202–240. See also G. L. Hendrickson, "Ancient Reading," *Classical Journal,* 25 (1929), pp. 128–196.

13. Euripides *Hippolytus* 856–886.

14. Ibid. 874–875. I examine this passage in greater detail below, p. 179.

15. Aristophanes *Knights* 115 f.

of drinking and asking for a drink while doing it!) in the company of a listener who does not seem accustomed to this practice and takes the words pronounced by the reader for words read by him, which in fact they are not.

The scene from the *Knights* seems particularly instructive, at first sight at least, as it implies that the practice of silent reading was not familiar to everybody in 424 (Plato was then five years old), even if it was assumed to be so to the comedy's audience. Consequently, we may suppose that silent reading, at this time, was practiced by a limited number of readers. Meanwhile, it was unknown to others, in particular to wholly illiterate people, familiar with writing only "from the outside."

In a culture that valued the sonority of the word as intensely as the Greeks did, the practice of silent reading required particular conditions even to be envisaged. If an inscription was a machine for producing *kléos*—"acoustic renown"—as I think it originally was to the Greeks, silent reading simply had no function.[16] In a culture where writing aimed at producing sound, silent reading had no raison d'être but appeared as something against nature, an anomaly. During the first centuries of Greek literacy, silent reading would have gone against the very purpose of writing, which was to produce and control a deferred oral statement. In such a culture, writing was inevitably perceived as something incomplete in itself, requiring a vocal supplement, a phenomenon alluded to by the Ionian verb meaning 'to read' (*epi-légesthai*), which implies that the reader adds (*epi-*) a sounding *lógos* to the letters that he sees.[17] Meaning could not yet be perceived without vocalization (I will return to this point later in this chapter). The act of reading aloud was the necessary "epi-logue" of the written word, of writing, of the graphic.[18]

It follows that, in the eyes of those early readers, writing did not

16. Above, p. 62.

17. See above, pp. 62–63.

18. Hence (probably) the scandal provoked among the Pythagoreans by the discovery of "irrational" or rather "unspeakable" numbers. The diagonal of a square (length × length) is a simple geometrical representation, but it becomes a *grammè álogos (árrhētos)* "unpronounceable line" when one tries to express it mathematically. Here, the "graphic" is impossible to "vocalize." See Hippasus frag. 4; Democritus frag. A 33 (VIII.1) Diels-Kranz; Plato *Republic* 7.534d, 8.546c.

by itself *represent* the voice that it, at least sometimes, was supposed to transcribe. Writing was not yet autonomous in relation to the voice, which it was supposed to trigger in order to become complete. Before its vocalization, writing did not represent something anymore than letters typed haphazardly by a monkey do to us. But writing would *produce* a representation if it but gave birth to a sound sequence that, unlike the written word, could be considered as the representation of the writer's voice (fictitious though that voice might be). Before the invention of silent reading, writing did not represent a voice. It was not yet the image of a voice; it only aimed to produce a voice that would "represent the same by means of the same."

Reading aloud does not separate the eye from the ear. And in early Greece it was only the ear that was capable of identifying the gestalt of what was written and read aloud, as is implied by the verb *anagignṓskein* 'to recognize, to read'. What is "recognized" in the act of reading is not the individual letter, as Pierre Chantraine suggests. A person may "know his letters" (*ta grámmata epístasthai*) without being able to "read."[19] What is "recognized" is, rather, the meaning of the sound sequence mechanically produced but not yet understood by the reader who pronounces the written signs for his own ear.[20] What seems meaningless to his eye (although he knows the

19. Chantraine, "Les Verbes signifiant 'lire,'" p. 115: "This verb [i.e., *anagignṓskein*] was well suited to signify 'to read', that is to say, to recognize characters and decode them." See Liddell–Scott–Jones, s.v. *anagignṓskō*: "of written characters, *know* them *again*, and so, *read*." See also D. J. Allan, "'Ἀναγιγνώσκω and Some Cognate Words," *Classical Quarterly*, 30 (1980), pp. 244–251, which does not tackle the problem of why *anagignṓskein* was chosen as the technical term for the activity of reading. On *grámmata epístasthai* see Hippocrates *On Regimen* 1.23.

20. See F. Bresson, "La Lecture et ses difficultés," in *Pratiques de la lecture* ed. R. Chartier (Paris, 1985), pp. 14–15: "As is now well established, the problem of reading has to do with the identification of individual letters and the rules of linking them together no more than the difficulties of arithmetic have to do with the way that the figures are written. . . . The difficulties of various forms of writing are thus not fundamentally those of recognizing graphic sequences, as forms in space. On the contrary, they lie in the system of correspondence between a graphic sequence and a spoken one. In other words, the graphic sequence is *a kind of* language." Although Bresson's remarks are concerned with reading acquisition in the twentieth century, they are pertinent to the interpretation of the Greek *anagignṓskein,* for they concern the moment when the graphic sequence, read aloud, is "recognized" as speech.

individual letters) is suddenly "recognized" by his ear, which is infinitely more accustomed to seize upon the gestalt of an unknown sentence than his eye is.

To illustrate the manner of reading implied by *anagignṓskein,* let us turn to a modern example, the first sentence of Raymond Queneau's novel, *Zazie dans le Métro.* It reads as follows: DOUKIPUDONKTAN.[21] This sentence is written in *scriptio continua,* that is, without word division (the absence of which is a characteristic of early Greek writing). Moreover, it is written phonetically, not in the etymological manner characteristic of French or English spelling (but alien to archaic Greek spelling, which is phonetic in principle). Finally, because of its syntax, the sentence belongs to spoken, not written language (which would be the case of any Greek sentence before the emergence of a written idiom perceptibly distinct from spoken language). For these three reasons, the French reader is at a loss when first confronted with this sentence. "Continuous" writing, phonetic spelling, and colloquial syntax are not phenomena normally found on the French printed page. The reader suddenly finds himself in a situation resembling that of the archaic Greek reader. Only by using his voice does he succeed in "recognizing" what is opaque to his eye. His eye (and here the analogy ends) would of course have preferred the following, normalized version of the sentence: "(C'est) d'où qu'ils puent donc tant?" (From where [is it] that they stink so much then?).

In this way, the Greek reader's ear "recognizes" the words that his vocal apparatus produces. Because of the *scriptio continua,* the eye had obvious difficulties in "recognizing" those same words. The ordinary reader had to rely on his voice if he wanted to decipher an inscription, and this ordinary reader was no doubt very much like the man "poor in letters" (*tà grámmata phaûlos*) alluded to by Socrates. He knew how to read, but hardly more, just enough for his own needs.[22] And for the most part, the ancient Greeks remained *tà grámmata phaûloi,* which means that they had to decipher the texts that they read with the help of their voices, a complex and cumbrous way of reading made necessary by the *scriptio continua* and

---

21. R. Queneau, *Zazie dans le Métro* (Paris, 1959).
22. Plato *Phaedrus* 242c. See Plutarch *Life of Lycurgus* 16.10.

encouraged by the high value given to the voice and by the fact that they read comparatively little, preferring a fluent reader to do the job for them.[23]

Only with the invention of silent reading did writing begin to "represent the same by means of the other" or, more concretely, the "voice by means of written signs" (*sēmêia anthrōpínēs phōnês*).[24] Only then could it be said purely and simply to represent. Only with the invention of silent reading did the written representation become a "pure" representation that no longer called for a vocal supplement of prolongation. From then on, the eye "saw" the sound.[25] What was previously perceived as one single continuous operation suddenly split into two: the written word was separated from the voice in the sense that it no longer called for any vocalization to become intelligible, "recognizable." From now on, the eye, and the eye only, would ensure the "recognition" of meaning. What was originally a "recognition" of something opaque at first sight had become an immediate visual identification of meaning.

Of course, the *scriptio continua* was an obstacle to this development, and it remained so. But it was not insurmountable, as one might surmise from the medieval evidence. According to Paul Saenger, word division was a necessary prerequisite for the development of silent reading in the Middle Ages.[26] For the Greeks really did practice silent reading, in spite of the fact that they kept on writing in *scriptio continua*. Knox suggests that it was probably the habit of reading large quantities of texts that was at the origin of silent reading in antiquity, as silent reading is considerably faster than reading aloud.[27] A writer like Herodotus probably abandoned the habit of reading aloud in the course of his work as a historian, and, well before him, those who worked on the Homeric text under the Peisistratids in sixth-century Athens—as perhaps Simonides

23. Consider the reader imagined by Mnesitheos' stele, or the *stratēgoí* readers of the siege of Potidaea in 479 (see above, pp. 50f. and 55), or the slave reading in Plato's *Theaetetus*.

24. Hippocrates *On Regimen* 1.23.

25. Cf. Aeschylus *Seven against Thebes* 103: *ktúpon dédorka* "I behold the din". We will return to both the *Seven* and this type of synaesthesia.

26. P. Saenger, "Silent Reading: Its Impact on Late Medieval Script and Society," *Viator*, 13 (1982), p. 378.

27. Knox, "Silent Reading in Antiquity," pp. 421–422.

did[28]—certainly had the chance to develop this new technique. True, it was the technique of a minority, but that minority was an important one—to which the dramatic poets certainly belonged— and its early history deserves our attention.

The mere introduction of word division in the manuscripts did not ensure the spread of silent reading in the Middle Ages. Something more was needed than this technical innovation introduced as early as the seventh century A.D. Scholasticism provided this impetus; it discovered the advantages of silent reading—rapidity and intelligibility—and exploited them on a large scale. Only in the scholastic context could silent reading catch on. In the rest of medieval society, it remained almost unknown.[29] In the same way, I would argue, the mere reading of large quantities of texts is insufficient as a factor to explain why silent reading appeared in fifth-century Greece. Extensive reading seems, rather, to have been the *outcome* of a qualitative innovation in the attitude to the written word, the outcome of a whole new and powerful mental framework, capable of restructuring the categories of traditional reading. The practice of silent reading could hardly have been structured by a purely quantitative factor. In truth, Knox himself quotes only post-classical authors—Aristarchus, Callimachus, and Didymus— when he wants to exemplify the vast readings of the ancient Greeks.[30] It could, however, have been structured by the experience of the theater.

What are the distinctive features of a theatrical representation— an eminently sonorous phenomenon—that are clear-cut enough and original enough to have structured the new practice of silent reading? The first that comes to mind is the marked separation between the stage and the public. This distancing delimits the fictitious acting on the stage and, in a way, constitutes the distinctive element of theater: the public is not supposed to participate in

28. See primarily pseudo-Plato *Hipparchus* 228b–c. The possibility of Simonides' putting a finishing touch to the Homeric text "imported" from Ionia by Hipparchus is suggestive, as the poet from Keos is cited as one of the artisans of the Greek alphabet (*Anecdota Graeca* 2.780.30–31, 781.2–4, 782.25–28 Bekker; Pliny *Natural History* 7.192).

29. Saenger, "Silent Reading," pp. 378–380, 383–384, 405.

30. Knox, "Silent Reading in Antiquity."

what is being played out. The spectator is not supposed to tell a person on the stage what he knows is going to happen.[31] He is not supposed to stop the course of events by telling the actors what to do. He is supposed to 'contemplate' (*theâsthai*) them as they move toward their own destruction. The tension created by this situation makes the action on the stage all the more fascinating. According to the rules of the 'game' (*paidiá*) that the tragic poet Thespis, in the sixth century, defended against the indignant criticisms of Solon, the play should take place in an autonomy that the public should not disturb.[32]

Even in Thespis' day, the public was supposed to *watch* and to *listen*. Passively. The spectators were not supposed to intervene on the stage nor to read the text that, although absent from the stage, nevertheless determined the action. Memorized by the actors, the text was not visible at the moment when it was pronounced.[33] The actors had, as it were, taken its place. They transposed it into a kind of "vocal writing."[34] They did not read it, but rather produced a vocal copy of it. In this, they differed from the ordinary reader, who lent his voice to the text in front of him. The ordinary reader, then, could not be said to produce another, vocal, piece of writing, for the simple reason that his voice was perceived as the "natural" prolongation of the writing, its fulfillment or necessary supplement. As we saw in Chapter 3, the reader's voice is the supplement of the writing, it belongs to the written word, and cannot for this reason be considered as a re-writing. The act of reading aloud presupposes the presence of the text (the completion of which is ensured by the voice), which means that a listener has no problem in grasping the contiguity of writing and voice. For unlike the words of the actor,

31. If the comic poets seem sometimes to be unaware of the existence of this separation, the reason is that its transgression produces a comic effect; the separation is in fact there. On the strict manner in which the tragic poets observe the demarcation between fictional space and the public, see D. Bain, "Audience Address in Greek Tragedy," *Classical Quarterly,* 25 (1975), pp. 13–25.

32. Plutarch *Life of Solon* 29.

33. See C. Segal, "Tragédie, oralité, écriture," *Poétique,* no. 50 (1982), pp. 131–154; "Greek Tragedy: Writing, Truth, and the Representation of the Self," in *Mélanges Hulley,* ed. H. Evjen (Chico, Calif., 1984), pp. 43–67; *La Musique du Sphinx. Poésie et structure dans la tragédie grecque* (Paris, 1987), pp. 263–298.

34. On the justification of the expression "vocal writing," see below, p. 180.

those pronounced by the reader are not memorized beforehand (although, of course, every reader is also free to memorize what he reads).

Conversely, the gap between dramatic text and performance is marked enough to justify our calling the performance a vocal re-writing of the text. The actors' performances are not a reading. They may have read the text to memorize it, but during the performance their voices replace it. The spectators *listen* to this vocal writing. They do not behave as traditional readers. They do not activate, or reactivate, the written word by means of their own voices, for the vocal writing of the performance speaks to them in total autonomy. They listen, passively, to this writing. And, as I have argued, listening to a vocal writing is not the same as listening to a reading made by someone who has a text in front of him: the reader's voice simply does not have the autonomy of the actor's voice. True, this autonomy is partly illusory, but it is also real, as the actor has to do without the text, materially speaking, once he stands on the stage.

The separation between the stage, from which this vocal writing is delivered, and the public was probably clear-cut enough to have suggested to the Greeks—or at least to certain Greeks—an analogous separation between what is written and the reader.[35] To put that another way, the separation was clear-cut enough to have suggested the possibility of a new attitude to the written word. The traditional reader, who needs his voice in order to "recognize" a text (a complex operation in which the eye first ensures the production of a sound sequence, which is then interpreted by the ear), has a manifestly active relation to what is written. He has to make an effort to understand; otherwise the letters will remain meaningless ("mere letters") to him.[36] Conversely, the silent reader, whose eye is capable of immediate word identification, has a relation to the written word that appears rather as a passive one. Or rather, the

35. To be more precise, the separation is more clear-cut than the one between rhapsode and public, which existed before the advent of theater and the implications of which I discuss below, p. 180. The practice of delivering speeches written and memorized beforehand developed after the establishment of theater.

36. See above, p. 165. The prefix *ana-* in *anagignṓskein* may express this effort of the reader: see Chantraine, "Les Verbes signifiant 'lire,'" p. 115.

activity of the silent reader is not thought of as an effort to decipher something, it is not a conscious activity (in the same way as the interpretative activity of the "ear" listening to a meaningful sound is not consciously an activity; rather, it seems a passive reception). The visual "recognition" of meaning here is immediate: it is not preceded by a moment of opacity. The reader who "reads in his head" does not have to (re-)activate the written word through the intervention of his voice. The written word simply seems to "speak" to him. He is "listening" to a writing—exactly like the spectator in the theater, who listens to the vocal writing of the actors. The text that is "recognized" visually seems to have the same autonomy as the acting on the stage. The letters, the *grámmata,* "read" themselves—or rather, "pronounce" themselves. The silent reader does not have to intervene on the "stage" of the written word. Since they are capable of "speaking," the *grámmata* can do without his voice. They already have one. The reader has simply to "listen"—inside himself. The reading voice is internalized.[37]

If this "passivity" of the reader is modeled on the passivity of the spectator in the theater, how far back can we trace it? George Thomson's analysis of the verb *hupokrínesthai* "to play a role" may help us to define the moment when this passivity was established. As Thomson observes, *hupokrínesthai* has two distinct meanings in the Homeric poems: 'to answer' and 'to interpret' (a dream or an omen).[38] Contrary to other scholars, who have tried to choose between these two meanings in order to explain the origin of *hupo-krités* 'actor',[39] Thomson asks why they have come to be covered by a single word, as in the passage in the *Odyssey* where Peisistratos asks Menelaos, "Is this omen intended for you or for us?" Homer continues, "At these words, Menelaos . . . pondered, wondering how he should answer [*hupokrínaito*] aright."[40] It would have been

---

37. I do not know whether the readers of antiquity arrived at the point where this internalized voice "was silent" and reading became purely visual, without recourse—even of a metaphorical nature—to vocalization.

38. G. Thomson, *Aeschylus and Athens,* 2d ed. (London, 1950), pp. 181–182.

39. A recent example is G. K. H. Ley, "ὑποκρίνεσθαι in Homer and Herodotus, and the Function of the Athenian Actor," *Philologus,* 127 (1983), pp. 13–29, which singles out the meaning "to answer" (Thomson's name does not appear in the notes).

40. *Odyssey* 15.167–170.

equally possible to translate the passage as "how he should *interpret* aright." The key to the problem is provided by a passage in Plato's *Timaeus,* where we read that "the *prophêtai* are the *hupokritaí* of enigmatical words and signs, but they are not *mánteis* [i.e., sooth-sayers pronouncing their words in ecstasy]."[41] Thomson concludes that *hupokritês* was originally the designation of a person who received questions concerning "enigmatical words and signs"; his *interpretation* constituted his *answer.* If such a person was the leader of a chorus performing a ritual in which the meaning was not perceived by those watching (perhaps newcomers to the city or simply new citizens), the *hupokritês* was in a position to "answer" possible questions by "interpreting" what was going on. He might say, "I am Dionysus, and those are the daughters of Eleuther whom I have driven mad."[42] Later on, when he began to give his "an-swers-interpretations" *without being asked,* he was suddenly no longer a *hupokritês* in the old sense. He had become an actor. The separation between the stage (from now on autonomous) and the spectator (from now on passive) was thereby a fait accompli.

Now, the verb *hupokrínesthai* is precisely what we find in an inscription belonging to a bronze statuette (now lost), dating from the late sixth century and found in Athens:

πᾶσιν ἴσ᾽ ἀνθρώποι[ς] ὑποκρίνομαι ὅστις ἐ[ρω]τᾷ
ὥς μ᾽ ἀνέθηκ᾽ ῎Ανδρων ᾽Αντιφάνους δεκάτην.

[To whoever asks me, I answer, *hupokrínomai,* the same thing, namely that Andron, son of Antiphanes, dedicated me as a tithe.][43]

A few remarks on this inscription are necessary. At the end of the sixth century B.C., theater already existed in its institutionalized form: the tragic contests began in 534 and the tragic representa-tions—before Aeschylus, with one actor and a chorus—go back

---

41. Plato *Timaeus* 72a–b.
42. According to Thomson, *Aeschylus and Athens,* p. 183. On Eleuther, see M. Detienne, *Dionysos à ciel ouvert* (Paris, 1986), pp. 51–56.
43. M. Lazzarini, *Le formule delle dediche votive nella Grecia arcaica,* Atti della Accademia nazionale dei Lincei. Memorie. Classe di scienze morali, storiche e filologiche, 8th ser., 19:2 (Rome, 1976), no. 658.

some thirty years before that date.[44] When the statuette received its epigram, the tragic poet Thespis was already in his heyday. The verb *hupokrínomai* consequently has a much richer meaning here than my translation "I answer" suggests.[45] In Attic Greek, *apokrínesthai* was used in that sense. If the author of the inscription had wished to write "I answer," he would have used *apokrínomai,* which is the perfect metric equivalent of *hupokrínomai.* He did not do so, which means that *hupokrínomai* was chosen to express more than the simple idea of "to answer."

Using the same verb, the Andron inscription singles itself out on another level, making its statuette a so-called "speaking object." Not because it uses the first person "I," in the manner of inscriptions like "I am the tombstone of so-and-so" (for, as we saw in Chapter 2, the faculty of speech is not a necessary attribute of the first person; otherwise, a mute person could not lay claim to an "I"). The statuette is a "speaking object" because of the vocal implications of the verb *hupokrínomai.* It is, in fact, our earliest clear example of an inscription using, with regard to itself, the metaphor of the voice.[46] By using the verb *hupokrínomai,* this inscription raises its "voice." It "speaks." And the Athenian context adds to this "speaking" a strong theatrical connotation; by means of its metaphorical voice, this inscription answers a question that is not asked but which the inscription anticipates, in complete autonomy. Exactly like the *hupokrités* on the stage. But if at the same time *hupokrínomai* means that it *interprets* what is perceived as an "enigma" (i.e., what meaning should be given to the inscribed statuette?), it "interprets" itself,

44. A. Pickard-Cambridge, *Dithyramb, Tragedy and Comedy,* 2d ed. (Oxford, 1962), p. 88.

45. The dialect of the inscription is clearly Attic, not Ionic: *anthrṓpois,* not *anthrṓpoisi* as in Ionic (the final - *s* is guaranteed by the meter, which would not allow -*si* in this position); *erōtâi,* not *eirōtâi* as in Ionic (the initial *e-* is equally guaranteed by the meter, which would not allow *ei-* here).

46. Although the Midas epigram evokes the metaphor of the voice with its use of *angeléō* "I shall proclaim", in the version given by Plato (*Phaedrus* 264c), the version given in the Hesiodic *Certamen* (p. 236.2 Allen) uses the variant *sēmanéō* "I shall indicate", which may well be the correct reading (as in G. Pfohl, *Greek Poems on Stones,* vol. 1, *Epitaphs: From the Seventh to the Fifth Centuries B.C.,* Textus Minores, no. 36 (Leiden, 1967), no. 24). The Mnesitheos epigram parallels that of Midas in several respects, but the voice metaphor is absent from it, as we learned in Chapter 3. The Midas epigram is known to us solely from the literary tradition.

it "deciphers" itself before the eyes of the spectator-reader, who does not have to make the effort of vocalizing the written word for the simple reason that here it "vocalizes" itself. Addressing the spectator-reader, who is not supposed to raise his voice, the inscription delivers its meaning directly to the eye: why read aloud if the inscription knows how to "speak" by itself? The meaning of the object reaches the eye of the reader through a kind of radiation or "flow." The object radiates its meaning on to the reader. The meaning of the object is no longer laboriously activated by the voice of the reader. Its writing is autonomous; it "speaks." This, I believe, is the logic of this Attic inscription, which in an indirect way (as opposed to the direct evidence in the *Hippolytus* and the *Knights* previously quoted) seems to attest to the existence of silent reading in late sixth-century Athens and, at the same time, the internalization of theatrical space within inscriptional space. From now on, inscriptional space is a "scene."

This new kind of reading, in which the reader is, as it were, turned into a passive spectator faced with an active piece of writing that radiates its meaning, is in conformity with the schema that is part of the theory of visual perception elaborated by Empedocles, Leucippus, and Democritus in the course of the fifth century. At first, in Empedocles, the situation seems somewhat confused. In Aristotle's words, "Empedocles seems sometimes to imagine that one sees because light issues from the eye."[47] So Empedocles' position is the reverse of that implied by silent reading, in which the writing projects meaning toward the eye. But interestingly enough, Aristotle adds, "At times, then, he explains vision in this way, but at other times he accounts for it by emanations [*aporrhoíais*] from objects seen [*tôn horōménōn*]."[48] This second position was to be adopted by his successors, the Atomists, who, starting with Leucippus, also considered vision to be the result of an emanation or a "flow" (*aporrhoḗ*) projected from the objects seen, toward the eye.[49]

47. Aristotle *De Sensu* 437b.
48. Ibid.; see Empedocles frag. B 89 Diels-Kranz.
49. See Plato *Phaedrus* 251b.

Alexander of Aphrodisias writes, "They attribute sight to certain images [*eídōla*] that, having the same form as the object, flow [*aporrhéonta*] ceaselessly from the objects seen and reach [*empíptonta*] the eye. Such was the position of the school of Leucippus and Democritus."[50] For the Atomists, then, vision is due to a continuous emission of corpuscles from the object seen, an emission that is finally received by the eye (in a manner that is more or less complicated on account of the constraints inherent in the Atomist theory[51]). The ambiguity of Empedocles' position can be explained by the fact that he was obliged to abandon one theory and elaborate another, more satisfactory, one. But the position of the Atomists— to whom that second theory was bequeathed—seems clear-cut from the outset, at least as regards the aspect in which we are interested. The eye does not emit a beam of light to see; it receives a flow from the objects seen. That flow is the direction in which visual information is believed to pass.

The analogy between visual perception and silent reading, in which the eye appears to receive passively whatever the writing radiates, does not acquire its full force until we connect it with a factor that is fundamental to the theory of the Atomists. They explain the combinations of *stoikheîa* in the physical world with the aid of an alphabetical model, in which words are formed from various combinations of the twenty-four *stoikheîa* of writing. *Stoikheîa* means both 'elements' and "alphabetical signs".[52] Leucippus remarks, "One writes tragedy and comedy using the same letters."[53] Similarly, in the physical world, the same elements are combined and recombined so as to change things. The word "ontography" has, justifiably enough, been used in connection with the Atomists. Indeed, Democritus is the author of a treatise on "physics" titled

50. Alexander of Aphrodisias *On Sensation* 56.12.

51. For not only the object seen emits a flow, but the eye that sees it does too. These two flows meet in midair and produce the image, the *émphasis* or *entúpōsis* (Democritus frag. A 135 Diels-Kranz).

52. On the alphabetical model see the remarkable passage in Lucretius *De rerum natura* 1.823–829, where *elementa* translates the Greek *stoikheîa*. See in general S. Sambursky, *The Physical World of the Greeks* (Oxford, 1956), pp. 126–128.

53. Leucippus frag. A 9 Diels-Kranz.

Kosmographíē.[54] What all this means is that, for the Atomists, visual perception was a reading—a silent reading of the physical world.

The statuette dedicated by Andron is an isolated example of a "speaking object" (in the sense that I have just given to this expression) as long as we remain in the sixth century, but the metaphor of the voice becomes more and more common in the course of the fifth. The change is not so much in the realm of inscriptions, but in authors who practiced a more prolific type of writing and who for this reason were more prone to change their habits of reading.[55] My first example is Aeschylus, whose precedence in this domain is ex-. tremely significant. In the *Seven against Thebes,* the use of the metaphor is suggested by the shields of three of the heroes, namely Kapaneus, Eteoklos, and Polyneikes.[56] Describing Kapaneus' shield, the messenger tells Eteokles: "His device [*sêma*] has a naked man that carries fire, in his hands, ablaze, a torch, all ready. In gold are letters [*khrusoîs . . . grámmasin*] through which he declares [*phōneî*] 'I'll burn the city.' "[57] In a play in which the remarkable synaesthetic expression, "I see the noise" occurs, it seems logical enough that objects should speak and also that a figure drawn on a shield 'speaks' (*phōneî*) as the above-mentioned one does, or 'cries out' (*boâi*) as does the one on Eteoklos' shield, through the *grámmata* inscribed alongside.[58] Polyneikes' shield, finally, displays a personification of Justice, iden-

54. H. Wismann, "Le Modèle graphique des atomistes," paper read at the colloquium *L'Écriture,* as mentioned in the Introduction. Democritus frag. A 33 (III.3) and B 5a Diels-Kranz. Democritus' *Ouranographíē* or "Celestial Writing" (frag. A 33 [IX.1]) is perhaps complemented by his *Astronomíē* or "Reading of the Stars" (frag. A 33 [VIII.3]).

55. But see the "poetic ostrakon" (dated 484 B.C.) from the Athenian Agora, published by A. E. Raubitschek, "The Ostracism of Xanthippos," *American Journal of Archaeology,* 51 (1974), pp. 257–262. See also S. G. Miller, *The Prytaneion: Its Function and Architectural Form* (Berkeley, Calif., 1978), p. 137: "The ostrakon agrees [*katá*]*phēsin,* that Xanthippos, son of Arrhiphron, is a transgressor in that he has especially abused [the privilege of] the prytaneion." I am indebted to François Lissarrague for this reference, as well as for those in n. 57, 58, and 59.

56. On this play, see P. Vidal-Naquet, "The Shields of the Heroes," in *Myth and Tragedy in Ancient Greece,* ed. J.-P. Vernant and P. Vidal-Naquet (New York, 1988), pp. 273–300.

57. Aeschylus *Seven against Thebes* 432–434. See L. Lupaş and Z. Petre, *Commentaire aux Sept contre Thèbes D'Eschyle* (Bucharest, 1981), pp. 144–145.

58. *Seven against Thebes* 103; see above, p. 167 and n. 25; ibid. 465–469.

tified not by her traditional attributes but by an inscribed legend: "She claims to be Justice, as the inscription says [*hōs tà grámmata légei*]. . . ."⁵⁹

My second example is Herodotus. For him, 'letters' (*tà grámmata*) begin to 'speak' (*légein*) all over the place; written oracles, steles, and tripods all raise their "voices," as does the stone statue of the Egyptian king Sethos, who "pronounces" his own inscription.⁶⁰ To the historian, who wrote extensively and had to read even more than he wrote, silent reading, made possible by the experience of the theater, came "naturally." (It is worth remembering that Herodotus was a friend of Sophocles.⁶¹) He was more or less forced to read fast in order to elaborate his own written work. And reading faster at a certain point necessarily means internalizing the reading voice. The reader does without the voice and reads in his head.

Many other writers of this period must also have needed to read more rapidly than reading aloud would permit. The tragic poet Achaeus, of the same generation as Herodotus, also uses the metaphor of a "speaking" inscribed object. It occurs in a fragment that sets on stage a satyr who is reading aloud, but is clearly "poor at reading" (*tà grámmata phaûlos*).⁶² "The *skúphos* of the god has been calling [*kaleî*] me for a long time, showing its inscription [*grámma*]: *délta, iôta,* and, in third place, *ó; nû* and *û* are there [*páresti*]; and in what follows, it is not their absence [*apousían*] that *sán* and *oû* proclaim [*kērússeton*]."⁶³ The author of this satyr play clearly took delight in presenting on stage a way of reading that seemed to him quite backward and, accordingly, suited to a satyr. In order to "recognize" the meaning of the graphic sequence *D-I-O-N-U-S-OU* "(I belong to) Dionysus", he has to pronounce the letters one-by-one yet as fast as he can, to enable his ear to seize the gestalt of the sequence of sounds thus produced. (One wonders whether he really does manage to decipher the inscription; but the spectators do, thanks to the letters that he provides for them.) The implication of

59. Ibid. 646–648, 660.
60. Herodotus 1.124.187, 2.106.136, 3.88, 4.91, 7.228, 8.22. Herodotus 2.133, 5.90.92, 6.77, 8.136, 2.102, 5.60.61. Herodotus 2.141: *légōn dià grammátōn táde.* . . .
61. See Plutarch *An seni respublica gerenda sit* 785b.
62. Plato *Phaedrus* 242c, cited above, p. 166 and n. 22.
63. Athenaeus 11.466f; Achaeus *Omphale* frag. 33 Nauck².

this scene is that Achaeus himself reads in a different fashion, as do his spectators, or the spectators that he imagines. And that other way of reading is implicit in the text. It is introduced quite discreetly, for a mind accustomed to the traditional reading aloud would not be expected to imagine writing to possess a "voice" of its own. Yet that is what the satyr believes: the inscription "calls" him, and its last two letters "proclaim" their presence—as 'heralds' (*kērukes*) would, that is to say, out loud. If he himself reads aloud, however, the satyr has no need of that metaphorical voice that, for its part, belongs to the practice of silent reading.[64]

The Andron inscription marks a decisive moment in the Greek experience of writing: it is no accident if Plato's *Phaedrus* echoes it, at a distance of more than a century, in a passage concerning the properties of the written word.[65] Comparing writing to painting, Socrates blames the written word for "always signifying the same thing," which is exactly what the Andron inscription takes pride in doing. The philosopher of course could have addressed the same reproach to an actor, whose voice is the mere instrument of an unchanging text, not that of someone in possession of 'knowledge' (*epistēmē*). And so he does, elsewhere.[66] It comes down to the same thing, for as we have seen, the written word and the actor are analogous, interchangeable. The actor takes the place of the written word on the stage, the written word takes the place of the actor in the Andron inscription. Producing what I have called a "vocal writing" on the stage, the actor opens up the possibility of a new attitude to the written word, the possibility of silent reading. In fact, the inscribed statuette dedicated by Andron defines itself as an 'actor' (*hupokritēs*), presupposing this new attitude to the written word. Inscribed space is a "scene" that borrows its logic from the theater in assigning the role of the spectator to the reader. It internalizes theater.

This view is justified not only by the Andron inscription but also by a passage like the one quoted from the *Hippolytus,* where the dead Phaedra's "writing tablet shouts, shouts things not to be for-

64. On a similar confusion, see Herodotus 8.136.
65. Plato *Phaedrus* 275d.
66. Plato *Ion* 532d.

gotten" (*boâi boâi déltos álasta*) (line 877).[67] As staged by Euripides, the written word not only "speaks" during an act of silent reading, it "shouts."[68] It may even "sing." "Such a song," says Theseus a few lines later, "have I seen crying forth through the writing" (*hoîon hoîon eîdon en graphaîs mélos/phthengómenon*).[69] The actor who *sings* the role of Theseus—the passage is in lyric meter—sings about a song coming forth through the written word, a song for the *eye*.[70]

On the stage, then, a singing actor; on the writing tablet (which is intended for silent reading and thus internalizes theatrical space), the "singing" letters. It is hard to imagine a more subtle staging of silent reading than this. The metaphorical voice of writing is presented here as the complement of silent reading; when one reads silently, letters raise their "voice." Thus, the evidence from the *Hippolytus* not only concerns the external facts—which do not make it possible to distinguish absolutely clearly between silent and merely noiseless reading—but also has an internal aspect that corroborates Knox's interpretation by adding elements that belong to the mental architecture of true silent reading.

But that is not all. In fact, the entire work of Plato could be added to our evidence. Plato had a well-known problematic relationship with the dramatic poets, a relationship marked by both emulation and hostility. The relationship began in his youth when, at Socrates' suggestion, in front of the theater of Dionysus, he burned a tragedy that he himself had written for a dramatic contest.[71] And it continued until his old age, when he defined the *politeía* "political constitution"—obviously the one proposed by himself—as "the truest tragedy of all."[72] In Plato's career, the sudden shift from the

---

67. See above, p. 166 and n. 22.

68. See Euripides *Iphigenia in Tauris* 641–642, 584–585.

69. Euripides *Hippolytus* 879–880. See Knox, "Silent Reading in Antiquity," p. 433; Segal, "Tragédie, oralité, écriture," p. 148 (= Segal, *La Musique du Sphinx*, pp. 289–290).

70. Musical notation in ancient Greece was alphabetical. See, for example, J. Chailley, *La Musique grecque antique* (Paris, 1979), p. 122. Thus, a reference to the silent reading of *music* cannot be excluded.

71. Diogenes Laertius 3.5.

72. Plato *Laws* 7.817a–c. Conversely, he calls the democratic constitution a comedy: *Scholia to Aristophanes*, pp. xxvii–xxviii (11.59–63) Dübner; see *Laws* 3.701a: *theatrokratía*.

dramatic genre to the dialogues may itself be seen as an internalization of theater in the book, for the dialogues have a dramatic form
without being intended for the stage.[73] If Plato's *politeía* had a
theatrical intention, its "stage" was the entire city-state, as opposed
to the illusory one of ordinary theater.[74] Despite all his hostility
toward the theater, his utopian thought may therefore have been
essentially theatrical.

With theater internalized in the book in this way, the book, for its
part, was internalized in mental space, called now *phrḗn,* now
psukhḗ. And this development occurred well before Plato.[75] Our
first example of the metaphor "the book of the soul" comes from
Pindar, who exclaims in his tenth *Olympian* (probably dating from
474 B.C.), "Read to me [*anágnōte*] the name of the Olympic victor
where it is written [*gégraptai*] in my mind [*phrenós*]!"[76] But it is the
tragic poets, notably Aeschylus, who most frequently employ this
metaphor before Plato. The reason seems obvious enough: the
dramatic poet, who writes texts intended for memorization by the
actors, is aware in a very concrete manner of the inscription of the
text in the mind of the actor. To the dramatic poet, the actor seems
to receive an inscription in the same way that a stone or a papyrus
leaf may receive one. The mind of the actor is a space for writing,
inscriptional space, which means that the dramatic text is "*inscribed*"
in the mind of the person who will *pronounce* it on the stage. "Vocal
writing," the formula that I have been using, in this way receives its

73. See in particular *Theaetetus* 143b–c.
74. Plato *Laws* 7.817c. This would be a typically Platonic structure: Plato's
politeía 'state', which is modeled on the theater, is nevertheless full of contempt for
the theater. In the same way, weaving is the paradigm of politics, but "no sensible
man would try to define weaving out of love for weaving itself" (*Statesman* 285d).
See n. 75.
75. Plato *Philebus* 38e–39a; *Phaedrus* 275d–276a. On the use of this metaphor
before Plato, see G. Nieddu, "La Metafora della memoria come scrittura e l'immag-
ine dell'animo come *deltos,*" *Quaderni di storia,* no. 19 (1984), pp. 213–219. If ordinary writing is considered the "simulacrum" (*eídōlon: Phaedrus* 276a) of metaphorical writing (i.e., writing in the soul), highly valued by Plato, this relation (central to
the analysis of Derrida, *Dissemination,* p. 149) has several parallels in Plato's thought.
For example, the craftsman, in spite of the depreciation in which he is held, serves as
a model for the metaphorical craftsman called the Demiurge. See P. Vidal-Naquet,
The Black Hunter (Baltimore, 1986), p. 287f.; see also above, n. 74.
76. Pindar *Olympian* 10.1–3. For the date of the tenth *Olympian* see C. M.
Bowra, *Pindar* (Oxford, 1964), p. 409.

full justification.[77] We also understand why Aeschylus, who introduced the second actor,[78] "writes" in the minds of his actors, whereas a writer such as Homer (if we assume for a moment that he was literate) cannot be considered as someone "writing" in the memory of his future reciters, the rhapsodes, for they were too distant from him in time and space for such a metaphor to have any relevance.

Aeschylus' work provides examples worth citing, although the metaphor also occurs in the other two great tragic writers.[79] In *Prometheus Bound* the protagonist declares, "To you, Io, I shall tell the tale of your sad wanderings: inscribe [*engráphou*] the story on the remembering tablets [*mnémosin déltois*] of your mind [*phrenôn*]."[80] Prometheus is a figure connected with the origin of writing. According to one tradition (though not an Aeschylean one), Danaos is another.[81] This is how he addresses his daughters: "And now, with foresight, I advise your taking care to have my words engraved [*deltouménas*] within your minds." And the same metaphor recurs further on in the same play, when Danaos says, "Now, to the many lessons of modesty inscribed [*gegramménois*] in you by your father, you will add the following inscription [*grápsesthe*]."[82] In the *Eumenides* the chorus compares the "memory" of Hades to a writing tablet. "Hades calls men to reckoning there, under the ground, sees all, and cuts it deep, in his tablet-writing [*deltográphos*] mind [*phrén*]."[83] In one last example from Aeschylus, Electra says to Orestes, "Hear, . . . and carve the letters [*gráphou*] of it in your mind [*en phresín*]."[84] The tragic poet might himself have used this expression when addressing one of his actors.

77. See above, p. 174. The fact that our earliest evidence for the metaphor of the "book of the mind" comes from Pindar does not invalidate my theory, as the choral poet "inscribes" his poem in the mind of the chorus that is going to perform it.

78. Aristotle *Poetics* 4.1449a16.

79. Sophocles *Triptolemos* frag. 540 Nauck², *Philoctetes* 1325, *Trachinian Women* 680–683, *Antigone* 707–709; Euripides *Trojan Women* 661.

80. Aeschylus *Prometheus Bound* 788–789.

81. *Anecdota Graeca* 2.783.7, 786.4–5 Bekker.

82. Aeschylus *Suppliants* 178–179, 991–992.

83. Aeschylus *Eumenides* 273–275.

84. Aeschylus *Libation Bearers*. Pindar and the tragic poets all use the word *phrén*, either in the singular or the plural, to refer to the place of the mental inscription. I have already stressed the silent nature of the *phrén* or *phrénes* (which is

The relation between theater and writing, as well as that between writing and the mind, thus takes the form of an internalization.

Andron inscription	Aeschylus and others
hupokrínomai	"the book of the mind"
────────────→	────────────→
internalization	internalization

THEATRICAL   /   ALPHABETICAL   /   MENTAL SPACE

But this double movement—from theater to writing, from writing to mind[85]—has its counterpart going in the opposite direction: a double movement of *externalization*. In the first place, mental space is of course externalized in the book. We may even postulate the existence of silent writing here, although it might prove impossible to document it positively. The written *hupómnēma* may replace a failing memory: it is an externalized, objective memory, or *aide-mémoire,* not to be confused with the living *mnémē* of a person.[86] Conscious of its limitations, the philosopher makes use of it, and so, of course, does the dramatic poet, whose text is a *hupómnēma,* written not for posterity but for a single performance, and probably constituting its necessary condition.

If mental space may be externalized in alphabetical space, writing may also be externalized—in theatrical space. The externalization takes place first of all, naturally, when a written text is performed on the stage, an operation that in a sense is unlike any other in this system of interdependent representations, as it gives rise to what I

---

particularly appropriate to the silence of the written signs): see above, Chapter 1, p. 15 and n. 34. In Pindar *Nemean* 4.6–8, the sonority of the vocal expression seems to stand in opposition to the silence of the *phrén,* the depository of the commemorative poem. The *glôssa* produces a sonorous *rhêma* that it has discovered in the "depths of" the *phrén.*

85. See Derrida's remark, *Dissemination,* p. 234 (on the subject of Mallarmé): "These propositions . . . *mime* the internalization of the theater in the book and of the book in the 'mental medium.'"

86. Plato *Phaedrus* 276d. Literally, *hupómnēma* means "memory support," in the same way as *hupopódion* means "foot support" or "footstool." In the singular *hupómnēma* may be translated as "memorandum," in the plural as "notes."

have been calling "vocal writing." But this externalization has even been represented, literally, on the stage in ancient Greece in a most unusual fashion, in the *ABC Show,* the *Grammatikḕ theōría,* by the Athenian poet Callias.[87]

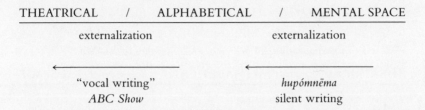

THEATRICAL	/	ALPHABETICAL	/	MENTAL SPACE
externalization		externalization		

← ←

"vocal writing"   *hupómnēma*
ABC Show   silent writing

The *ABC Show* (or the *ABC Tragedy,* as Athenaeus also calls it) poses difficult problems as to the date of its composition and its relationship, on the musical and metrical levels, to Euripides' *Medea* (which dates from 431 B.C.) and to Sophocles' *Oedipus Rex* (a little after 430). Hermann Koller's view is that Euripides and Sophocles adopted innovations introduced by Callias, who (according to Athenaeus) was writing between 455 and 426.[88] Egert Pöhlmann believes that the play dates from 403 for two reasons. First, despite his declarations regarding the relationship between Callias and the two tragic poets, Athenaeus explicitly attributes to him a date slightly earlier than Strattis (active between 409 and 375).[89] And second, only Archinos' decree establishing the Ionian alphabet (the one used in the *ABC Show*) as the official alphabet of Athens in 403 can have prompted the play by "Callias," who cannot be the same person as the tragic poet called Callias.[90] True, the alphabetic signs H, Ξ, Ψ, and Ω, said to have been invented by Simonides, were officially

87. Athenaeus 7.276a; 10.448b, 453c–454a (= Callias frag. 31 Edmonds). See F. D. Harvey, "Literacy in the Athenian Democracy," *Revue des études grecques,* 79 (1966), p. 632n.13.

88. H. Koller, "Die Parodie," *Glotta,* 35 (1956), pp. 17–32. Athenaeus 10.453e. For the dates for Callias see J. M. Edmonds, *The Fragments of Attic Comedy,* vol. 1 (Leiden, 1957), cited by E. Pöhlmann, "Die ABC-Komödie des Kallias," *Rheinisches Museum* 114 (1971), p. 232, n.14.

89. Pöhlmann, "Die ABC-Komödie," pp. 230–240. Athenaeus 10.453c. On the dates of Strattis, see Edmonds, *The Fragments of Attic Comedy,* pp. 813, 815. The poet was active between 409 (the date of the *Anthrōporaístēs*) and 375 (the date of the *Atalante*).

90. The evidence is quoted by Pöhlmann, "Die ABC-Komödie," p. 233n.17.

adopted as Athenian at this date, although they were already in use in Athens during the first half of the fifth century.[91] Pöhlmann is consequently obliged to discount a number of Athenaeus' views. For example, he quite rightly regards the *ABC Show* as a comedy, not a tragedy; and, more important, he believes that the play did not inspire *Medea* and *Theseus,* but rather *parodies* them.[92]

Because of these problems in dating and the improbability of resolving them definitively, I simply date the play very approximately to the second half of the fifth century. All the dates so far proposed fall within this period, and this approximation should amply serve the purpose here.

What does the *ABC Show* offer to the 'contemplation' (*theōría*) of its 'spectators' (*theataí*)? Nothing less than a chorus of twenty-four women representing the Ionian alphabet, introduced in the following manner in the Prologue: "Alpha, beta, gamma, delta, ei [which is Apollo's letter], zeta, eta, theta, iota, kappa, lambda, mu, nu, xei, ou, pei, rho, sigma, tau, u, phei, and khei next to psei—and finally ō!"[93] Next, the chorus, disposed in pairs, makes us attend a lesson in elementary school: "Beta alpha: ba; Beta ei: be; Beta eta: bē; Beta iota: bi; Beta ou: bo; Beta u: bu; Beta ō: bō."[94] Following this stanza, the answering stanza runs: "Gamma alpha: ga; Gamma ei: ge; Gamma eta: gê," and so on, which gives us a total of seventeen stanzas, all sung to the selfsame tune.

After this "syllabic chorus," which should horrify modern specialists of reading acquisition, comes a dialogue between a schoolmaster, it seems (?), and two women.

> SCHOOLMASTER: You must pronounce *alpha* by itself, my ladies, and secondly *ei* by itself. And you there, you will say the third vowel!
> FIRST WOMAN: Then I will say *eta.*
> SCHOOLMASTER: Then *you* will say the fourth one by itself!
> SECOND WOMAN: *Iota.*

91. *Anecdota Graeca* 2.781.2–4, 782.27–28 Bekker. Pöhlmann, "Die ABC-Komödie," p. 234.

92. Athenaeus 10.454b. *Theseus* appeared a little before 422.

93. Athenaeus 10.453d.

94. Ibid. See H. I. Marrou, *A History of Education in Antiquity* (London, 1956), p. 151.

SCHOOLMASTER: The fifth one!
FIRST WOMAN: *Ou.*
SCHOOLMASTER: The sixth one!
SECOND WOMAN: *U.*
SCHOOLMASTER: But the last of the seven vowels, *ō,* I will pronounce
for you. So now all seven are put into verse. When you have
pronounced them, say them to yourselves![95]

In the subsequent fragment, Callias amuses himself by giving
detailed descriptions of two letters without pronouncing their
names—descriptions that are so precise that the audience is able to
identify them. In his *Theseus,* Euripides does just the same thing:
an illiterate shepherd describes the letters that form the name
"Theseus," without knowing what they mean.[96] In Callias' play,
the same operation is not undertaken as a result of ignorance, for
reasons that are made plain. "I am pregnant, my ladies," announces
a woman (possibly *Grammatikē,* a personification of the Art-of-
writing). "But out of shame, my dear friends, I shall tell you the
name of the baby by describing the shape of the letters. There is a
long straight stroke; at the side of it, on each side, stands a small
reclining stroke. Next comes a circle with two little feet."[97] The
letters are Ψ and Ω, two letters of the Ionian alphabet and therefore
foreign, even "illegitimate" in an Athenian context—a joke that
was clearly meaningful well before 403. These two letters are the
ones with which the seventeenth and last stanza of the "syllabic
chorus" quoted above must have ended. Unfortunately, we do not
know the exact meaning of *psō* (undoubtedly it was obscene). In one
way or another, *psō* must refer to something that the woman is
embarrassed to say; and given that the joke is made on the stage, we
may add that these two letters have a pictographic character that
could well be exploited for obscene purposes. After all, Sophocles is
reported to have used an actor who *danced* the shapes of the letters (*tà
grámmata orkhoúmenon*) in his satyr play *Amphiaraos.*[98]
However that may be, the fragments of Callias' play show that

95. Athenaeus 10.453f.
96. Ibid. 10.454b (= Euripides frag. 382 Nauck[2]).
97. Athenaeus 10.454a.
98. According to Athenaeus 10.454f. (= Sophocles frag. 117 Nauck[2]).

the Ionian alphabet was staged in the theater of Dionysus in the second half of the fifth century, a remarkable fact. Precisely at this time the *grámmata* began to 'speak' (*légein*) on a large scale in the works of Herodotus (who, as I have said, was a friend of Sophocles). This fact testifies, albeit indirectly, to the existence of silent reading (and, one might add, to that of silent *writing*). Through a ploy that is the exact opposite of that used in the Andron inscription, which precedes it by a century (at most), the *ABC Show* makes visible what is normally concealed in the theater—that is, writing. The major character absent from the stage finally makes her appearance. The very title of the play emphasizes this fact: *theōría,* a word derived—like *théatron* itself—from *theáomai* 'to see, contemplate', means literally "a show for the eye." What it announces is that the alphabet will be *seen* in the theater, not just heard (through the "vocal writing" of the actors). The *grámmata* will actually appear on the stage, not just be inscribed in the memory of the actors. The whole scene will make clear that this is a fundamentally inscriptional space, capable of pronouncing itself, of reading itself, and of interpreting itself aloud.

The idea of such a play could arise only in the mind of someone to whom the *grámmata* seem already autonomous and to whom their vocalization no longer constitutes a necessary condition for their deciphering. In other words, it only arises in the mind of someone to whom the letters have become the "pure" representations of a voice (transcribed or fictitious, as in the case of silent writing) and for whom their original purpose—that is, to produce *kléos* "audible renown"—is no longer the only one.

CHAPTER 10

The Reader and the *erómenos:*
The Pederastic Paradigm of Writing

Pederasty, a "sore point" for Greek society, gave rise to a whole body of moral problems, recently studied by Michel Foucault in his book, *The Use of Pleasure.*[1] Masculine love, prized and practiced throughout the history of the Greek city, brings into play two irreconcilable structures, and the clash between them constitutes a perpetual source of questioning as to the behavior of lovers and loved ones—to stick to the Greek words—the *erastés* and the *erómenos.*

The first of those structures is that which defines the two partners in a pederastic relationship in terms of domination and submission. The adult partner, who is dominant and active, is set in opposition to the adolescent partner, who is dominated and passive. To penetrate is necessarily to dominate, to overcome; to submit to penetration is to submit to a master, a conqueror. The second structure is that which defines the citizen—and, in anticipation, whoever is destined to become one—as subject to no one (except, as we have seen, to the *nómos,* which is "king" of the city). To exercise one's political rights, to participate in the life of the city and take on civic functions, the citizen must be *eleútheros* 'free'. That is an *essential* condition. An extreme but nonetheless extremely revealing example is the citizen who prostitutes himself and thereby forfeits his

1. M. Foucault, *The History of Sexuality,* vol. 2, *The Use of Pleasure* (New York, 1985), pp. 187–227.

right to speak in the Council or the Assembly. If he does so, he is condemned to death.[2] To be of advantage to the city, the use of speech must be subject to no constraint, whether overt or underlying; the citizen must express himself freely.

This conflict between masculine love and citizen status introduced problems, particularly in relation to the behavior of the *erómenos,* the boy who was the object of love for the *erastés.* If the *erómenos* was not the son of a citizen and hence himself a future citizen, there was no problem. The duty of a young slave was to submit, to be dominated by his master: that was part and parcel of his condition. In contrast, a future citizen to whom an *erastés* had attached himself was clearly faced with a dilemma. If he submitted to the *erastés,* he found himself in the position of one dominated, a slave or a woman—a position at odds with his future destiny as an adult man subject to nobody, in other words, a citizen. If he did not submit but resisted the advances of the *erastés,* he ruled out a particular way of transmitting knowledge within Greek society—a way whose importance has been emphasized by Henri-Irénée Marrou and Eric Havelock.[3] He would never learn to behave as a man should, for it was first and foremost from the *erastés* that he could hope to learn these lessons, since his father would have been too taken up with his civic activities to be able to devote himself to the task.[4] Usually the favors, promises, and gifts of the *erastés* would overcome any resistance. But at this point the *erómenos* had to behave in such a way as not to endanger his future reputation. In itself, the act of submitting to an *erastés* was not shameful. What would have been shameful would have been for the boy to take pleasure in his passive role; he was not supposed to identify with that role. What he was supposed to receive from the *erastés* was not sexual pleasure but favors of a different order—material gifts, for instance. The *erómenos* was supposed to content himself with *procur-*

2. Aeschines *Against Timarchus,* analyzed by K. J. Dover, *Greek Homosexuality* (London, 1978), p. 27.

3. H.-I. Marrou, *A History of Education in Antiquity* (London, 1956), pp. 26–36; E. A. Havelock, "Why Was Socrates Tried?" in *Festschrift Norwood* (Toronto, 1952), pp. 95–109.

4. See Marrou, *A History of Education in Antiquity,* p. 31, citing Plato *Laches* 179c–d.

ing pleasure for the *erastés*. In a pederastic relationship, pleasure was not supposed to be mutual. Consequently, the shameful thing for a boy was to submit for the sake of pleasure, to submit too often and to too many *erastaí*. And any *erómenos* who forsook his *erastés* for another (or several others) risked hearing and reading comments about himself that could only harm his reputation. Instead of singing his praises by calling him *kalós* 'beautiful', an adjective to which every courted *erómenos* could lay claim, his abandoned *erastés* might take his revenge by henceforth calling him *katapúgōn* 'buggered'.

The role of the *erastés,* on the other hand, contained no element that might endanger his condition of citizen. To be dominant and active was to behave as a free man. There was nothing shameful about conquering. That seemed to go without saying. All the same, even if the behavior of the *erastés* did not conflict with the civic ideal, we must necessarily characterize this behavior by a certain sense of seemliness: the *erastés* had to demonstrate responsibility in his relationship with the boy. He was expected not to corrupt him, but to improve and educate him.

Dwelling on the pederastic relationship may seem perverse in a study devoted to reading in ancient Greece. On the face of it, that relationship and the conflict that it perpetuated have nothing to do with the relationship between the writer and the reader—apart from the purely practical fact that the *erastés* would write graffiti intended to be read by his beloved. Yet by resorting to the pederastic model the Greeks themselves tried to understand the relationship between writer and reader, apparently at a very early date. One of the earliest known definitions of the relationship between the writer and the reader presents the writer in the role of the *erastés* and a reader in the role of the *erómenos*. It takes the form of an inscription scratched upon a black Attic kylix discovered in Gela, Sicily, and dating from 500–480 B.C. (according to Marialetizia Lazzarini).[5] The date of the inscription itself is only slightly later, as determined by Bernhard Forssman.[6]

5. M. Lazzarini, "I Nomi dei vasi greci nelle iscrizioni dei vase stessi," *Archeologia classica,* 25–26 (1973–1974), p. 356.
6. B. Forssman, *"ANNEMOTA in einer dorischen Gefässinschrift,"* Münchener *Studien zur Sprachwissenschaft,* 34 (1976), p. 39.

τοῦτον τὸν σκύφον Πόρκος ἀποδίδωτι
ἐς τὸν θίασον τῶν π[αῶ]ν.
αἰ δ' ἐφίλει Φρύναν, οὐκ ἄλλος κ' ἄγ', ὁ δὲ γράψας
τὸν ἀννέμο⟨ν⟩τα πυγίξει.

[This *skúphos,* Porkos sends it to the *thíasos* of the parents [of the husband]. If he [the husband, Porkos' rival] loves Phryna, nobody else will marry her; all the same, the writer of this inscription will 'bugger' the reader.][7]

A certain Porkos sends a kylix—which he calls a *skúphos*—to what seems to be the parents of the man who is about to marry Phryna, with whom Porkos has himself been in love. To show that despite his failure in that love, he is not finished yet, Porkos adds, "The *grápsas* will bugger the *ananémōn.*" At a stroke, the reader is reduced to the role of "the one who is buggered" (*katapúgōn*). His eagerness to read betrays his despicable nature, but only at the very last moment of the reading. Not for nothing is the word *pugíxei* positioned right at the end. It defines the action that is completed by this very word, without giving the reader a chance to break off. The writer wins the day; the reader has been had.

The credit for showing that this inscription is in no way exceptional must go to Forssman, for he has compared it to a series of Latin inscriptions that, though more recent, are clearly related to the Gela inscription. In one of these, the four terms of the analogy are set out clearly: *amat qui scribet pedicatur qui leget* "the one who will write is the lover, the one who will read gets buggered".[8] In another, discovered at Meaux, the reader is again forced to identify himself: *ego qui lego pedicor* "I, who am reading, am buggered."[9] Clearly the inscription is a veritable commonplace, and it reappears in Catullus: *pedicabo ego vos* "I will bugger you" (in a poem addressed to malevolent readers).[10]

The reader is thus cast in the role of the *erómenos,* or the one "buggered," while the one who does the writing is identified with

7. I follow the normalized text of C. Gallavotti, "Letture epigrafiche," *Quaderni Urbinati di Cultura Classica,* no. 20 (1975), pp. 172–177.

8. *Corpus inscriptionum latinarum,* 4.2360 (Forssman, "ANNEMOTA in einer dorischen Gefässinschrift").

9. Ibid. 13.10017.40 (Forssman, ibid.).

10. Catullus *Carmina* 16.

the *erastés*. The reader is at the service of the writer, a point that has already been made in Chapters 2 and 3 in particular. For the *erómenos* is understood to "serve"—*therapeúein, hupēreteîn,* or *hupourgeîn*—his *erastés,* by submitting to the sexual act.[11] Likewise, there can be no satisfaction for the writer without the collaboration of the reader who, on that account, must not be insulted lightly or too frequently. On the contrary, he must be cosseted even if, deep down, the writer despises the one upon whom he seeks to impose his power and without whom he cannot manage.

This model is found not only in Dorian Sicily and in Latin-speaking countries, but also in Athens. Two Attic inscriptions, contemporary with the Gela inscription, fall into the same category. The first runs as follows: *Sōsías katapúgōn: Euphróniós phēsin ho grápsas* "Sosias buggered: the one writing this, Euphronios, says so" (485 B.C.; found in Athens). The second runs: *Sōs[ías] kastapúgōn: ho grá[psas phēsín]* "Sosias buggered; the one writing this says so" (found in Cumae).[12] An extremely ancient inscription, possibly dating from the mid-eighth century, is also worth mentioning here, even though it does not contain the word *gráphein:* "Nikodemos [illegible patronymic name] *Katapúgōn*" (found in Athens).[13] Clearly these inscriptions produced their maximum effect if they came to the notice of the person insulted in them. Very early on, writing seems to have been used to insult the reader who, reading aloud and with some difficulty, would slowly discover, after "recognizing" his own name, the nature of his own activity. Once he arrived at the word *katapúgōn,* he would realize that he had been had and that the writer had made his point. The two inscriptions that mention Sosias (probably, but not necessarily, the same individual[14]) follow more

11. Dover, *Greek Homosexuality,* p. 44; Foucault, *The Use of Pleasure,* p. 223.

12. See M. J. Milne and D. von Bothmer, "Καταπύγων, καταπύγαινα," *Hesperia,* 22 (1953), pp. 217–218, nos. 3 and 4.

13. C. W. Blegen, "Inscriptions on Geometric Pottery from Hymettos," *American Journal of Archaeology,* 38 (1934), p. 11. See H. A. Thompson, "Activities in the Athenian Agora: 1955," *Hesperia,* 25 (1956), pp. 63–64: "Titas, Olympic victor [*katapúgōn*]" (before 500).

14. See Milne and von Bothmer, "Καταπύγων, καταπύγαινα," p. 218. Sosias was a common name for slaves: see O. Masson, "Les Noms des esclaves dans la Grèce antique," in *Actes du Colloque 1971 sur l'esclavage,* Centre de recherches d'histoire ancienne, 6 (Paris, 1972), pp. 15, 19 (I am indebted to Pierre Vidal-Naquet for this reference).

or less the same schema. "X buggered: the one who writes this [Y] says so." It seems to have been a quite common schema, because it can also be found in the same period on the island of Lesbos: *Phaéstas kálos, ōs phási o grápsais Ogesthénē[s]*, "Phaestas beautiful; so says the one writing it, namely Ogesthenes."[15] The only difference here is that *kalós* takes the place of *katapúgōn*. Ogesthenes is not insulting Phaestas, but courting him, so he uses *kalós*, not *katapúgōn* or *kakós*, another possible substitute for *kalós*.[16]

Kalós is the usual qualification for the *erómenos* in inscriptions and graffiti. That is what an *erastés* would write on the doors and walls of the city to make known his love for a particular boy.[17] If, however, he called the boy *katapúgōn*, it was because he wanted to insult the one who, having been his *erómenos*, left him for another or others. In both cases the *erastés* was, literally, the writer. And his writing, which was more or less public depending on where it appeared, was clearly intended to capture the attention of the boy in question, who was thereby placed, quite literally, in the role of the reader.

But this analogy between the *erastés* and the *erómenos* on the one hand and the writer and the reader on the other involves far more than the fact that someone writes "so-and-so *kalós*" and someone else reads that inscription, as the graffiti that set up an opposition between a *grápsas* and a *katapúgōn* demonstrate. In truth, the analogy concerns the entire activity of writing and its destination: reading. To put it in schematic terms, to write is to behave as an *erastés*; to read is to behave as an *erómenos*, either *kalós* or *katapúgōn* as the case may be. To write is to be dominant, active, triumphant, as long as one finds a reader prepared to be amenable. To read is to submit to what the writer has written, to be dominated, to occupy the position of the one overcome, to submit to the metaphorical *erastés* in the person of the writer (that is, if one decides to read, for the reader, if he is not a slave, is clearly free to refuse to read). Although writing is honorable, reading may present problems, for it is per-

15. *IG* 13.2.268.

16. See Dover, *Greek Homosexuality*, p. 121n.30.

17. Aristophanes *Acharnians* 142–144, *Wasps* 97–99. See Dover, *Greek Homosexuality*, p. 111 f. See also Y. Garlan and O. Masson, "Les Acclamations pédérastiques de Kalami (Thasos)," *Bulletin de correspondance hellénique*, 106 (1982), pp. 3–22.

ceived as a servitude and as "passivity" (the one who submits to the writing is "passive"). To read is to lend one's body to a writer who may be unknown, so as to make the words 'of a stranger', 'another' (*allótrioi*), sound forth. If it is to succeed in transmitting its meaning, the activity of writing needs this loan from the reader. Only the metaphorical *erómenos,* who is the reader, can ensure the success of the writing. The ambiguity of the reader, who is at once necessary and inferior (or servile, in relation to the writer who makes use of him), is similar to the ambiguity of the *erómenos.* So it seems reasonable to suppose that reading, a task that the Greeks tended to leave to slaves, as in Plato's *Theaetetus,* had to be practiced only in moderation if it was not to become a vice.[18] Or, rather, whoever did the reading had to be sure not to identify with the role of reader if he wanted to remain a free man, that is to say, one unaffected by the constraints imposed by the Other. It was better to remain *tà grámmata phaûlos* "poor at reading", that is to say, capable of reading but no more.

In a collective work titled *Pratiques de la lecture,* Jean-Marie Goulemot suggests elaborating a history of the reading body, or a history concerned with the physical positions adopted by readers. "We ought to establish a history of the representations (of positions) that have served as models for the act of reading. The history of bodies and books contains a dialectic. We are presented (by whom?) with reading attitudes: dreamy reading (Baudelaire, Hugo), absorbed reading (head buried in hands), distracted reading (Jean Lorrain, with carefully made-up face, stretched languidly upon his sofa)."[19] In such a history, clearly the bodies of boys engaged in reading (as represented on Greek vases[20]) would have a place. The vases show reading lessons that constitute a physical training for future citizens, an orthopaedy in the etymological sense of the term.

18. The slave's reading begins at 143c and continues right to the end of the *Theaetetus* (210d). See I. Dühring, *Aristotle in the Ancient Biographical Tradition,* Studia Graeca et Latina Gothoburgiensia, 5 (Göteborg, 1957), p. 108: "The status of an ἀναγνώστης in the Academy was that of a servant; he was probably a slave trained for his task." Aristotle, in contrast, read for himself, voraciously.

19. J. M. Goulemot, "De la Lecture comme production de sens," in *Pratiques de la lecture,* ed. R. Chartier (Paris, 1985), p. 92.

20. See F. A. G. Beck, *Album of Greek Education: The Greeks at School and at Play* (Sydney, 1975).

The images are of well-brought-up boys characterized by an air of *sōphrosúnē* 'moderation'. In contrast, one red-figure Attic vase, dating from about the same period as the Gela inscription and the two inscriptions referring to Sosias, cited above, carries an image of a different kind of boy engaged in reading.[21]

The cup carries a single painting, on the inside, of a beardless boy, draped in a cloak that reveals the contours of his body. The boy is certainly the age of an *erómenos* and, significantly enough, he is engaged in reading an inscription on a stele, bending forward to do so. In this position, the boy's behind is much in evidence. Although draped in a cloak, it is clearly the behind of an *erómenos:* the reading boy is ready to be "buggered." His position is that which, in iconography, suggests *katapúgōn*. It is the very same position as that of the Persian depicted on a vase cited by Kenneth Dover: "A man in Persian costume, informing us, 'I am Eurymedon, I stand bent over,' suits his posture to his words, while a Greek, half-erect penis in hand, strides towards him with an arresting gesture. This expresses the exultation of the 'manly' Athenians at their victory over the 'womanish' Persians at the river Eurymedon in the early 460s; it proclaims, 'We've buggered the Persians!' "[22]

21. *Corpus vasorum antiquorum,* Germany (Adolphseck, Schloss Fasanerei), 16.2, no. 62. I am indebted to François Lissarrague for bringing this picture to my attention and for providing me with the references given in the following note.

22. Dover, *Greek Homosexuality,* p. 105. The vase is published by K. Schauenburg, "Εὐρυμέδων εἰμί," *Athenische Mitteilungen,* 90 (1975), pp. 97–121, pl. 25.

From the Greek point of view, the perversion of the reading boy lies in the fact that he seems to be entering fully into the role of reader-*erómenos*. He seems to take pleasure in offering himself to an unknown writer-*erastés*, whose scorn for him is such that the letters that he has written on the stele make no sense. What emerges from the boy's mouth will therefore be meaningless babble. The humiliation of the reader-*erómenos* is at its peak here; the boy is prepared to make the effort "to read," only to discover that he is being cynically mocked and that, in a sense, he is useless. We can easily imagine a situation in which an *erastés* forsaken for another (or even others) by his *erómenos* might send him this painted cup instead of simply writing *katapúgōn*, which would not be nearly as original. Our hypothetical *erastés* presents his erstwhile *erómenos* as someone who offers himself for the pleasure of doing so, as would the reader of a meaningless public inscription—meaningless because the author of an inscription addressed to the first comer cannot know the identity of that "first comer." And if he does not know the boy, he cannot love him—unlike the *erastés* who commissioned the cup and who, being wounded in his love for his faithless *erómenos*, takes his revenge in this deliberate fashion.

If the boy on the vase is an *erómenos* who reads only to learn nothing, he is probably the victim of disappointed love, as are so many of the *katapúgones* of archaic and classical epigraphy. Normally an *erastés* would write "so-and-so *kalós*," since his writing would be intended to attract the *erómenos*. He was out to seduce him, not insult him. And normally, the *erómenos* who capitulated did so not in order "to learn nothing" but, on the contrary, to become *sophós* 'wise' and *agathós* 'noble' thanks to the *erastés*.[23] As Dover observes, "acceptance of the teacher's thrusting penis between his thighs or in the anus is the fee which the pupil pays for good teaching."[24]

Pederasty was a fundamental element in the Greek *paideía* "system of education". Pederasty and education went hand in hand; in *sunousía* 'intercourse'—in every sense of the term—with an adult

23. See Plato *Symposium* 184d–e and 185b; Dover, *Greek Homosexuality*, pp. 90–91. See also G. Nagy, "Theognis and Megara: A Poet's Vision of His City," in *Theognis of Megara: Poetry and the Polis*, ed. T. J. Figueira and G. Nagy (Baltimore, 1985), pp. 54–56.

24. Dover, *Greek Homosexuality*, p. 91.

man a boy received his education. Havelock has written a number of memorable pages on the subject, and Marrou has devoted a whole chapter to it in his *A History of Education in Antiquity*.[25] So I will limit myself to a few remarks on Greek elementary instruction that can also be charged with considerable pederastic significance.

One gets some idea of it by leafing through Frederick Beck's album devoted to Greek education.[26] The images, which show bearded men with boys in pedagogic situations, are all of a kind that could easily take on an erotic significance by virtue (in my view) of the very fact that the figures depicted are engaged in reading and writing. Corroborative evidence is provided by the epigrams to be found in Book 12 of the *Greek Anthology*. Admittedly, these date from the Hellenistic or Roman periods, but, as Dover points out, the continuity in this field is quite remarkable.[27] Consider, first, an epigram by Strato: "You even ask for payment, you schoolteachers! What ingratitude on your part! Is it not enough to look at the boys, speak to them, embrace them when you meet them? Is not that privilege, in itself, worth as much as gold? If any of you has beautiful boys, let him send them to me! Let them embrace me! Let them claim any remuneration they like from me!"[28]

From the point of view of the pederast, a schoolteacher was a privileged being. His privileges, however, incorporated dramatic upheavals of their own, as another epigram, by the pseudo-Skythinos, makes clear: "I am the victim of great pain, great strife, great passion: Elissos. Having reached the age of love, that is to say the fatal age of sixteen, he is furthermore endowed with every charm, both slight and great, a voice like honey for reading [*pròs anagnônai phōnèn méli*], lips for kisses and an irreproachable thing to receive me within [*kaì tò labeîn éndon amemptótaton*]. What will become of me? He tells me to do nothing but look. In truth, I shall remain awake at night, battling with my love deprived of a body."[29]

25. Havelock, "Why Was Socrates Tried?"; Marrou, *A History of Education in Antiquity*, pp. 26–36 ("Pederasty as Education").

26. Beck, *Album of Greek Education*.

27. Dover, *Greek Homosexuality*, p. 112.

28. *Greek Anthology* 12.219.

29. Ibid. 12.22. On Elissos, see (*an-*)*elíssein* 'to read' (Xenophon *Memorabilia* 1.6.14; *Greek Anthology*, 12.208).

The schoolmaster derives great pleasure *from hearing the boy read*. The beloved's reading voice is the foremost of his charms. To make the boy read is to act upon his body, to force him to follow the written signs. For the schoolmaster, this "manipulation" of the pupil's body gives him intense pleasure. And since he refers to the boy's vocal organ, this is no "Platonic" love, as is amply borne out by the remainder of the epigram. The schoolmaster copes badly with chastity, dreaming of kisses; in his thoughts, he has already arrived at the moment of penetration.

Here, writing takes the place of a penetration that is out of the question. The schoolmaster cannot 'do it' [*diapráttesthai*], but must content himself with the pleasure derived from the power that he "legitimately" exercises over the boy's body, namely over his vocal apparatus, an internal—one might almost say intimate—organ. The pleasure stems from the exercise of power. The same fantasy surfaces again in another epigram, by Strato, one not directly situated within a pedagogic context. "Fortunate little book, I am not jealous of you [meaning 'would not be, even if you deserved it']. Reading you, a boy will touch you, hold you close to his cheek, or press you to his lips, or perhaps he will unfold you upon his tender thighs, O most fortunate of books! Often, you will be carried within his shirt or, flung down upon a chair, you will dare to touch those particular things (*keîna*) without fear. You will speak much with him, alone with him. But, O little book, I do implore you, from time to time do speak of us!"[30] The boy-reader imagined by the poet and mentioned in the text will manipulate the book in a way that gives pleasure in anticipation to the one who writes it. And this boy, unlike Elissos, has no identity. He is an *erómenos*-reader about whom the writer as yet knows nothing and perhaps never will. He is a "first-comer" whose role is defined in the poem. Strato's perfect reader will be one who acts out the very scenario the poet imagines. It is the possibility of such a submission to what is written that procures pleasure for the poet; he himself will never come into direct contact with this future reader, but he enjoys thinking about him. He derives pleasure from this future reading, a pure, impersonal pleasure with no love involved. He is not jeal-

30. *Greek Anthology*, 12.208.

ous—*ou phthonéō,* as he says—of the little book, despite the fact that, in a way, it is his rival.[31]

All these sources of evidence—epigraphical, iconographical, and literary—show that pederasty was one of the models the Greeks used in order to think about writing and reading. I say "one of the models" advisedly, for the pederastic model was clearly not the only one in this field. I have already studied two others, one in which the reader is seen as the suitor of the writing, which is the daughter of the writer, and another in which the reader is seen as the spectator of written theater. To assess what I believe is the profound relevance of the pederastic model, let us turn to the work of Plato.

In the dialogues of Plato, people are sometimes presented in the act of reading. In the *Parmenides* Zeno reads out his own *grámmata* to his listeners, among them Socrates, who also has his moments as a reader.[32] In the *Theaetetus,* a slave of Euclid's reads out the *lógos* that his master has set down in writing.[33] Terpsion and Euclid himself are the two listeners to this *lógos,* which is a transcription—revised and corrected—of a conversation between Socrates, Theodorus, and Theaetetus.[34] But when one thinks of reading in Plato's works, the first example to come to mind is the *Phaedrus.* From the point of view of the present study, that is for two reasons: (1) the starting point of this dialogue is provided by the reading of Lysias' speech, and (2) the subject of that speech is, precisely, pederastic love. The two themes of *Lógos* and *Érōs* (masculine, of course) in fact jointly dominate the dialogue in such a way as to have perplexed many of its commentators, even in antiquity, since it is hard to decide which of the two constitutes the principal subject of the dialogue. Some have wondered if the dialogue in fact *lacks unity,* attributing the disunity either to the author's youth or to his great age.[35] The

31. On *phthoneîn* in this sense, see Plato *Phaedrus* 232d. Another three-cornered situation (above, p. 151) may be compared to this. Sappho is jealous of the future reader of her poem, as if of a suitor who is to marry her daughter.

32. Plato *Parmenides* 127c–d. On Socrates as a reader see F. D. Harvey, "Literacy in the Athenian Democracy," *Revue des études grecques,* 79 (1966), p. 629n.8.

33. Plato *Theaetetus* 143b–c.

34. Ibid. 143a.

35. J. Derrida, "Plato's Pharmacy," in his book *Dissemination* (London, 1981), pp. 65–67.

matter seems all the more serious since in this dialogue Plato insists on an organic composition for a *lógos gegramménos* "written speech".[36] Can he have forgotten that principle of "organic composition" in that dialogue in which he produces his most meticulous definition of it, a passage that has become the foundational text of an entire rhetorical tradition?[37] Scholars today no longer believe that possible. Jacques Derrida draws attention to the admirable *sumplokḗ* 'intertwining' of the dialogue and G. J. De Vries concludes in his commentary that its "two principal themes are interwoven."[38] What remains to be seen, however, is exactly how they interact. We must try to discover the logic that makes it possible for them to do so. And here the analogy between writing and pederasty may prove particularly useful.[39]

"Yes, my dear, when you have first shown me what you have in your left hand, under your cloak. For I suspect you have the actual discourse [*lógos*]," Socrates says to Phaedrus, who has been hiding the *biblíon* that contains Lysias' speech.[40] Clearly, Phaedrus has been going about with a little book concealed beneath his clothes, close to his body. In this, he resembles the boy conjured up by Strato in the epigram considered above. Lysias' pamphlet could thus be an object already eroticized simply by the way that it has been carried about, by the "erogenous" zone that it has occupied.[41] The point is confirmed by Hermias in his commentary on the dialogue: Phaedrus was Lysias' *erómenos*. A little further on in the text Socrates also suggests as much, at the beginning of his first speech. The dates of birth of the two men also provide corroboration: Lysias was born around 460, Phaedrus around 450.[42]

36. Plato *Phaedrus* 264c.

37. See J. Svenbro, "La Découpe du poème. Aux origines sacrificielles de la poétique grecque," *Poétique,* no. 58 (1984), pp. 221–223.

38. Derrida, *Dissemination,* p. 67. G. J. De Vries, *A Commentary on the Phaedrus of Plato* (Amsterdam, 1969), p. 23.

39. Derrida, *Dissemination,* p. 153, writes: "One could cite here both the writing *and* the pederasty of a young man named Plato."

40. *Phaedrus* 228d.

41. In this connection see *Charmides* 155c–d, the importance of which for the *Phaedrus* has been emphasized by Derrida, *Dissemination,* pp. 124–125.

42. *Phaedrus* 237b. The fact that Socrates describes Phaedrus as an *erastḗs* at 236b, 257b, and 279b means that in Socrates' view only an *erastḗs* could improve Lysias: see *Symposium* 222b, together with Foucault's commentary, *The Use of*

Phaedrus, then, has been going about with the *biblíon* of his *erastés* beneath his cloak, pressed against his body. Indeed, as soon as the book is discovered, Socrates pronounces Lysias to be 'present' (*paróntos dè kaì Lusíou*). He is "present" through the intermediary of his pamphlet, which stands in for him, the *erastés*. That very morning, Phaedrus has listened to Lysias delivering his speech. Socrates suggests that Phaedrus may even have betrayed overinterest in the speech by requesting the pamphlet itself even after hearing the speech several times.[43] Phaedrus now sets about reading the pamphlet in Socrates' presence. You could say that, even though Lysias, the *erastés,* is absent, he continues to act upon the body of his *erómenos* through the intermediary of his writing. And Phaedrus is only too ready to comply.

The first thing we notice about Lysias' speech is the strangeness of its subject, its artificial and contrived character.[44] For it is devoted to singing the praises of the lover without love. It suggests that the *erómenos* should submit, not to the *erastés* who feels love for him, but to the one who does not, the *erastés* who is coldly interested in nothing but sexual pleasure and feels no passion for the *erómenos* personally. Lysias stresses the advantages of such a relationship: no jealousy, no conflict with parents, no social isolation for the *erómenos*. The lover without love introduces a kind of serenity into his relationship with the *erómenos;* unbridled passion does not come into it. The liaison causes no neglect of personal affairs, no friction with the family, no adverse publicity, and, above all, no regrets when the sexual liaison comes to an end. The *erómenos* must make the most of it and retain the friendship of his nonpassionate lover, whose 'merit' (*aretê*) alone, not love, induced the *erómenos* to grant him sexual relations.

Lysias declares that he is this man without love to whom the

Pleasure, p. 240 f. Even if Socrates is joking in these passages, there is a serious— indeed a very serious—side to the joking. For Hermias' statement, see his scholia printed in F. Ast's edition of the *Phaedrus* (Leipzig, 1810), p. 64. On Lysias' dates, see Plutarch *Lives of Ten Orators* 835c; on Phaedrus' dates, see L. Parmentier, "L'Âge de Phèdre dans le dialogue de Platon," *Bulletin de l'Association Guillaume-Budé* (January 1926), p. 10, and L. Robin, the "Notice" in the Collection des Universités de France edition of the *Phaedrus, Phèdre* p. xiii.

43. *Phaedrus* 228e, 228a–b.
44. Ibid. 230e–234c.

erômenos should grant that act. That is the very first thing he says.[45] Now the subject no longer seems so strange, for this passionless lover is the very man who wrote the speech that Phaedrus, his *erômenos*, carries upon his person and reads out, after Socrates has invited him to take up the position (*skhêma*) that he considers to be "the most comfortable for reading."[46] Lysias is the writer and, as we now know, also the *erastés* of Phaedrus, his reader. Phaedrus' reading of Lysias' speech thus becomes an allegory of itself: the subject is the passionless lover, an artificial figure that coincides with the figure of the writer to whom the *erômenos*—Phaedrus, the reader—grants the favor of his reading the speech aloud. That is "the act." Phaedrus performs it willingly, agreeing with ill-disguised eagerness to assume the role of reader.[47] By reading the pamphlet of the writer who is absent, he grants that act to the man who does not love him and who therefore keeps his distance.

Phaedrus knows how to read; that is to say, he is technically capable of conveying the meaning of the speech he has brought along. But while he may be deeply impressed by its rhetorical qualities, he is not—as he later shows—capable of defending the speech once Socrates sets about criticizing it. He has not even been able to learn it by heart. And that is why he needs the *phármakon* 'drug' represented by the writing: only the writing can "cure" his forgetful soul. Lysias' *phármakon* provokes speech; it is accompanied by a reading voice, a voice the *Charmides* compares to an 'incantation' (*epōidé*).

Let us read that passage from the *Charmides*.[48] At Critias' request, Socrates suggests "a cure for a headache" (*tò tês kephalês phármakon*) for Charmides. Actually, this English translation is more precise than the Greek, which means "cure for the head," as one might say "cure for the memory" (*mnémēs phármakon*) or "cure for forgetfulness" (*léthēs phármakon*).[49] What Socrates says is, "However, when he asked me if I knew the cure for headache, I somehow contrived

45. Ibid. 231a.
46. Ibid. 230e. See above, p. 193 and n. 19.
47. See *Phaedrus*, 228c.
48. Plato *Charmides* 155e–156a.
49. *Phaedrus* 274e; Euripides frag. 578.1 Nauck[2].

to answer that I knew. 'Then what is it?' he asked. So I told him that the thing itself was a certain leaf [*phúllon*], but there was a charm [*epōidḗ*] to go with the remedy and if one uttered the incantation at the moment of its application, the remedy made one perfectly well; but without the incantation there was no efficacy in the leaf. 'Then,' said he, 'I will take down the incantation from you in writing [*apográpsomai*].' " The presence of the words *phármakon* and *apográpsomai* in itself indicates the possibility of a metaphorical reading for this passage, for both in Plato and elsewhere, writing is, as we know, a *phármakon*. If that is the case, *phúllon* may be considered as a synonym for *biblíon* and, in view of the existence of the verb *epilégesthai*, with the sense of 'to read' (literally, "to add a *lógos* [to the writing]"), the *ep-ōidḗ* may here take on the meaning of 'reading'— "reading" understood as an incantation added (*ep-*) to the leaflet (of writing!).[50] The principle behind this little joke lies in a quasi-behaviorist view, according to which the incantation over the sheet of writing is in no way different from a reading of the sheet of writing. Yet, Socrates says, on its own that incantatory reading cannot cure Charmides' headache. The head cannot be cured unless one addresses oneself to the soul. In other words, reading on its own will not make Charmides better. To be effective, it must be accompanied by knowledge; in fact, with knowledge reading is not necessary.

Thus, the *phármakon* prepared by Lysias makes for speech. Even someone with nothing to say on the subject of love will be able to hold forth: the *phármakon* produces loquaciousness. Phaedrus, who has not been able to memorize the speech, is able to deliver it, thanks to the *phármakon*. He is "drugged." He speaks under the influence or constraint of the *phármakon*, which decides in advance what he will say. He will follow the written signs set down by Lysias, down to the last detail, syllable by syllable, thereby willingly satisfying the inscriptional desires of his *erastés*.

If this interpretation of the reading of Lysias' speech hits upon the essential point, it should provide the key to Socrates' first speech, which follows hard upon it.[51] Here, Socrates develops Lysias'

50. See above, pp. 62–63.
51. *Phaedrus* 237a–238c, 238d–241d.

theme, but from a different angle. Instead of singing the praises of the lover without love, he blames the *erastês* who is moved by passion. The theme is complementary to that of Lysias' speech, indeed in a sense identical to it.[52] Socrates declares that the passionate *erastês* is not concerned about the education of his *erómenos;* on the contrary, he concentrates on debasing and diminishing him, the better to control him. The passionate *erastês* is jealous, he keeps his beloved away from others—his friends and his family—isolating him in ignorance so that he shall have eyes for no one but his *erastês*. In fact the *erómenos* is put under *constraint;* he is at the service of the *erastês*.[53] If the *erastês* is harmful while he is in love with the boy, he will be equally so when the relationship is over. He will not keep any of the promises that he has made to his *erómenos*.

Now this speech, known as Socrates' first speech, is not really *his* speech. He himself tells Phaedrus as much. This is a speech "which was spoken by you through my mouth that you drugged [*dià toû emoû stómatos katapharmakeuthéntos hupò soû elékhthē*]."[54] Socrates has not in fact been reading. He has not read "a speech by Phaedrus." Yet the text insists that he has spoken under 'constraint' (*anánkē*) from Phaedrus. He has not spoken as a 'free agent' *idiótēs*), of his own volition.[55] But Socrates has taken his own precautions. In the exordium, he places the speech in the mouth of an *erastês* who, in order to win the favors of an *erómenos* courted by many *erastaí,* pretends that he himself feels no love and, on that account, is more worthy of the favors of the *erómenos* than the others are.[56] The implication is clear: Socrates is suggesting that the thesis defended by Lysias in *his* speech is simply a cunning ruse on the part of an *erastês*—who is in love—seeking to win over a much courted *erómenos*. So the speech that Phaedrus extorts from Socrates should be placed within quotation marks. The blame heaped upon the passionate *erastês* no more comes from Socrates than the praise for

52. In this connection see *Parmenides* 128b, *Phaedrus* 241e.
53. *Phaedrus* 240c: *anánkē*.
54. Ibid. 242d–e; see 242b and 244a.
55. Ibid. 236d, e, 237a, 242b, d. On *idiótēs* see ibid. 228a, 236d, and 258d, and, for example, *Ion* 532d. The *idiótes* is regularly set in opposition to the "professional writer" (*poiētês*), who works for others (see J. Svenbro, *La Parole et le marbre. Aux origines de la poétique grecque* [Lund, 1976], pp. 211–212).
56. *Phaedrus* 237b.

the lover without love comes from Phaedrus. Both speeches are to be placed within quotation marks, the one because it is read aloud by someone who is not its author, the other because it is delivered by someone forced to do so by his interlocutor. Both speakers are subject to constraint. Phaedrus, as he reads, is constrained to do so by the letters written by Lysias; Socrates, as he delivers "his" speech, is constrained to do so by the words of Phaedrus.

Moreover, we should be quite clear about a fact unmentioned in Derrida's analysis: in both cases it is a *phármakon* 'drug' that produces the speaking. The *phármakon* makes for speech. In the case of Phaedrus, the writing does it. In the case of Socrates, whose mouth has been 'drugged' *kata-pharmakeuthén,* the *phármakon* is not a piece of writing but a *lógos,* an unwritten *lógos,* a *lógos* that imposes a constraint, an oath. "I can say something that will force you to speak," says Phaedrus to Socrates, who replies, "Then pray don't say it," whereupon Phaedrus declares, "Oh, but I will. And my saying shall be an oath [*ho dé moi lógos hórkos éstai*]."[57] This is the *phármakon* that makes Socrates speak, that "drugs" him and forces him to deliver a speech that, in truth, ought to be called "Phaedrus' speech" (delivered by Socrates) or even "Lysias' second speech."[58] Socrates himself is really not involved. All he does is set out a thesis that is not his own choice and with which he is not in agreement (as can be seen from what follows). In a sense, the difference between the *lógos* that is read and the one that is spoken is negligible. In both cases 'constraint' (*anánkē*) is behind the words that are pronounced. And to tell the truth one must be free from all constraint, one must speak not as a *poiētēs* 'poet' but as an *idiōtēs* 'free agent'.[59]

So the speech on the passionate *erastēs,* who clings to his *erómenos* and uses force to achieve his ends, may be read as an allegory of himself, with Phaedrus in the role of the *erastēs* who constrains his *erómenos,* Socrates, forcing him to do his will, namely despite himself to express blame for the passionate *erastēs.*[60] And all to give

57. Ibid. 236d. The oath runs as follows: "I swear to you by . . . this plane tree. I take my solemn oath that unless you produce the discourse in the very presence of this plane tree, I will never read you another or tell you of another!" (236e).

58. According to the argument given in the *Parmenides* 128b.

59. See *Ion* 532d and above, n. 55.

60. *Phaedrus* 240d. See *Symposium* 222b.

pleasure to Phaedrus. When Socrates expresses that blame, he is thus the victim of a lover who seeks to keep him in ignorance, for in truth Socrates does not for a moment believe what he is forced to say.[61] The trouble is that Phaedrus has discovered the *phármakon* through which he can act upon Socrates' body, upon his vocal apparatus. Phaedrus uses Socrates as he would an instrument, an *instrumentum vocale,* an *órganon émpsukhon,* in other words, an object. The point is, though, that as Plato sees it, one cannot take part in the search for the truth if one is forced into the role of an object. To reach knowledge and declare the truth, one must act as a subject, which is exactly what Socrates proceeds to do in his "second speech," his Palinode.[62]

If one regards Lysias' speech and Socrates' first speech (i.e., "Phaedrus' speech") as allegories of themselves and, as such, as presentations of two ways to deliver speeches (reading/improvisation on a given theme), one soon realizes that, according to an ABBA schema, they correspond to the sections devoted to the reform of rhetoric and the critique of writing in the second half of the *Phaedrus*. Furthermore, if one considers Socrates' Palinode—his great speech on Love—to be the central section of the dialogue (which is not the same as saying that Love is *the* subject of the *Phaedrus*), one discovers a strikingly symmetrical schema, which certainly does not explain all the thematic connections in the dialogue but appears coherent enough to show that it is not simply the product of a series of accidents.[63]

61. See *Phaedrus* 243c.
62. See Foucault, *The Use of Pleasure,* p. 240: "In Platonic erotics, the beloved cannot settle into the position of object in relation to the other's love, simply waiting to receive, by the terms of the exchange to which he is entitled (since he is loved), the counsel he needs and the knowledge to which he aspires. It is right that he should actually become a subject in this love relation," for, as Foucault goes on to point out, "the love is the same for both of them since it is the motion that carries them toward truth." Socrates' Palinode is described as "belonging to Stesichorus" (*Phaedrus* 244a), in reference to the Palinode of Stesichorus (fr. 15 Page), and also, no doubt, on account of its "choral" character (see 252d, etc.). As is well known, *Stēsíkhoros* was a choral poet whose true name was Tisias, according to the *Suda,* s.v. *Stēsíkhoros*.
63. See, for example, A. Philip, "Récurrences thématiques et topologie dans le 'Phèdre' de Platon," *Revue de métaphysique et de morale* (1981), pp. 452–476. See p. 198.

Let us concentrate on the basic essentials of this schema. Lysias' speech, which is written and is read out in the absence of its author and introduces a metaphorical lover who can be identified as the writer, corresponds to the section devoted to a critique of writing. What is praised by Lysias is censured in the section on writing, if one recognizes that the speech on the unpassionate lover may be taken as allegorical. One indication of that relationship of correspondence is constituted by the fact that while Lysias is said to be "present" (in that Phaedrus carries his speech on his own person) it is precisely the "absence" of the writer which constitutes one of the gravest shortcomings of writing in the final section.[64] Without the presence of its "father," the speech cannot defend itself. The "presence" of Lysias is illusory and Phaedrus is not up to taking on the role of "father" of the speech when Socrates attacks it.

Both these sections (A and A' respectively) also contain an explicitly "pharmaceutical" myth: on the one hand the myth of Oreithyia, on the other that of Theuth. In the first, Oreithyia is raped by Boreas while playing with a dangerous nymph called Pharmakeia.[65] In the second, Theuth presents the *phármakon* of writing to the Egyptian king Thamous.[66] Nor is that all. The mention of Sappho in the first section seems to correspond to the mention of Adonis in the last, for Sappho is particularly associated

64. *Phaedrus,* 228e, 275e.
65. Dangerous indeed. In this connection see Timaeus the Sophist, *Appendix platonica,* p. 207 Hermann. Pharmakeia is the name of a deadly spring. Pharmakeia is believed to have played a role in Simonides' poem celebrating the victory at Artemision, during which Boreas intervened to help the Greeks (Simonides frag. 27f Page). Soon after the victory, this poem was reportedly sung at the inauguration of the altar of Boreas, close to Ilissos (Herodotus 7.189; Pausanias 1.19.5), a spot familiar to readers of the *Phaedrus* (229a f.). For Simonides, the reputed inventor of four letters of the Greek alphabet (see above, Chapter 9, p. 168, n. 28) as well as memorizing techniques (Cicero *De oratore* 2.86.352–353, a passage that ends with a reference to writing; on the mnemonic space as an alphabetical space, see Xenophon *Economica* 8.14), writing was probably already a *phármakon* for, according to Ammianus Marcellinus (16.5.8), to develop his memory in such a remarkable fashion he used a *remedium* (which the Latin author understands literally as 'drug'), a Latin word that precisely translates *phármakon*. Simonides thus stands as a background to "Plato's Pharmacy," clearly by reason of the analogy between painting and poetry that this poet from Keos is attested to have drawn: see Plutarch *On Whether the Athenians Shone Most with Glory* 346f.
66. *Phaedrus* 274e.

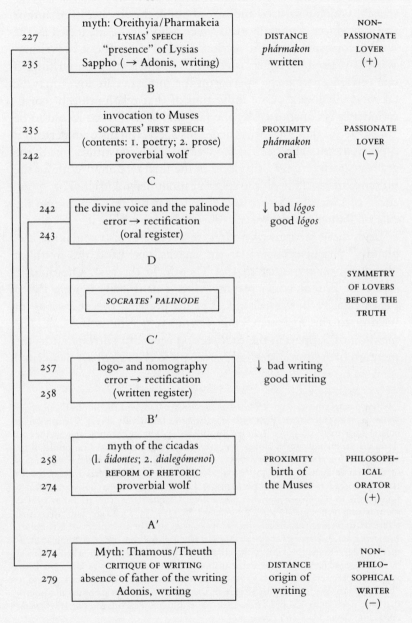

with the cult of Adonis, as she is with writing, and on Socrates' lips the "gardens of Adonis" become a metaphor for, precisely, writing.[67]

But the fundamental element in this correspondence remains the figure of the lover without love, used as a metaphor for the writer. This figure, praised (+) by Lysias (A) and criticized (−) by Socrates (A'), establishes the link between the two sections. And in the sections containing Socrates' first speech and the project for the new rhetoric (B and B' respectively), the identification of the passionate lover (in the sense of Lysias and Phaedrus) with the bad orator makes it possible to see the correspondence between these two sections. In the first, the characteristics of the bad orator are distinguishable in the figure of the passionate lover, who is violently criticized. In the second, rhetoric is analyzed at length, eventually to be totally redefined as philosophical rhetoric. The blame apportioned to the passionate lover (−) thus corresponds to the definition of the philosophical orator. These two sections (B and B') are furthermore introduced by an invocation to the Muses and by the myth of the cicadas respectively.[68] What is the connection here? Those who, at the birth of the Muses, became passionate about words are changed into cicadas as a result of forgetting to eat and drink. The cicadas thus become the *prophêtai* 'spokesmen' of the Muses. They will tell the Muses which men, here on earth, honor them. Just as Socrates declares himself to be inspired by poetry and prose when he begins his first speech, the cicadas devote themselves to both song and dialogue [*áidontes kaì allélois dialegómenoi*].[69] Then at the end of each of these sections, the figure of the wolf provides an extra sign. In the first case, Socrates uses a proverb that is applicable to the *erastés/erómenos* relationship: "Just as the wolf loves the lamb, so the lover adores his beloved."[70] The second case also involves a proverb: "Even the wolf, you know, Phaedrus, has a right to an advo-

67. See Sappho frag. 140.1, 168.140b, and 211 Lobel-Page; Dioscorides *Greek Anthology* 8.407. For Sappho's association with writing see Chapter 8. The quotation is from *Phaedrus* 276b–d.

68. Ibid. 237a, 258e f.

69. Ibid. 262d; 259c–d; 235c–d, and 258e.

70. Ibid. 241c–d. See G. Luck, "Kids and Wolves," *Classical Quarterly,* 9 (1959), p. 35.

cate, as they say."[71] Here, the wolf is not the passionate *erastés* but his double, the orator who rates oratorical success above the desire for truth, in other words, a man who is concerned to convince rather than to speak the truth, a man who, to borrow the terms used in the *Phaedo,* "loves to win" (*philoníkōs ékhei*) rather than "to behave as a philosopher" (*philosóphōs ékhein*).[72]

Next comes the correspondence between the section immediately preceding Socrates' Palinode and the one immediately following it (C and C' respectively). In the first, Socrates discovers the nature of the speech that he has just delivered; he says that his internal voice tells him that he has wronged the deity.[73] The wrong must be rectified by a palinode. The "internal law" represented by the voice of conscience demands that amends be made. Now, in the section following Socrates' Palinode, Phaedrus hastens to attribute the cause for what he regards as Socrates' triumph over Lysias to the fact that Lysias writes—something that suddenly seems essentially dubious to Phaedrus. He reminds Socrates that Lysias has been insulted and "abused . . . as a speech-writer" and goes on to declare that truly great men do not desire to leave writings behind them "through fear of being called sophists by posterity."[74] To this Socrates replies that a lawgiver, who uses writing, would not reproach Lysias for being a writer, for, he continues (and this is particularly important), "writing is not in itself a disgrace."[75] By referring to "external law" Socrates corrects Phaedrus' over-hasty conclusion. The first correction was applied to an oral speech (Socrates' first speech); this second correction is applied to a written speech. In the first case, we progress from a bad *lógos* to the idea of a good one; in the second, we move from the written speech, which Phaedrus regards as bad in itself, to the idea of a written speech that is not bad.[76]

71. *Phaedrus* 272c.
72. *Phaedo* 91a. Those who "behave as philosophers" stand as equals before the truth; similarly, citizens should stand as equals before the law: Plato *Letters* 7.337c–d (see above, p. 187).
73. *Phaedrus* 242b–c.
74. Ibid. 257c–d.
75. See *Laws* 10.891a; *Phaedrus* 258d.
76. See ibid. 278c–d.

The symmetrical schema also reveals correspondences between consecutive sections, correspondences between sections A and B and between sections B' and A'. A and B set up an opposition on the level of modes of communication and also on that of space: Lysias' written *lógos* is opposed to Socrates' nonwritten one. Phaedrus delivers the former, whose author is absent, and Socrates delivers "his," whose author is close at hand (Phaedrus). A similar relation links B' and A': the birth of the Muses, poetry, and speeches as well as the origin of the cicadas are set in opposition to the origin of writing, just as what is native (near) is opposed to what is foreign (distant). The Muses are Greek, and Theuth is a foreigner (as indeed is Lysias, the metic). Thus, not only do A and B correspond to A' and B', but the relationship between A and B corresponds to that between A' and B'.

All these elements are arranged around the central section of the *Phaedrus*, namely Socrates' Palinode. And if the interplay of correspondences, the logic of which is revealed by the *diaíresis* 'dissection' of the dialogue, [77] turns out to be serious, that is precisely because of their relationship to this central section of the dialogue, which produces a profound and extraordinary transformation of the relationship between the *erastḗs* and the *erṓmenos*. Lysias certainly would like to see a more satisfactory relationship than the kind in which shortcomings are expounded by Socrates in his first speech. But in that he considers the loveless relationship to be the ideal one, he is not only guilty of blasphemy against the god of Love but also incapable of seeing where the real problem, according to Socrates, lies. An *erṓmenos* who is nothing but an object of pleasure for the *erastḗs* is incapable of seeking the truth. To do so, the *erṓmenos* must become a subject of love, just as the *erastḗs* is. The real problem, therefore, lies in the fact that the *erṓmenos* allows himself to be penetrated, an act that, for a Greek, is inextricably linked with the role of one conquered, enslaved, or subjected, or with the role of a woman, that is to say, the role of an object, which is what the *erṓmenos* assumes in the pederastic act. What Socrates, in contrast,

77. See ibid. 265e–266b (the word *diaíresis* 'dissection' reappears at 266b4). The *Phaedrus* could thus be said to encompass the theory of its own "anatomy" (see Svenbro, "La Découpe du poème").

proposes in his great speech on Love, is a love that has no room for conquerors or conquered, masters or slaves, dominators or dominated—if it is the case that those conquered, enslaved, or dominated occupy the position of objects whose function is to satisfy the desire of the *erastés*.

Michel Foucault has given us a memorable analysis of this transformation that turns the *erastés* and *erómenos* into symmetrical subjects of love, so I need not dwell on it.[78] I emphasize, however, that this transformation of the loving relationship into a "Platonic love"—involving no penetration—implies the possibility of a similar transformation of the relationship between writer/reader and speaker/listener, in the sense that both these relationships are, as in the *Phaedrus,* invested by pederastic values.

What the central section of the *Phaedrus* renders possible is a new way of thinking about writing and rhetoric. Once the Palinode has been pronounced, the way is clear for a redefinition of rhetoric and a critique of writing based on new foundations—a critique that, while condemning its abuses, does not totally deny to writing a respectable status.[79] For Socrates writing is not an evil in itself. The important thing is to recognize its limitations.[80] One must take the addressee into consideration and likewise, as with the spoken word, the relationship within which the writing plays its part.[81] Writing possesses properties that call for vigilance. Left on its own, it may go off track. We must accordingly take special steps to make sure that it is used only in the context of a search for the truth.

The pederastic model constitutes the organizing principle of the theory of *lógos* in the *Phaedrus,* a fact that in itself testifies to its

78. Foucault, *The Use of Pleasure,* pp. 227–247.

79. For a critique of the written speech in Alcidamas, a contemporary of Plato, see S. Gastaldi, "La Retorica del IV secolo tra oralità e scrittura. 'Sugli scrittori di discorsi' di Alcidamante," *Quaderni di storia,* no. 14 (1981), pp. 189–225. See also the "Notice" by Robin in the Collection des Universités de France edition of the *Phaedrus,* pp. 164 ff., and Derrida, *Dissemination,* p. 112n.47, and p. 148n.70.

80. *Phaedrus* 271e–272b; see also 276d.

81. With the invention of silent reading the instrumental character of the reader is diminished. Apparently effortlessly, he receives the meaning by way of his eyes, just as the listener receives the meaning by way of his ears (see above, p. 170). Silent reading, therefore, tends to encourage a redefinition of the writer/reader relationship, or at any rate it certainly does not present an obstacle to such a redefinition.

importance and that makes it possible for us to recognize in Socrates' two fundamental gestures (not writing and not penetrating)
one single gesture that might be described as writerly *abstinence*.
Socrates does not write, nor does he seek to perform "the act" in his
(many) relationships with boys. He presents himself as an *erómenos*,
not an *erastés*, an *erómenos* who resists all seductive advances.[82] What
is the meaning of that double gesture? Simply, that writing could all
too easily become a facile and misleading means of victory instead
of being an instrument in the search for truth, the search that two
may engage in, in the chastity of a reformed love.

Plato thus makes a clear distinction between himself and the
"master who does not write." For Plato does write, abundantly. In
his merciless critique of writing, he assesses the risks run by written
lógoi, and makes the opposite choice from his master. Not through
some monstrous aberration, nor because he has had enough of him.
At no point in Plato's work is writing "parricide," as Derrida would
have it.[83] For the *graphé* 'denunciation' that sends Socrates to his
death is, quite simply, not signed by anyone who could claim to be
the "son" of Socrates. Plato's writing does not kill his "father," it
simply *moves away* from the one who wrote it and from the *lógos*
that it transcribes. And that is quite dramatic enough, so far as Plato
is concerned. Writing is liable to go off "rolling to the right and to
the left." So it is absolutely essential for Plato to find a means of
control that will enable him to deploy writing addressed to a reader
who is known and who is engaged in the same search as he is.[84] He
needs a kind of writing that is controlled, protected, and responsi-
bly taken care of by someone who, no less than its author, will be
capable of defending it against all attacks. In short, writing in itself
is neither good nor bad; everything depends on the relationship

82. *Symposium* 222b. See also the analogy suggested by P. Bourdieu in his
discussion with R. Chartier, "La lecture: Une pratique culturelle," in Chartier,
Pratiques de la lecture, p. 238: "Just as there are weapons such as judo for physical self-
defense, I believe that a certain type of historical analysis of the secret strategies for
manipulating the reader may have a liberating effect." *Mutatis mutandis,* that could
well be considered to be a Socratic position.

83. Derrida, *Dissemination,* pp. 145–146, 147, and 163. Derrida seems to wish
Western philosophy to be founded upon a parricide—that of Socrates (who does not
write) by Plato (who writes down what Socrates says). I would ascribe this to an
"ideology of the foundational murder."

84. *Phaedrus* 275e, 271e–272a, 276d.

within which "she" (in Greek the noun is feminine) functions.[85]

Or rather, "he"; for Plato prefers the periphrastic expression *lógos gegramménos* "written speech" to the word *graphḗ*, despite the fact that the latter is shorter and certainly easier to use (two syllables as opposed to six). Why is that? Because, as Derrida points out, Plato's view is that there is no "written thing." The *lógos* is left "open," just as is *nómos*, which, unlike a *rhḗtra* or a *lex*, can be either oral or written.[86] Here, Plato is faithful to a particular Greek tradition that refused to regard writing as a separate phenomenon. We have noted how *némein* can mean 'to cite (from memory)' as well as 'to read'. We have also noted how *ananémesthai* can mean 'to recite (from memory)' as well as 'to read'. The fact is that the opposition that we of the twentieth century are accustomed to draw between the oral and the written was not yet established. It was, if anything, discreet, invisible, possibly masked, in Plato's case perhaps already *deconstructed,* that is if it ever had been constructed before him (for example, by the sophists). Whatever the case may be, in Plato there is no *lógos/graphḗ* opposition, simply *lógoi* of different levels. In fact, one could say that there are only two kinds of *lógoi:* those characterized by constraint (active or passive) and those pronounced in the "free love" (*eleútheros érōs*) of those who seek the truth.[87]

Thus, Plato declines to attribute any autonomous status to writing. He is in a position to do that because he does not believe that evil—or good—is inherent in it. "Writing speeches is not in itself a disgrace," declares Socrates.[88] And he sticks to that opinion. Addressing Lysias, Homer, and Solon, he says: "If he has composed his writings with knowledge of the truth, and is able to support them by discussion of that which he has written, and has the power to show by his own speech that the written words are of little worth [*phaûla*], such a man ought not to derive his title from such writings, but from the serious pursuit that underlies them."[89] At this,

---

85. It is hard to imagine circumstances in which Plato would prefer an oral speech improvised by a sophist solely concerned with gaining the upper hand to a letter sent him by a friend engaged in the same search as himself.

86. Derrida, *Dissemination*, p. 143. See above, Chapter 6, in particular p. 115.

87. *Phaedrus* 243c.

88. Ibid. 258d.

89. Ibid. 278c–d. On the sense of *phaûla,* see T. A. Szlezák, *Platon und die Schriftlichkeit der Philosophie. Interpretationen zu den frühen und mittleren Dialogen*

Phaedrus asks him what "title" Socrates would apply to him, and Socrates replies, "I think, Phaedrus, that the epithet 'wise' [*sophós*] is too great and befits the god alone; but the name 'philosopher' [*philósophos*], that is, 'lover of wisdom', or something of that sort would be more fitting and modest for such a man." He then goes on to say, "On the other hand, he who has nothing more valuable than the things he has composed or written, turning his words up and down at his leisure, adding this phrase and taking that away, will you not properly address him as poet [*poiētḗs*] or writer of speeches [*lógōn sungrapheús*] or of laws [*nomográphos*]?"[90] Phaedrus feels bound to agree.

This point means that Plato rejects a certain fetishism about writing, a fetishism that makes writing not simply the name for the relation between the writer and his reader but something distinct, separate, with its own intrinsic properties that belong to it, in itself—something that impresses the reader, who is powerless to withstand this seduction. It is precisely to that fetish—abolished by Plato—that the word *graphḗ* corresponds. The very gender of the word distinguishes a *graphḗ* from a *lógos gegramménos*. A *graphḗ* is a daughter, not a son. And for that reason it is invested with attributes that do not suit the exercise of deconstruction undertaken by Plato. A daughter has to leave her father. Unlike a son, who is a *lógos* that is an extension of his father (as *Tēlé-makhos* is an extension of Odysseus[91]) and who will ensure the continuity of the paternal hearth, a daughter's destiny is to be espoused by Another. In that respect, she is exactly what the *lógos gegramménos* should not be, according to Plato. She is destined for separation, a separation that of course represents a danger for the *lógos gegramménos,* albeit not an inevitable one. For Plato hopes that the *lógos gegramménos* will be able to remain in the paternal house.[92]

(Berlin, 1985), pp. 18–19. Only from the point of view of the aid that their author might provide are written texts *phaûla.*

90. Ibid. 278d–e. On the "sticking together" of pieces of writing, see *Menexenus* 236b (Aspasia, the 'sticker'). On the *nomográphos,* see *Statesman* 295b f. and the passage cited above, p. 127.

91. See above, pp. 68–69, 71–78.

92. In a way, the *"epíklēros"* writing of a figure such as Phrasikleia (above, pp. 8–9) answers the same need: it will never leave the paternal house. But that is just what Kallirhoe does do; she is the girl who ought to have remained in her father's house but who escapes in a dash for freedom (above, p. 93).

A *graphḗ* may indeed intervene between the writer and the reader. Between Phokos, the writer, and the thirty suitors, who are ill-intentioned readers, Kallirhoe fills the role of a *graphḗ* that they must deserve in order to marry, that is, to read. Between Sappho, the writer, and her future reader, there is the written poem, the smiling "daughter" whom Sappho cannot outlive.[93] The case of Sappho seems particularly illuminating. Unlike Plato (and Epimenides[94]), Sappho is reconciled, although not without jealousy, to the fact that her own writings must inevitably leave her. They are her daughters and are destined by their sex to be separated from their "mother." Despite his deep admiration for Sappho,[95] Plato clearly cannot accept a feminine writing of this kind, for it implies that not only is it destined to go off on its own but also that it is alien to the world of masculine love. And there is another reason for his resistance: the jealousy that develops between Phokos and his daughter's suitors and between Sappho and her future readers (who will be alive when she is dead) has no equivalent in "Platonic love." For in Platonic love, the master, who is engaged in the same search as his pupil, is "master" only in the sense that he knows how to guide the beloved, without jealousy, toward the truth.

One problem remains, however, and it is a fundamental one. The reason that Socrates does not write is that he does not think that he could control a *lógos gegramménos* once it became separated from him.[96] He would be no more able to control a written *lógos* than Sappho is. Plato is the first to defend this position adopted by his master. Yet Plato himself not only writes, but writes prolifically. Can it be that what applies to Socrates does not apply to Plato and, if so, why not? What can be the reason for Plato's ability to write when the reasons for not writing produced by Socrates appear to be universally valid? The difference is that Plato truly has foreseen how to defend and control his writings, even well after his own death.

93. See above, Chapter 8, p. 153 and n. 26.
94. See above, pp. 140–141, and 143–144.
95. *Phaedrus* 235c.
96. The living *lógos* that is written in the *psukhḗ* may be the "legitimate brother" (*adelphòs gnḗsios: Phaedrus* 276a) of the *lógos gegramménos,* but that does not necessarily mean to say that the *lógos gegramménos* is a 'bastard' (*nóthos*), as Derrida, *Dissemination,* p. 148n.70, would have it. Plato does not say so; and the speech described as a "legitimate son" at 278a has "brothers" who, for their part, are certainly not bastards. In my opinion, by not describing the *lógos gegramménos* as

Like Epimenides, he has concerned himself with the *location* of his inscriptions and, in particular, with the location where his writing will be deposited. Plato was the founder of the Academy; and what was the Academy if not the institution that, for close to a millennium, guaranteed the protection of Plato's works?[97] His oeuvre constituted first and foremost the kernel of the library of the Academy, whose members received an education (still founded upon pederastic love, as Marrou points out[98]) that rendered them capable of "coming to the aid" (*boētheîn*) of Plato's writings, just as Socrates was capable of "coming to the aid" of his own *lógos* in the *Phaedo*.[99] That was no doubt exactly what Plato had intended. His works were not abandoned to the perils of the public domain (even if they ended up there eventually) but were protected by those who succeeded him as directors of the Academy.[100] Once the Academy had been founded, Plato could risk doing something that Socrates could not. He could commit his words to writing, in the firm conviction that he had made sure that his readers would be engaged in the same quest as himself and that, after the appropriate training, they would be ready to come to the aid of his *lógos gegramménos*.

'*nóthos*', Plato left the question open. We cannot disqualify a *lógos* purely on the grounds that it is written.

97. The Academy, founded by Plato in about 385 B.C., continued to function until it was closed by the emperor Justinian in 529 A.D.

98. Marrou, p. 33.

99. See J. N. Findlay, *Plato: The Written and the Unwritten Doctrines* (London, 1974), pp. 157–158; Szlezák, *Platon und die Schriftlichkeit der Philosophie,* pp. 16–23, 66–71. *Phaedo* 88e. I find myself in agreement with the "esoteric" position of Szlezák, pp. 400–405.

100. 'To fall' (*ekpíptein*) is the verb used by the pseudo-Plato, *Epistles* 2.314c: "For it is not possible that what is written down should not fall into the hands of the public." On the inauthenticity of Letter 2, see Szlezák, *Platon und die Schriftlichkeit der Philosophie,* pp. 386–388. Plato's strategy is to be found *in nuce* in Theognis 21, where the poet declares that the sense of his poetry will not be falsified "if a worthy man is present when it is recited [*tousthloû pareóntos*]" (see above, p. 147 and n. 8).

Index

Greek entries are glossed in English with single quotation marks when the English word represents one word (for example, *bállein* 'throw, pour out'). The gloss receives double quotation marks when the English represents more than one word (for example, *ágalma* "honorific offering, statue").

ABC Show, 5, 183–186
absence, absent, 3, 30–31, 44–45, 47, 123, 140, 150–153, 169, 186, 200–201, 206
Abu Simbel, 38n55
Academy, 216
accusative, 95
Achaeus, 177–178
Achilles, 26, 66, 113. *See also Akhileús*
active, activity, 2, 13n25, 14, 59, 170–171, 174, 187
actor, 169–172, 178–181, 185. *See also hupokritês*
Adeimantos, 77
adelphós 'brother,' 215n96
Admetos, 73
Adonis, 206, 208
aeídein 'sing,' 116, 208
Aelian, 135n64, 146
aénaos "which always flows," 91n45
Aeneas, 66, 113
Aeschines, 118, 188n2
Aeschylus, 15, 21n62, 36, 50n19, 75n55, 121, 167n25, 172, 176–177, 180–182; *Persians,* 36, 37n49; *Seven against Thebes,* 167n25, 176–177
affiliation, 3
ágalma "honorific offering, statue," 32–33, 39–40, 57, 148
Agamemnon, 26–28

Agariste (*Agarístē*) "by far the best," 76–77, 86, 91n48, 92
Aglauros, 8, 81, 82n6
Agostiniani, L., 29n16, 39n57
ágraphos "not written," 116, 120
Aiakos, 143
aídontes. See aeídein
Aineias, 111n8
air, 138–139, 142, 144
Aithon, 79n69
Ajax, 26, 73, 96, 101
akámatos 'indefatigable, inextinguishable,' 52, 54
Akhileús, 69n15
akoé, 'hearing,' 159
akoúein 'listen,' 14, 46n8, 55, 114, 123, 159, 161
akroatês 'listener,' 46n8, 55
Akrothínion, 77
Aktaia, 81
Aktaíōn, Aktaîos, 81n5
Aktê, 81
Aktaion (grandson of Kadmos), 81–83
Aktaion (king of Attica), 8–9, 81–86
Alcaeus, 147n7, 156–158
Alcidamas, 125, 161, 211n79
Alcmaeonids, 12–13, 77, 136
Alcman, 111, 117
Alcmeon, 25n76

Alḗtēs, 75
alḗtheia 'truth,' 24
Alḗtheia 'Truth,' 140n98, 146n4
aletrís "woman who grinds wheat," 100
áleuron 'flour,' 100
Alexander of Aphrodisias, 175
Alexibía, 77
Alkinoos, 105
Alkmene, 93n57
Allan, D. J., 165n19
allegory, allegorical, 152, 156–158, 201,
    204–206
Allen, T. W., 112
álogos 'unpronounceable, irrational,' 62,
    164n18
alphabet, alphabetic, 1, 5, 8–9, 45, 64–65,
    81–82, 85, 114, 141n99, 159, 168n28,
    175, 179n70; Ionian, 5, 183–184
ámata. See êmar
Ammianus Marcellinus, 206n65
aná 'through, across,' 112n14
anabállein, anabállesthai "put off," 91
anabálleto. See anabállesthai
anabolḗ 'delay,' 91n47
anagignṓskein 'recognize, read,' 4, 35n47,
    51n21, 110, 160n2, 163–166, 170n36,
    180, 196
anagnô, anagnônai. See anagignṓskein
anagnṓrisis 'recognition,' 17–18
anágnōsis 'reading,' 17–18, 24, 44
anagnṓstes 'reader,' 61, 193n18
anagnôte, anágnothi. See anagignṓskein
analégesthai 'read,' 35n47, 160n2
anáneimai. See ananémesthai
ananémein 'distribute, read,' 35n47, 51,
    110, 116, 190
ananémesthai 'distribute, recite, read,'
    35n47, 51–52, 63–64, 110, 114, 160n2,
    213
ananemómenos. See ananémesthai
ananémōn. See ananémein
anánkē 'constraint, necessity,' 203–204
anatithénai 'dedicate,' 32–33, 38, 42, 57,
    148n10
Anaxagoras, 138n86
Anaximander, 138
Anaximenes, 138n86
Anchises, 66
Andocides, 118, 120–121
Androkles, 31
Andron, son of Antiphanes, 28–29, 172–
    173, 176, 178, 182, 186
Andron of Halikarnassos, 81n3
(an-)elíssein 'unroll, read,' 196n29
anéthēke(n). See anatithénai
angéllein 'proclaim, announce,' 173n46

Aníkētos, 75
animist, 41
anneim-, annem-. See ananémein
"Anonymus Iamblichi," 125
Antenor, 12n18
antí 'in place of,' 19–20, 93n57
Antigone, 19–20, 93, 153n28
Antikleides, 120
Antiphanes, 100n82, 158–159
Antoninus Liberalis, 93n57
aoidḗ 'song,' 112, 153, 155
aorist, 16n38, 23
áphōna 'consonants, silent,' 141n99,
    159n47
Aphrodite, 19, 66, 154, 156
áphthitos 'imperishable,' 23, 66, 97,
    153n28
áphthongos 'voiceless,' 16, 60
apográphein 'copy,' 202
apokrínesthai 'respond,' 173
Apollo, 61, 74, 92, 96–97, 101–102, 104,
    106, 118, 121, 131
Apollodorus, 58, 68n14, 70n20, 75nn51,
    53, 82n6, 110n4
Apollonius of Rhodes, 74n49, 75n54, 83–
    84, 101nn86, 89, 102n92
aponémein 'attribute, distribute, read,'
    19n54, 111
aporrheîn, 175
apórrhēta "secret instructions," 140, 147n9
aporrhoḗ, apórrhoia 'emanation,' 174
apótheta "things hidden, kept aside," 137,
    140, 142, 147n9
Apseudḗs, 73
ápsukhos 'inanimate,' 133–134, 139, 144–
    145, 159n47. *See also nómos ápsukhos*
Archandros, 71, 78
Archelaos, 138n86
Archias (of Athens), 34, 36–37, 46
Archias (of Sparta), 78
Archilochus, 118n34, 157
Archinos, decree of, 183
archon, 61
pseudo-Archytas, 128, 134
aretḗ 'virtue, excellence,' 67, 200
"Arignota," 154n32
Aristaîos, 74
Aristarchus, 15, 21n62, 168
Aristeas, 138n83
Aristeús, 77
Aristion of Paros, 12, 25n75
Aristocrates of Sparta, 131
Aristolochos, 40
Aristophanes, 52n23, 163, 192n17;
    Knights, 163–164, 174
Aristotle, 16n41, 23n67, 58n41, 60n50,

84n19, 92n50, 110n5, 118nn34, 36,
    125–127, 130n40, 133, 135, 137n74,
    139, 144, 146n5, 159nn46–47, 174,
    181n78, 193n18
Aristylla, 35
árkhein 'lead, rule,' 121, 124, 126–128
Arkhéptolis, 77
árkhōn 'archon, magistrate.' *See árkhein*
árotos 'ploughing,' 99
ároura "arable land," 99n77
árrhētos 'unpronounceable,' 164n18
Artabazos, 55
Artemidorus, 22n65, 85, 99nn76–77,
    159n48
Artemision, 77, 89, 206n65
ásbestos 'inextinguishable,' 23, 53–54
Ashbery, John, 155
Asía, 77, 82n8
Aspasia, 214n90
áspermos 'sterile,' 66
astrología, 160n2
astronomía, 160n2
Astronomíē, 176n54
Astyanax, 71–72
athánatos 'immortal,' 67, 153n26
Athena, 101, 106
Athenaeus, 82n6, 100n82, 101n87,
    111nn10–11, 116, 120n42, 136n71,
    146n5, 177n63, 183–184, 185nn95–98
Athens, Athenian, 9, 12, 28, 30, 38n55,
    39, 55, 77, 81–84, 116, 135–136, 172–
    174, 183, 185, 191
Atomists, 174–176
Attica, 81
audé 'voice,' 58–62
audire 'listen,' 123
autodeictic, 29, 34
Autolykos, 69
Autonóē, 82
autonomy, autonomous, 123, 135, 146,
    169–173, 186
autónoos, 82

Bacchylides, 150n16
Bain, D., 169n31
bállein 'throw, pour out,' 112n14
Balogh, J., 163n12
basileús 'king,' 72. *See also nómos basileús*
Bechtel, F., 14n26
Beck, F. A. G., 193n20, 196
Bellerophon, 73, 85
Benveniste, Emile, 19n53, 27nn5, 7,
    30n20, 52n22, 94n59, 95n62
Bias, 125
biblíon 'book,' 52, 199, 202

Blegen, C. W., 191n13
Blepsídēmos, 13
blēstrízein 'throw,' 112n14
blood, 96, 139
Blümner, H., 58n43
boân 'shout,' 176, 179
Boeckh, August, 10n8
Boeotia, Boeotian, 82, 86, 101–102; con-
    federation, 107
boēthein "bring assistance," 216
Bömer, F., 96n68
book, 180–182, 197–200. *See also biblíon*
book of the *psukhé,* 180–182
Boreas, 206
Borecký, B., 19n53, 20n55, 112n12
Boring, T. A., 115n25
boundary marker, 38n55
Bourdieu, P., 47, 212n82
Bowra, C. M., 111n10, 156n39, 180n76
Bréal, Michel, 109
Bremmer, J., 138n85
bréphē 'babies,' 159n47
Bresson, F., 165n20
bride, 83n14
Brisson, L., 87n29
Brugmann, K., 42
Buck, C. D., 49n16, 50n19
burial (vs. cremation), 133, 137
Burnet, J., 123n2, 162n8
Burns, A., 55n32
Burzachechi, M., 29, 32, 38n55, 41

Calame, C., 27n5
Callias, 5, 183–185
Callimachus, 74n49, 168
Camassa, G., 2n2, 109n2
Cameron, A., 156n39
carmen 'song,' 107
Carmenta, 106–107
"catalogue of gifts," 26–27
Catalogue of Ships, 110n3
Catullus, 190
Cerri, G., 148n10
Certamen ("Contest of Homer and
    Hesiod"), 173n46
Chailley, J., 179n70
chanter, 116–117, 121
Chantraine, P., 2, 13, 15n34, 18n48, 62,
    86n26, 94n58, 138n85, 160n2, 162n9,
    165, 170n36
Chariton of Aphrodisias, 88n33
Charles, Michel, 44, 45n2
Charondas, 116, 135
Chartier, R., 47n9
child, 66–81, 94, 103, 153n26, 159n47

Chirassi, I., 89n36
chorus, 172, 181n77; Dionysiac, 118, 121;
    "syllabic," 184–185
cicada, 208, 210
Cicero, 9n4, 62n57, 82n6
circle, 25
Clader, L., 69n15
Claus, D. B., 138n85
Clearchus, 82n6
Cleisthenes the Athenian, 13, 76–77, 86
Cleisthenes the Sicyonian, 76–77, 86
Clement of Alexandria, 127
coding/decoding, 17, 82
coins, 38n55
Colonna, G., 29n16
comedy, comic, 169n31, 179n72, 184
commemoration, commemorative, 9,
    53–54, 79–80, 84, 86, 94–95, 98
compression/expansion, 70n18
consonants, 141n99
contaminatio, 'contamination,' 32
Cook, A. B., 21nn60–62
corpse, 93, 132, 136–138, 140, 143
cremation, 131, 133, 137
Crete, 130–131
Critias, 125
Criton, 161
crown, 25

daíesthai 'distribute,' 162n9
daímōn 'distributor,' 162n9
daimónion, 162
damnánai 'subjugate,' 157n43
Damon, 116
dative, 39n57
daughter, 3, 18, 20n59, 22, 70, 73–77, 81–
    87, 90–95, 97–100, 102–105, 107, 153–
    154, 157–158, 214–215. See also koúrē
Daux, G., 10nn7, 10, 12n12, 19n50
deafness, 159n46
Debrunner, A., 30n20, 61n51
dedication, 9, 32
dédorka. See dérkesthai
defer, 45, 91, 95, 164
Defradas, J., 120n46, 121, 136n70
Deianeira, 20
dēloûn 'show,' 15
deltográphos "one who writes on a déltos,"
    181
déltos "writing tablet," 54n31, 179, 181
deltoûn "mark on a déltos," 181
Demeter, 100
Demiurge, 180n75
democracy, democratic, 29n15, 125,
    179n72

Democritus, 139, 174–176
Demodokos, 70
demonstrative, 32–34, 36, 38, 40–41
Demosthenes, 22n64, 52n25, 118
pseudo-Demosthenes, 119, 120n44,
    136n71
dérkesthai 'see,' 167n25
dérma 'skin,' 137, 140
Derrida, Jacques, 3n4, 42n67, 63n58,
    160n2, 182n85, 199, 211n79, 212,
    215n96
des Places, E., 67n6, 68n12, 70
despótēs 'master,' 124–125, 128, 132
Detienne, Marcel, 8n1, 12n19, 14, 24n72,
    68, 83n12, 84n15, 145n1, 148n10,
    156n38, 172n42
De Vries, G. J., 199
Dexíklea, 14
dhyāma 'thought,' 17
Dí. See Zeus
Diagoras of Rhodes, 90
diaíresis 'dissection,' 210
dialogue, 57–59, 60n49, 61, 161, 180
dianomḗ 'distribution,' 126n25
Dicaearchus, 135n66
Didymus, 168
Diels, Hermann, 49–50
Dienstverhältnis, 61n51
díkaion 'just,' 126–127
dikaiosúnē "sense of justice," 132, 162
dikastḗs 'judge,' 126
díkē 'justice,' 114, 121, 125, 162
Díkē, 140n98
Diodorus Siculus, 135n65
Diogenes Laertius, 124n4, 135n66,
    136n72, 141n101, 143n106, 147n9,
    148n10, 179n71
Diogenes of Apollonia, 138–139, 159n47
Dionysius of Halikarnassos, 133n52
Dionysius Thrax, 8n1, 81n3
Dionysos, 177
Diós. See Zeus
Dioscorides, 97n69
Dioscorides the Epigrammatist, 153,
    208n67
Diotima, 67, 144n107, 153n26
Diotogenes, 128, 134
discus, 96–97, 101
distribution, 19, 51–53; of land, 109
document/monument, 13
Dodds, E. R., 138n83, 139n93
domestic cult, 22
domination/submission, 187–189, 192–
    193, 210–211
Dorian, 49–50, 51n21, 110
dōristí "in the Dorian manner," 51n21

doûlos 'slave,' 61, 125
Dover, K. J., 188n2, 191n11, 192nn16–17, 194–195
drân 'do, perform,' 136
drômena 'rites.' *See drân*
Dühring, I., 193n18
Dumézil, Georges, 61, 106, 121
dunástēs 'master,' 161

eating habits, 156n38
ear, 46, 52, 123, 165–166, 170, 177
Edmonds, J. M., 183nn88–89
Edwards, R., 8n1, 82n7
ēérios "made of air," 142
★eg(h)om 'hereness,' 42
egô 'I,' 27, 29–34, 36, 40n62, 41–43, 104, 140–141, 149–150
"egocentric," 29–30, 34–43
égrapse. See gráphein
eídōlon 'image, simulacrum,' 175, 180n75
eîdon. See horân
ēídonto. See aeídein
eíē. See eînai
eimí. See eînai
eînai 'be,' 18n48, 19n51, 31–41
eipeîn 'speak, talk,' 15–16, 50–53, 60, 93, 110n3
eírein 'speak,' 115
ekeî 'there, over there,' 30, 43, 149
ekeînos 'that,' 30, 43, 140, 149, 151–152, 197
ékgona 'children, descendants,' 153n26
ékhein 'have, hold, behave as,' 24, 72, 152n21, 209
Ekhéphrōn, 72
ekhétōr "he who holds, governs," 72
ekpíptein "fall into the hands of the public," 216n100
élege, elékhthē. See légein
elementa, 175n52
elementary education, 184–185, 193–198
Eleusinium, 118–120
Eleusis, Eleusinian, 120–121
eleútheros 'free,' 187
eleútheros érōs "free love," 213
Elissos, 196–197
Ellinger, Pierre, 87n28
ellipse, elliptical, 39, 60, 65, 70, 90, 107
êmar 'day,' 49–50, 53
emiméeto. See mimeîsthai
emmeléōs 'harmoniously,' 115n23
Empedocles, 20n59, 174–175
émphasis 'image,' 175n51
empíptein 'reach,' 175
émpsukhos 'personified,' 127, 139, 145. *See also nómos émpsukhos*

enántios "seated before," 156
engráphein 'inscribe,' 181
enoplion, 25n75
entháde 'here,' 43
enthúmēma 'meaning,' 140
entunkhánein 'meet, have sex with, read,' 22n65, 86, 98
entúpōsis 'image,' 175n51
épea, epéōn. See épos
epenenkeîn. See epiphérein
éperse. See pérthein
epéthēke. See epitheînai
Ephorus, 82n7, 131n46
éphrase. See phrázein
epic, 28, 148, 151
Epicharides, 41
Epicharmus, 51n21
epígamos 'nubile,' 91
epíklēros 'heir, heiress,' 20, 22, 74, 85–86, 91, 93, 98–99, 104–105, 214n92
epilégesthai 'read,' 35n47, 62–63, 160n2, 164, 202
Epimenídeios 'Epimenidean,' 137, 140
Epimenides, 129, 135–138, 140–146, 147n10, 150, 153, 215–216
epinémein 'read,' 111
epiphérein 'carry,' 119
epísēmos "carrying an inscription," 93
epístasthai 'know,' 165
epistḗmē 'knowledge,' 178
epistolé 'letter,' 159
epítagma 'prescription,' 125
epitheînai 'set up,' 37
epithet, 68n14, 69–79, 81–82, 87, 91, 94
epithumía 'desire,' 126, 135
epōidé 'incantation,' 201–202
epoíēse. See poieîn
épos 'word,' 113–114, 142
éranos "feast of which the cost is shared," 91–92
Erasíklea, 14
erastḗs 'lover,' 2, 97, 187–204, 208–212
eréei, ereî. See eipeîn; légein
Eretria, 34, 48, 55, 111
Ernout, A., 62n57
erṓmenos 'beloved,' 2–3, 97, 187–204, 208–212
érōs 'love,' 198
erōtân 'ask,' 173n45
error of versification, 54
éskheto. See ékhein
éspete. See eipeîn
éssesthai, éstai. See eînai
éstēse. See histánai
esthlós "worthy man," 147, 216n100
estí. See eînai

Eteokles, 176
Etymologicum Magnum, 71n25, 72n31, 74n46, 75n50, 136n68
Eubulus, 100n82
Eukosmides, 34
Eumares, 30
Eúmēlos, 72
Eumolpos, 120
Euphronios, 191
Euripides, 5, 16n40, 32, 33n35, 45n5, 58n43, 73, 81n5, 82n7, 84n19, 96n67, 117, 125, 152n24, 163, 179, 181n79, 183, 185, 201n49; *Hippolytus,* 6, 163, 174, 178–179; *Iphigenia in Tauris,* 16, 117, 179n68; *Medea,* 117; *Theseus,* 185
Eurymedon, 194
Eurysákēs, 73
Eurytos, 73
Eustathius, 68n13, 72, 74n46
exárkhein 'dictate,' 117–118, 121
exegeîsthai 'dictate,' 117–122
"exegesis," 118–121, 145
Exēgētēs, 121
exeipeîn 'tell, say aloud,' 56, 60–61, 64
expounder (*exēgētēs*), 116–122, 129, 135–136, 142, 143n106
external, 161–162, 209
externalization, 182
eye, 5, 20n59, 29, 164–167, 170, 174–175, 179, 186

Fantasia, U., 137n77
father, 3, 18n49, 20n59, 22, 23n67, 29, 68–79, 82–85, 87–88, 91–94, 99, 101, 103–105, 138, 144, 153, 188, 206, 212, 214
feminine, 24, 84, 159, 215
Festugière, A. J., 99n77
"fetishism," 214
Fick, A., 14n27
figura etymologica, 15n34
Findlay, J. N., 216n99
fire, 20–24, 53–54. *See also pûr*
first comer, 195, 197
first person, 24, 29–33, 35, 37, 39–42, 46, 103–104, 140n98, 148–150, 173
Flacelière, R., 93n57
flour, 100–101
flow, flowing, 174–175
flower, 10, 21–25, 96–97
foedus 'treaty,' 107
formula, formulary, 18n49, 27–28, 32, 37–38, 99, 118–120, 147n7, 152n21
Forssman, B., 189–190
Foucart, P., 120n46, 121n47

Foucault, Michel, 2, 6, 13, 97n69, 187, 199n42, 205n62, 211
Fourmont, Michel, 10
Fournier, H., 15n34, 52n24
Frame, Douglas, 25n75
funerary, 9n4, 81, 93, 95, 97, 120, 136. *See also* inscription: funerary

gaîa 'earth,' 90n43
Galen, 96n64
Gallavotti, C., 31n22, 190n7
gámos 'wedding,' 19–20, 91–92
gardens of Adonis, 208
Garlan, Y., 192n17
Gastaldi, S., 211n79
gegramménos, gégraptai. See gráphein
Gela, Doric epigram from, 2–3, 51n21, 189–192, 194
gems, 38n55
generic (poet, philosopher, legislator), 129–130
génesis 'procreation,' 65–68, 70, 78
genitive, 60–61, 95
Gentili, Bruno, 148n10
Georgoudi, S., 2n2
géras 'honorific portion,' 19–20
Gernet, Louis, 138n84
gerousía, 61
Gerth, B., 33nn32, 34
gestalt, 166, 177
gestures, language of, 16, 23
Gigante, Marcello, 124
gilding, 89–90, 96, 103
Glaukos, 3, 30–31, 36
Glaukos (Homeric hero), 75
Gleukitas, 37
Glisas, 90
glôssa 'tongue,' 113nn17–18, 181n84
gold, 89
Gorgias, 59n47, 161n3
Gorgo, 90
Gorgophónē, 75
Gorgophónos, 75
Goulemot, Jean-Marie, 193
Gow, A. S. F., 51n21
graffiti, 148, 189, 192
grain, 99–101
grámma "written word," 128, 145n2, 177
grámmasi(n). See grámmata
grámmata 'letters [of the alphabet],' 8–9, 41n65, 58, 81, 127, 131, 133, 134n60, 137–140, 142, 144, 158–159, 165–166, 171, 185, 193, 198
grammatical forms: accusative, 95; aorist,

16n38, 23; dative, 39n57; genitive, 60–
61, 95; imperative, 57, 60, 120; infinitive, 119–120
Grammatikḕ [tékhnē] "the Art-of-writing,"
185
grammatikós "having to do with writing,"
183
grammḗ 'line,' 164n18
grandfather, 22, 69, 74, 76, 83, 85
grandson, 22n65, 71, 82–83, 86, 103
graphaîs. See graphḗ
graphḗ 'writing,' 16, 22n65, 84, 153–155,
159, 179, 212–215
gráphein 'write,' 42, 89, 93, 114, 116, 127,
149, 153n26, 180–181, 190–192, 199
graphic sequence, 4, 177
graphthénta. See gráphein
Greek Anthology, 58n40, 85n22, 89n40,
97n69, 101n84, 196
Groeneboom, P., 37n49
Guarducci, M., 9n5, 30n19, 31n21,
38n55, 149n12
gunḗ 'woman,' 20, 93n57

haîma 'blood,' 90n43, 93
Haimon, the "Bloody One," 93
hair, hair growth, 97
Halikarnassos, 56, 58, 62
Halirrhóthios, 68n14, 75
Halliday, W. R., 112
hálōs 'threshing floor,' 98–99
Harvey, F. D., 183n87, 198n32
hátis (hátis). See hóstis
Häusle, H., 29n16, 36n48
Havelock, E. A., 1, 114n19, 162, 188, 196
"head," 87, 201
hearth, 19–23, 93
Hecataeus, 149
hḗde. See hóde
hēgeîsthai 'guide, dictate,' 116, 121
hēgemṓn "one who guides, dictates," 117,
124–125
heir, heiress. See epíklēros
Hektor, 16, 53, 71–72, 102n91
Helen, 110
Hellanikos, 8
Hellquist, E., 15n31
hēmeîs 'we,' 32, 40
Hendrickson, G. L., 163n12
Hḗra (vocative), 39n57
Heraclitus, 91n45, 124, 126n25, 132,
147n9, 148n10
Heraclitus the Allegorist, 156–157
Herakles, 75

herald, 118
Hermes, 96, 154
Hermias, 199
Hermippus, 111n11, 116
Hermogenes, 139
Hermokrates, 88
Herodotus, 9n3, 16, 32, 33n35, 41n65, 51,
55, 62, 76n60, 77–78, 81n4, 82n7,
91n48, 92n50, 93n55, 114n22, 124,
130n39, 135n64, 149–150, 167, 177,
178n64, 186, 206n65
Herse, 9, 81, 82n6
Hesiod, 15n34, 23n67, 33n30, 71n23, 73,
87n30, 88, 96n67, 112–114, 140n98,
148n10, 150, 154, 160
Hestia, 19–21
hestiân 'entertain,' 91
hestiátōr 'host,' 116
Hesychius, 51n21, 72n33, 94n60, 100,
110–111
hḗtis. See hóstis
heurétēs 'inventor, discoverer,' 82n7
hexameter, hexametric, 34, 54, 67n8, 137,
140, 142, 159n46
Hicks, E. L., 61n52
Hierheit ("hereness"), 42–43
hiketēría 'bough held by suppliant," 119
Hiller von Gaertringen, F., 61n52
Himerius, 153n26
Hipparchus, 168n28
Hippocrates, 165n19, 167n24
Hippodameia 'horse-breaker,' 91
Hippotai, 90, 102, 106
hippótēs 'horseman,' 106n97
Hippotes, 74
histánai 'put, place,' 38, 42, 49
historíē 'inquiry,' 150
ho 'the, this,' 33, 35, 38, 52, 61
hóde 'this,' 31, 34, 36–40, 43, 60, 84
hód' egṓ, 33–34
hoi. See ho
hoîde. See hóde
hoi ekeî "those there, those beyond (i.e.,
the dead)," 43n71, 152
Homer, 14–15, 24, 26, 28, 33, 65, 69–71,
74n47, 88, 100, 112, 114, 139, 167, 171,
181, 213
Homeric Hymn to Aphrodite, 18n49, 19,
53n27, 66n2
Homeric Hymn to Apollo, 18n49, 53n27,
112
Homeric warrior, 152
Homeridai, 137
Hondius, J. J. E., 56n36
hópou 'where,' 50

horân 'see,' 174
hórkos 'oath,' 204
hóstis 'whoever,' 49–50
hoû 'where,' 50–53
hoûtos 'this, that,' 33–34
Humbert, Jean, 112
hupakoúein 'hear, listen,' 155
hupēretein "serve, perform an office," 118, 191
hupērétēs 'officer,' 118n36, 126
hupogrammateúein 'act as *hupogrammateús*, clerk,' 118
hupokrínesthai "respond, play a role," 28, 171–173, 182
hupokritēs 'interpreter, actor,' 171–173, 178
hupómnēma 'note, *aide-mémoire*,' 127, 148, 182–183
hupourgeîn 'serve,' 191
husband, 153
hyacinth, 96–97
Hyakinthia, 101
Hyakinthos, 96–97, 101
Hymen, 95

"I," 3, 16n41, 27, 40–41, 46, 102, 148–152, 155, 157, 173. *See also egō*
iconography, 194
ídios 'own,' 46
idiōtēs "free agent," 203–204
Iliad, 13n23, 14, 15n34, 16, 18n49, 21, 23n69, 24n73, 26, 27n4, 53, 54n30, 66, 70n17, 71n28, 72nn30, 32, 73, 75, 90n43, 93n56, 100, 101n90, 102n91, 110n3, 112, 113n16, 114n19, 118n34, 138n85, 139n87, 141, 152n23
Ilissos, 206n65
illiterate, 60, 164
immortality, immortal, 65–68, 78–79, 123, 153n26, 156
imperative, 57, 60, 120
infinitive, 119–120
inheritance. *See epíklēros*
inner. *See* internal
inscription, inscribe, 28–30, 40–43, 46, 61–62, 79, 84, 89–90, 93, 97, 103–104, 140–144, 148–156, 172–174, 176, 180–181, 189–192, 194–195, 216; funerary, 28, 31–32, 34, 38, 40, 48, 53, 140, 148; votive, 33n31, 37–41, 48, 140, 148
inscriptional, 79–80, 89n39, 98, 174, 180, 186
instrument, instrumental, 2–3, 46–47, 52, 56, 61, 63–64, 83, 85, 104, 106, 110, 142, 160, 178, 205

instrumentum vocale, 110, 139n90, 142, 161, 205
internal, 8, 36, 42–43, 62–63, 113, 161–162, 209
internalization, 5, 162–163, 171, 174, 177–178, 180, 182
Iobates, 85, 105
Ionian, 49, 62
Isaeus, 22n64
Isandros, 73
Isocrates, 12
isonomía "equality before the law," 29n15
isonumía, 75–78, 80
ísos 'equal,' 28–29, 41n65

Jacoby, F., 8n2, 120n46
Jason, 83, 101
Jeffery, L. H., 8n1, 9n5, 12n13, 25n75, 31nn22–23, 32, 38n55, 39n58, 41n63, 43n69, 48n13, 58n39
Jocasta, 153n28
Jones, H. L., 117
pseudo-Julian, 159n49
jurisconsult, 116
Justice, 176–177. *See also Díkē*
Justinian, 216n97

Kadmos, 8n1, 82–83
kakós 'ugly, ignoble,' 192
kaleîn 'call,' 18, 20n58, 36–37, 39n58, 53n28, 79, 177
Kallirhóē, daughter of Okeanos, 73
Kallirhoe (*Kallirhóē*), daughter of Phokos, 86–88, 90–96, 98–106, 214n92, 215
kallírhoos "that which flows beautifully," 73, 88
kalós 'beautiful,' 189, 192, 195
Kapaneus, 176
Karo, G., 56n36, 58n40
Karousos, C., 48n13, 59
Kassel, Rudolf, 58n40
katalégein 'enumerate,' 26n1
kataleîn 'grind, mill,' 100
kataleúein 'stone [to death],' 101
kataphánai 'agree,' 176n55
katapharmakeúein "drug, treat with medicine," 203–204
katapúgōn "one who is buggered," 189–192, 194–195
katastízein "cover with punctures, tattoo," 137
katéleusan. See kataleúein
keîna, keínou. See ekeînos
keklēsetai, keklēsomai. See kaleîn
Kekrops, 9, 81, 82n6
keleúein 'order,' 56

kēnē (= ekeínē), kênos. See ekeînos
kerkís "weaver's shuttle," 58
kḗrukes 'heralds,' 178
kērússein 'proclaim,' 177
Kerykes, 119, 121
kheír 'hand,' 15
khélus 'tortoise,' 141n99
khṓra 'country, district,' 86, 103
khrusoûs "golden, in gold," 176
king, 124, 130, 132–134
Kirk, G. S., 147n9
Kleidemos, 120
Kleimachos, 30, 64, 149
kleín "celebrate, make renowned," 13n23,
   53n28, 79
kleinós 'renowned,' 66
kleís 'key,' 153n28
Kleis (*Kléïs*), 153, 154n32, 157
Kleisas, *Kleísas*, 90, 92–94, 97, 103, 106
Kleisthenes. *See* Cleisthenes
Kleite (*Kleítē*), 83
kléomai. See kleín
kléos "resounding renown," 4, 12–16, 20–
   24, 37n49, 44, 53–54, 61–62, 64–68,
   70, 76, 78–79, 83–84, 86, 89n39, 91n45,
   92, 97, 103–106, 141n99, 153–154, 164,
   186
"Kleos-town" (= Kleisas), 91–93, 98,
   105–106
klêros 'land, property,' 98
klēthêi. See kaleín
Knox, B. M. W., 2, 5, 18n45, 35n47,
   47n11, 163, 167–168, 179
Koller, H., 183
kolossós 'image, statue,' 93
Kontoleon, N. M., 10n9, 19n50
Kopreus, 73
Korakos, 30
kore, *kórē. See koúrē*
Kore, 19
Koroneia, 101
Kosmographíē, 176
koúrē "girl, young girl," 18–20, 22, 32,
   100, 154
Kourouniotis, K., 48n12, 50
krateín 'reign,' 125
Kreon, 93–94
Krites, 32–37
krokízein "resemble saffron," 89
krókos 'saffron,' 89–90, 94, 96, 98
Krokos (*Krókos*), 96–97
krúptesthai "conceal oneself," 98
ktáomai. See ktâsthai
ktâsthai 'acquire,' 95
ktêma "that which is acquired, possession," 95

ktêma es aieí "possession for all time,"
   148n10, 150n17
ktúpos 'noise,' 167n25
kûdos 'strength,' 83
Kühner, R., 33nn32, 34
kulindeîsthai "roll to right and left," 29,
   138, 144, 147, 212
kúrbeis 'tablets,' 133
Kyzikos (*Kúzikos*), 83–84, 101

lakhoûsa(n). See lankhánein
"land," 99
lankhánein "receive by lot," 19–20, 24
Laodámeia, 73
Laomedon, 72
Larfield, W., 89n41
Laroche, E., 4n5, 109n2, 112
law. *See lex; nómos; rhêtra*
lawgiver, 128–135, 209
Lazzarini, M., 9n5, 28nn9, 11, 30n17, 33,
   38–39, 40n59, 43n70, 56–58, 172n43,
   189
Learete, 35
légein 'say, read,' 15, 35n47, 41n65, 52,
   56–57, 59–60, 62–63, 102–103, 109,
   160, 177, 186, 203
legere 'read,' 62, 109, 115
legitimate (*gnḗsios*), 22n65, 85, 99, 215n96
légō. See légein
lego. See legere
Lehrs, K., 15n32
leípein 'leave,' 141n100, 152n23
Leonardos, B., 50n18
Leonidas, 124
Lesbos, 192
lḗthē 'oblivion,' 24n72, 154, 201
letter (*epistolḗ*), 152
letters, 4–5, 8–9, 81, 89–90, 96, 103, 143–
   144, 164–166, 170, 176, 185–186;
   "speaking," 5, 177–179. *See also grámmata*
Leucippus, 174–175
Lévêque, P., 12n18, 13n20, 29n15
Lévi-Strauss, Claude, 82n11
lex 'law,' 109–110, 115–116, 123, 213
léxis 'word, diction,' 109, 148n10
Ley, G. K. H., 171n39
Liddell-Scott-Jones, 18n48, 20n59, 46n8,
   50n19, 52n24, 99n77, 106n97, 146n6,
   165n19
Lindos, 90
lípe. See leípein
"liquid" character of speech, 88n35
Lissarrague, F., 176n55, 194n21
listener, 46, 55, 63, 169. *See also*
   speaker/listener

literacy, 55
líthos 'stone,' 58–61, 93n57
lógos 'word, discourse,' 3–4, 22n65, 23,
    46, 62–63, 83, 85–86, 89n39, 92, 95,
    106, 109, 135, 139, 145n2, 160–161,
    164, 198–199, 202, 204, 209–216
lógos gegramménos, 213–214. *See also grá-
    phein; lógos*
Lokros, 76
Lolling, H. G., 25n75
Longo, O., 55n32
Loraux, Nicole, 101n90, 130n37, 133n55,
    141n102, 150n16
Lord, A. B., 54n31
lotus, 10, 20–21, 23–25
lover: passionate, 203, 208; without love,
    200, 203, 206, 208
Luck, Georg, 208n70
Lucretius, 175n52
Lupas, L., 176n57
Lycophron, 100
Lycurgus, 129–137, 143
lyric, 147–148, 151
Lysias, 120, 124, 198–210, 213

McEvilley, T., 153n25
Magdelain, André, 109, 118n37
mákhaira "sacrificial knife," 101
mákhesthai 'fight,' 68n13
male love, 187–188, 198, 215
Mallarmé, Stéphane, 182n85
malthakóphōnoi 'sweet-voiced,' 155n35
manteîon 'oracle,' 102n92
Mantiklos, 30, 39n57
mántis 'soothsayer,' 172
marriage, 81, 95, 99, 153
Marrou, H.-I., 184n94, 188, 196, 216
Martin, P. M., 134n61
Masson, O., 191n14, 192n17
"master of truth," 145–146
Mastrokostas, E. I., 9n6, 10nn8 and 11,
    11, 12n15, 25n75
Mazakenoi, 116
me 'me, myself,' 31–34, 36–38, 40n62
meaning, 24–25, 62, 142, 155, 164–165,
    167, 174. *See also enthúmēma*
Megakles, 13, 77
Megas, 41
Meillet, A., 62n57
Meletus, 162
méli 'honey,' 196
memnēménoi. See mnâsthai
memorization, 169–170; memorizing
    techniques, 206n65
memory, 4, 51, 53, 78–79, 114, 120–121,

    128–129, 146, 148n10, 180, 182; collec-
    tive, 23
Menander, 99n76
Menecrates of Olynthus, 81n3
Menelaos, 74, 87n30, 110, 171
mental, 5, 179, 182–183
Merenda, 9
Méridier, L., 117
méros 'share, portion,' 20, 126
méson, mésson 'middle, publicity,' 101, 126
Metanastes, 71, 78
meta-narrative, 107
metaphor, metaphorical, 5, 20–22, 24, 41,
    50, 58, 83–84, 117, 123–124, 127–128,
    157, 160, 171n37, 173, 176–181, 192–
    193, 206, 208
metempsychosis (*metempsúkhōsis*), 123,
    143
metensomatosis (*metensōmátōsis*), 123, 143
meter, 25n75, 54, 173n45
Meuli, K., 138n83
Midas, epitaph on, 59, 173n46
Middle Ages, 167–168
mill, millstone, 100–101; collective,
    101n89
Miller, S. G. 176n55
Milne, M. J., 191nn12, 14
mimeîsthai 'imitate,' 77
mimesis, 23, 69
Minos, 111
mnâma. See mnêma
mnáomai, mnásasthai. See mnâsthai
mnâsthai "ask in marriage, remember,"
    94–95, 154
mnêma "funerary monument," 30, 32, 35,
    38–39, 48–49, 54, 67, 76–77, 88–90,
    93–98, 101–104, 150n17, 154n32
mnếmē 'memory,' 67, 182, 201
mnêmōn "one who remembers, secretary,"
    58, 62, 181
mnēmosúnē 'memory,' 146
mnēmósunon 'memorial,' 93n57
Mnesiepes, 14
Mnēsíklea, 14
Mnēsiptoléma, 77
Mnesitheos, 48–50, 52–56, 60, 63, 114,
    152, 167n23, 173n46
mnēstếr "suitor, one who remembers," 94–
    95
model, 198
Moon, 75
Moranti, M., 25n75, 33n31
Morpurgo(-Davies), A., 36n48, 58n39
mother, 3, 147, 153–154, 215
mourning, 97, 101
múlē 'millstone, kneecap,' 101

mulḗphatos "murdered by the mill," 100
Muleús "of the mill," 100
Muse, 110n3, 118, 140n98, 154, 208, 210
music, musical, 18, 116, 179n70
mutheîsthai 'recount,' 149
muteness, 159n46
Myles, 101

Nagy, Gregory, 12n19, 14, 17, 19n53, 23n69, 25n75, 44, 65, 66n1, 68–70, 82, 84n16, 130n37
name, 12–14, 18–19, 22, 38, 60–61, 64–65, 68n14, 69–80, 86–88, 91, 93–97, 107, 142, 153–154; periphrasis of, 68n14. *See also ónoma*
name-giving. *See* onomatothesis
nati natorum "children's children," 66n2
Nausiníkē, 77
Nausíthoos, 13
Neanthes of Kyzikos, 84, 146n5
neîmai. See némein
neîsthai 'return,' 25n75, 78n67
némein 'distribute, read,' 4, 29n15, 35n47, 109–116, 160, 213
Nēmertḗs, 73
neógamos "newly married," 96n66
Neokles, 77
néomai. See neîsthai
Neoptolemus, 23
Nereus, 73
Nestor, 72
Nestor's cup, 38n55, 64
newborn, 69, 80, 139, 144. *See also bréphē*
Nieddu, G., 180n75
Nikasippos, 111n8
Nikódēmos, 191
Nikomákhē, 77
Nikostrate (*Nikostrátē*), 87–88, 106–107
Nikóstratos, 87n30
nóēsis 'thought,' 17, 45, 47
nomeús 'apportioner,' 111
nomikós, nomikṓtatos "conforming to the *nómos*, jurisconsult," 111, 116–117
nómimos "conforming to the *nómos*," 119, 128
nominative, 34n37, 36n48
Nómios, 74
nomode (*nomōidós*), "singer of laws," 117
nomographer (*nomográphos* "one who writes *nómoi*"), 214
nomophúlax "guardian of the law," 126
nomós 'pasture,' 112–113
nómos 'law, melody, nome,' 4, 29n15, 61, 94, 109–132, 134–136, 143n106, 160–162, 213

nómos ápsukhos "*nómos* deprived of *psukhḗ*, soulless *nómos*," 128–129, 134–135
nómos basileús "*nómos* reigning as king," 4, 123–125, 128–130, 132, 134–135, 160–161, 187
nómos émpsukhos "*nómos* personified, living *nómos*," 127–130, 134–135
Nonnos, 75n52
nóos 'intelligence, reason,' 25n75, 78n67, 126, 132
nóstos 'return,' 25n75, 78n67
nóthos 'bastard,' 22n65, 85, 215n96
noûs. See nóos
nubile, 85, 91, 95, 99
Numa, 129, 133–135, 137–138, 140–144, 147n9
nuptial rites, 120
Nylander, C., 12n14
nymph (*númphē*), 83, 96n66

oblivion, 24
odussámenos 'angered,' 69
Odysseus, 15, 17, 26–27, 32, 33–34, 59, 68–71, 73, 78–79, 85, 100, 214
Odyssey, 15, 18n49, 21n63, 23nn67–68, 24n73, 27n6, 32n24, 33nn30, 33, 53n27, 59nn46–47, 69–70, 72n35, 73n38, 74n47, 75n55, 79n69, 100, 171
Ogesthenes, 192
oîkos 'house,' 31, 34
Oinomaos, 91
Okeanos, 73
Oliver, J. H., 120n46, 136
Olympia, 39
ómphē 'voice,' 121n52
ónoma 'name,' 20, 49
onomastic system, 14, 18n46
onomastós 'renowned,' 67
onomatothesis, onomatothete, 22n66, 64–65, 71, 75, 78–79, 87–88, 105–107, 153n28
ontography, 175
Opous, 76
oral/written, 1–2, 4, 28, 54–55, 65, 89n39, 110n3, 114–116, 120–122, 132, 146–150, 166, 209–210, 212–213
Orchomenus, 102–106
"order" of written discourse, 148–149
Oreithyia, 206
Orestes, 74, 121
órexis 'desire,' 126, 132
organic composition, 199
órganon émpsukhon "living instrument," 110, 142, 205
orkheîsthai "dance, represent choreographically," 185

orkhoúmenon. See orkheîsthai
Orpheus, 138n86
Orphic Hymns, 73, 75n54
Orsilokhos, 75
orthopaedy, 193
Ouranographíē, 176n54
Ovid, 95n63, 96n68, 134n61
oyster, 141n99

paideía "educational system," 131, 134,
  143, 195
paîdes paídōn "children's children," 66n2,
  67–68, 70
paidiá 'game,' 169
painting, 29, 178, 206n65
Palamedes, 8n1, 59
palingenesía 'reincarnation,' 143
Palinode, 205, 209–210
Panamyes, 56–57, 60–64, 149, 155
Pandora, 154
Pandrosos, 8, 81, 82n6
"papponymie" 75n56
parádeigma 'example, paradigm,' 131
pareînai "be present," 32, 102, 147n8, 177,
  200
pariénai "pass by," 50–52
parióntes. See pariénai
Pários 'Parian,' 93n57
parioûsi. See pariénai
Parmenides, 25n76
Parmentier, L., 199n42
"parricide," 212
Parry, Milman, 146, 147n7
Partheneia, 37
Parthenios, 51n21
parthénos "virgin, young girl," 8, 19n51,
  20n58, 153n26
Pasipháē, 75
passive, passivity, 2–3, 59, 169–172, 174–
  175, 187–188, 193
páthē 'passions,' 134
pathētikón "emotional element," 126, 135
Paton, W. R., 61n52
Patroclus, 152
Pausanias, 23n67, 70, 74n45, 75nn55, 57,
  78, 81n5, 82n6, 97nn70–71, 101nn87–
  88, 115n25, 135n67, 206n65
pederast, pederasty, pederastic, 2–3, 6,
  96, 187–189, 195–199, 211, 216
pedicare 'bugger,' 190
Peek, W., 48, 50, 97n72
pēgḗ 'spring, fount,' 99n66
Peisistratids, 167
Peisístratos, 72

Peisistratus, 12
peíthesthai 'obey,' 124
Peleus, 69n15, 97
Pelops, 91
pémpein 'send,' 150n16
Penelope, 15, 17
penetration, penetrate, 187, 197, 210–211
pentameter, 54
pentathlon, 101
péphrade. See phrázein
performance, 147, 181n77
Perikles, 13
Perimḗlē, 72
Periphḗtes, 73
pérramos 'king,' 72
Persephone, 19
Persepolis, 71
Perseus, 75
personification, 59, 107, 146n4, 176
pérthein 'destroy,' 70–71
Petre, Z., 176n57
Pfohl, G., 9n5, 23n69, 25n75, 28n9,
  29n16, 30n18, 31nn21–23, 32nn25, 28,
  34, 35nn41–46, 36n48, 37nn50–52, 38–
  39, 46n7, 48, 50, 80n1, 93n57, 97n72,
  114n22, 141n99, 152n20, 173n46
Phaestas, 192
Phaidimos, 34
Phaîdra, 75
Phaedrus, 199–206, 208–210, 214
phaínesthai 'appear,' 158
phánai 'say,' 191–192
Phanodikos, 25n75, 36n48
pharmacopeia, 96
Pharmakeia, 206
phármakon 'drug, cure,' 201–202, 204–206
phaûlos 'weak,' 166, 177, 193, 213
phēsí(n). See phánai
Philip, A., 205n63
Philolaos, 139n93
Philomela, 58
philónikos "he who loves to win," 209
Philo of Alexandria, 127
philósophos "he who loves wisdom," 209,
  214
Philostratus, 96n67
Phoenicia, Phoenician, 8, 80–83
Phoïdos (*Phoîdos*), 87–88, 102, 105–107
Phoinike (*Phoiníkē*), 8, 81–82, 85–86
phonikḗïa "Phoenician letters, letters,"
  9n3, 81
Phoinix (Homeric hero), 26
Phoînix, father of Kadmos, 82
Phokos (*Phôkos*), father of Kallirhoe, 86–
  94, 96, 102–106, 215

Phokos of Aegina, 88, 97
phōnáessa. See phōnḗeis
phonation, 45–46, 61, 112–113, 136–139
phōnḗ 'voice,' 15, 24, 58, 102, 139,
    152n21, 161–162, 167
phōnḗeis 'vocal, sounding,' 141n99
phōnḗenta 'vowels,' 141n99
phōneîn 'speak,' 176
phōnēma "pronounced word," 102–103
phónos 'murder,' 100
Photius, 9n3, 96n66
phrásai. See phrázein
phrásasthai. See phrázein/phrázesthai
Phrasídēmos, 13
Phrasikleia (*Phrasíkleia*), 9–14, 17–25, 37,
    64, 84, 96n68, 214n92
Phrasiklês, 14n27
phrásis 'diction, expression,' 140
phrázein/phrázesthai "show/pay attention
    to," 13–17, 18n47, 21, 23
phrḗn 'thought, attention,' 13–15, 17n44,
    92n49, 113n17, 180–181
phthéngesthai 'speak,' 179
phthínein 'wither, perish,' 23n69. *See also
    áphthitos*
phthoneîn "be jealous," 198
phúllon 'leaf,' 202
pinakís "writing tablet," 159n48
Pindar, 15n34, 23n69, 66, 74n49, 75–76,
    88n35, 90, 91nn47–48, 95n61, 111,
    113n17, 118n34, 121, 124–125, 155,
    157n43, 180, 181n84
pistós 'faithful,' 36
Pithecussae, 38n55
Pittakos, 115
Plain of Aletheia, 84n15
Plato, 3n4, 6, 15n34, 16n39, 21n63,
    22n64, 29nn12, 14, 35n47, 45nn5, 6, 52,
    61n52, 62, 66, 70n22, 72n31, 84n15, 85,
    87, 89n39, 103n94, 110, 111n11,
    115n24, 118n36, 121n48, 123nn1–2,
    124–125, 126nn20, 24, 127, 132,
    136n71, 137–139, 142, 143n106,
    144n107, 145n2, 146n5, 147, 160–162,
    164, 166n22, 167n23, 172n41, 173n46,
    174n49, 177n62, 178nn65–66, 179–180,
    189n4, 193, 195n23, 198–199,
    200nn43–44, 202, 203nn52–56,
    204nn57–60, 205, 206nn64–66,
    208nn67–70, 209nn71–76, 210n77,
    211nn79–80, 212–216; *Charmides*, 201–
    202; *Phaedrus*, 3n4, 6, 29, 62n55, 178,
    198, 205, 210–211; *Theaetetus*, 35n47,
    52, 103n94, 167n23, 193, 198
pseudo-Plato, 111, 168n28, 216n100

pleasure, 188–189, 191, 194, 197, 200–
    201, 205
pleonasm, 33
Pliny the Elder, 96
Plutarch, 21, 77–78, 84n15, 86–92, 98–
    99, 100n78, 101n85, 106–107, 115n25,
    116n28, 125, 128–133, 134nn56, 60–61,
    135nn62, 67, 136nn68, 70, 73, 137n81,
    140n96, 146n5, 147n9, 166n22, 169n32,
    177n60, 199n42, 206n65
Pöhlmann, Egert, 183
poem, 146, 148–149, 151–156, 215. *See
    also* epic
poet, 14, 153n26
poieîn 'make, do,' 42
poiētḗs "poet or writer employed by an-
    other," 203n55, 204, 214
poimaínein 'pasture,' 113n18
pólemos 'war,' 23, 150
pólis 'city,' 61, 70–71
politeía "political constitution," 179–180
Polydoros, 82n7
Polyneikes, 176
Polynoe, 31
Ponge, Francis, 4
Porkos, 190
Porphyry, 147n9
Poseidon, 66, 75
Potidaea, 55, 167n23
power, 47, 142, 161, 197
praeire in verbis, 117
prapídes 'diaphragm,' 138, 145
Praxilas, 31
Praxiteles, 39
presence, present, 31, 38, 42–45, 103,
    132, 140, 147, 150, 153, 155, 169, 178,
    200, 206
Priam, 13n23, 72
Proclus, 22, 143n106
production of meaning, 62
production of sound, 5, 45–46, 62, 65,
    142, 164–165, 186. *See also kléos*
proem (*prooímion* 'prelude'), 126, 132,
    136n68
Prokleidas, 36–37, 39n58, 68n14, 80
proodopoieîn "clear the way," 130, 136
prophêtai 'interpreters,' 172, 208
prostitution, 155n35, 187
Protogeneia, 76
proverb, 91, 98–99, 137, 208
psō, 185
psóphos 'sound, noise,' 139
psukhḗ 'spirit,' 126–127, 129, 137n76,
    138–144, 153, 155, 180
psúkhein 'breathe,' 138

psychological depth, 42
ptolíethron. See pólis
Ptoliporthe, 70
Ptoliporthes, 70–71
ptolipórthios "destroyer of cities," 70
public, publicity, 98–99, 101–104, 147,
    168–170, 192, 195, 216
Pucci, Pietro, 42n66
pugízein 'bugger,' 2, 190
punthánesthai 'ask,' 102, 106n98
pûr 'fire,' 21, 54
purêphatos "murdering the grains of
    wheat," 100–101
purification, 120, 135–137
púthesthai 'rot,' 102n92
puthésthai. See punthánesthai
púthomai. See púthesthai
puthómenoi. See punthánesthai
puzzle, 93
Pythagoras, 2, 134, 145, 156n38
Pythagorean, 139, 145n2, 147, 164n18
Pythian (*Púthios*). *See* Apollo
Pytho (*Puthố*), 102n92

quadrifunctional, 106–107
Queneau, Raymond, 166

Raubitschek, A. E., 28n10, 176n55
Raven, J. E., 147n9
"read," 2, 4, 35, 45, 51–52, 60, 62, 86, 98,
    103, 110, 114, 164–165
reader: scorned, 5, 190–191, 195; solitary,
    52
reading: inaudible, 5, 179; silent, 2, 5, 18,
    47, 159n46, 163–165, 167–168, 170–
    171, 174–175, 177–179, 186, 211n81;
    speed, 167–168, 177
reciter, recite, 27, 181
recognition, recognize, 4, 24, 165–167,
    191
reference, referent, 62, 155
refusal: to read, 46–47, 103, 192; to write,
    145n2, 156n38, 212, 215
reincarnation, 123n2, 143
reizianum, 25n75
remedium (phármakon 'drug, medicine'),
    206n65
re-naming, 75, 83, 86
representation, represent, 4, 165, 167–
    168, 186
réson 'resonance,' 4
return, 24, 78, 105, 142–143
reversibility, 149, 155
rhapsode, 170n35
rhée. See rheîn

rheîn 'flow,' 88, 90, 94. *See also rhêma*
rhêma 'statement,' 15n34, 113n17, 115,
    124, 181n84
rhetoric: legal, 101n90; reform of, 205,
    208, 211
rhêtra 'law,' 115–116, 124n9, 131–133, 213
rheûsai. See rheîn
Richter, G. M., 25n75
riddle, 158–159
Rilke, R. M., 24
Rissman, L., 152n22, 156n39
Robert, L., 89
Robin, L., 199n42, 211n79
Roesch, P., 90n44
Rohde, Erwin, 138n85
Rose, H. J., 56, 58
Russo, Joseph, 55n33, 56n34
Rydbeck, L., 155n36

Sabines, 133
Saenger, P., 167, 168n29
saffron, 89–90, 95–96, 98. *See also krókos*
sákos 'shield,' 73
sâma. See sêma
Sambursky, S., 175n52
Samios, 78
Samos, 78
Sappho, 72, 141n99, 142, 145–159,
    198n31, 206, 215
Sarpedon, 141, 152
Schachermeyr, F., 12n16
Schmidt, J. H. H., 15n33
Schofield, Malcolm, 147n9
Scholasticism, 168
Schwyzer, E., 30n20, 61n51
scriptio continua, 45, 166–167
secondary character of writing, 89n39,
    212–213
seed, 22, 24. *See also spérma*
Segal, Charles, 169n33, 179n69
sêma "sign, funerary monument," 9, 15–
    18, 23–25, 31–32, 34–37, 39n58, 40,
    44, 46–47, 53, 68n14, 80, 84, 102n91,
    139, 141–143, 176
sēmaínein 'signify,' 15–16, 88, 102–103,
    139, 173n46
sēmantikós 'signifying,' 139
sēmêïa 'signs,' 167
semiliteracy, 55
Semites, Semitic, 1, 141n99
separation, 29, 138, 140–141, 145–147,
    153, 155, 157, 168, 170, 172, 214–215
service, servitude, 60–62, 64, 85–86, 110,
    123, 142, 145, 191, 193, 203
Servius, 134

Sêthos, 177
shaman, shamanistic, 138, 141
shell, 141n99
shield, 176
ship of state, 157
Shipp, G. P., 109n2
sigân "be silent," 16, 45, 84
sign. *See sêma*
signature, 30n19, 38n55
signifier/signified, 69, 88, 91–93
sigôsa. See sigân
Sikes, E. E., 112
silence, silent, 15–16, 23, 25, 45, 61, 64,
    84, 159n46, 161, 174, 181n84. *See also*
    reading: silent
Simonides, 59, 91n45, 115, 167, 168n28,
    183, 206n65
Sinos, D., 68n14
sîtos 'grain, wheat,' 99
Skamon of Mytilene, 8, 81
skhêma 'position,' 201
Skopas, 115
Skutsch, Franz, 109
pseudo-Skythinos, 196
slave, 110n5, 123, 128, 137, 142, 160, 188,
    191n14, 192–193, 210–211. *See also*
    doûlos
sociology, sociological, 1, 3
Socrates, 2, 6, 29, 62, 125, 145n2, 154n32,
    156n38, 161–162, 166, 178, 198–216
Solon, 86n98, 133n55, 135–136, 144n107,
    146–147, 169, 213
sôma 'body,' 136, 137n76, 141–142
son, 3, 22, 23n67, 68–75, 77–79, 83–86,
    93–94, 212, 214, 215n96
son-in-law, 3, 22n65, 85, 92, 98–99, 103–
    105
sophist, 209, 213
Sophocles, 19–20, 33n35, 58, 73n40,
    74n45, 84n19, 89n40, 93, 96, 110, 177,
    181n79, 183, 185
sôphrōn 'virtuous,' 92n49
sōphrosúnē 'modesty,' 92, 194
Sosias, 191, 194
Sosibios of Sparta, 136
Sōsíkleia, 14, 21n63
sound, sonorous, 3–4, 14, 15n34, 23–25,
    44–46, 61–63, 85, 91–92, 94–95, 103–
    104, 121, 142, 144, 155, 165, 168
sound sequence, 4, 142, 165, 170, 177
sowing, 99, 101
spark, 24, 54. *See also zôpuron*
Sparta, 115–116, 136–138, 145
Spartans, 124
speaker/listener, 33, 211

speaking object, 16n41, 29, 38n55, 41, 50,
    173, 176
spectator, 5, 24, 42, 169–172, 174, 177–
    178
Spensitheos, 58n39
spérma 'seed,' 21, 66, 101
spirit. *See psukhê*
spondee, 54
stâse. See histánai
stele (*stêlē*), 48–49, 52, 54, 89, 93, 140,
    143, 194–195
Stephanus of Byzantium, 81n5
Stesichorus, 59n47, 205n62
'sti = estí. See eînai
Stobaeus, 111n11, 117, 128nn32–33,
    135n64, 146n5
stoikhēdón, 25n75
stoikheîa "letters of the alphabet," 175
stóma 'mouth,' 141n99, 203
stoning, 100, 103
Strabo, 116–117, 121
Strato, 196–197, 199
Strattis, 183
subject, 205, 210–211
submission, 47, 197. *See also* domination/
    submission
Suda, 8n2, 15, 72n31, 81n2, 137–138, 140
suitor, 3, 76–77, 89–92, 94, 100–104, 110,
    215
Sulzberger, M., 22n66, 23n67, 69n15, 71,
    72nn34–35, 73nn36–41, 43, 74,
    75nn50–56, 88n32
súmphōna 'consonants,' 141n99
sumplokḗ 'intertwining,' 199
sun, 75
sunégrapse. See sungráphein
sungráphein 'write,' 150
sungrapheús 'writer,' 214
sunousía 'intercourse,' 195
supplement, 63, 164, 167, 169
symbolic topography, 105–106
symmetry, symmetrical, 51, 54, 105, 205,
    210–211
symposium (*sumpósion* 'banquet'), 91–92,
    116, 146
synaesthesia, 5, 167, 176
synecdoche, 60–61
syntax, 31–34, 166
Szegedy-Maszak, Andrew, 129, 135nn64–
    65
Szlezák, T. A., 213n89, 216nn99–100

tá. See ho
Tacitus, 9n4, 82n6
táde. See hóde

tagálmata. See ágalma
táphos 'tomb,' 100
tattooing, 29, 137–138, 140–142, 150, 153
taûta. See hoûtos
táxis 'order,' 126
têi. See ho
têide 'here,' 38, 43, 60. *See also hóde*
teisámenos "who has avenged," 74
tékhnē 'art,' 59–60
tekhnḗeis "artfully worked, artful," 57–60
têle "far off," 68n13
Telemakhos (*Tēlemákhos*), 34, 68–69, 71, 74, 78, 214
télos 'goal, end,' 87
tḗn. See ho
tension, 3, 104, 106
tês. See ho
têsde. See hóde
text, 3–4, 10, 44–47, 150, 169–170, 178, 182
thalerós 'flowering,' 24, 152n21
Thaletas (Thales), 130, 132, 135–136
Thamous, 206
theâsthai 'observe,' 169, 186
theataí 'spectators,' 184
theater, theatrical, 168, 171–172, 174, 178–183
theatrokratía "dictatorship by the theater," 179n72
théatron 'theater,' 186
Thebes, 90, 94
thémis 'law,' 73, 93
Themistius, 128n32
Themistḗ, 73
Themistocles, 77, 82n8
Theocritus, 51n21, 74n49, 136n68
pseudo-Theocritus, 20n58
Theognis, 16n41, 60, 97n69, 112n14, 147, 216n100
Theophrastus, 21, 96n65
theōría 'show, contemplation,' 183–184, 186
theory of the sign, 24
theory of visual perception, 174–176
theós 'god,' 38, 57, 117, 126, 153
therapeúein 'serve,' 191
Thermopylae, 124
Theseus, 5, 163, 179
Thespis, 169, 173
Thessalia, 38
Theuth, 85, 206, 210
third person, 30–31, 34–37, 39–43, 46, 104, 140, 149–150, 152, 156
thôkos 'seat,' 31
Thompson, H. A., 191n13

Thomson, George, 118n34, 171–172
Thoúrios "from Thurii," 149–150
Thrason, 40
Thrasumḗdēs, 72
threshing, 101
threshing floor, 98–99, 106
Thucydides, 33n30, 37n49, 89n41, 148n10, 149–150
thugátēr 'daughter,' 18n49, 20n59, 35, 153, 157
thumós 'heart, desire,' 126
Timaeus the Sophist, 206n65
timḗ 'honor,' 9, 19n54
Timoxenos, 55
Tisamenos, *Tisamenós*, 74
tó. See ho
tóde. See hóde
toí, tôi. See ho
tôide. See hóde
tón, tôn. See ho
tónde me. See hód' egó
tónos "tone of voice," 146
toû. See ho
toûde. See hóde
tousthloû. See esthlós
toût(o). See hoûtos
Toxeús, 73
tragedy, tragic, 169n31, 172–173, 179
transcription, transcribe, 5, 27–28, 30, 35–36, 41, 141, 144, 146, 148, 150–152, 165, 212
trifunctional, 106–107
trimeter, 34, 159n46
Troy, 70
truth, 24, 145–146, 204–205, 209–212, 215
túpoi 'imprints,' 159n48
túrannos "absolute ruler," 124–125
Tyrtaeus, 75n53
Tzetzes, 75n50, 91n48

upakoúei. See hupakoúein

Van der Valk, M., 69n15
Varro, 110n5
vase paintings, 193–194
vengeance, 100
Vernant, Jean-Pierre, 6n7, 19n52, 21n63, 22nn64–65, 85nn23–24, 93, 99n76, 137n75, 138n84
Vidal-Naquet, Pierre, 12n18, 23n67, 29n15, 110n3, 176n56, 180n75
violence, 3, 103–104, 106
Virgil, 66n2
Vlastos, Gregory, 29n15

vocal apparatus, 2, 46, 128, 142–143, 145, 166, 205
vocal function, 106
vocalization, 4, 120–122, 164–165, 171n37, 174, 186
vocative, 39n57, 60
voice: appropriation of, 46, 103, 106, 142–145, 154–155, 169, 203–204; of conscience, 4, 162, 209. *See also phōnē*
von Bothmer, D., 191nn12, 14
Vorsänger, 118, 121
vorsprechen, 117
vowels, 141n99

Warren, Austin, 24n71
weaving, 180n74
"web" of the text, 45n4
wedding, 20, 91, 153. *See also gámos*
Wellek, René, 24n71
wife, 85–86, 91, 98
Wilamowitz-Moellendorff, Ulrich von, 56, 58, 60n49
Wisman, H., 176n54
wolf, 208–209
woman, 99n77, 158, 188, 210. *See also gunē*

writer, 2, 36, 45–46, 54, 83–86, 97–98, 142–143, 151–153, 156, 164–165, 206, 208, 210–212
writer/reader, 2–3, 5–6, 44, 46–47, 85–86, 104, 106–107, 140–141, 189–193, 195, 197–198, 200–201, 214–215
writerly abstinence, 212
writing: critique of, 205–206, 211; etymological, 166; phonetic, 166; silent, 182–183, 186; "vocal," 169–171, 178, 180–181, 183, 186
writing in the *psukhē*, 154n32, 180n75, 215n96. *See also* book of the *psukhē*

Xanthippos, son of Arrhiphron, 176n55
Xenophanes, 112n14, 138n86, 146

"you," 35, 62, 149, 151, 155–157

Zaleukos, 135
Zeno, 198
Zeus, *Zeús*, 32, 41, 72, 100
zôion 'living thing,' 139
zōós 'live,' 23n69, 141n99
zṓpuron 'spark,' 21n63

MYTH AND POETICS

A series edited by

GREGORY NAGY

The Ravenous Hyenas and the Wounded Sun:
Myth and Ritual in Ancient India
by Stephanie W. Jamison

Poetry and Prophecy:
The Beginnings of a Literary Tradition
edited by James Kugel

The Traffic in Praise:
Pindar and the Poetics of Social Economy
by Leslie Kurke

Epic Singers and Oral Tradition
by Albert Bates Lord

The Language of Heroes:
Speech and Performance in the Iliad
by Richard P. Martin

Heroic Sagas and Ballads
by Stephen A. Mitchell

Greek Mythology and Poetics
by Gregory Nagy

Myth and the Polis
edited by Dora C. Pozzi and John M. Wickersham

Knowing Words:
Wisdom and Cunning in the Classical Traditions of China and Greece
by Lisa Raphals

Homer and the Sacred City
by Stephen Scully

Phrasikleia:
An Anthropology of Reading in Ancient Greece
by JESPER SVENBRO
translated by JANET LLOYD

Library of Congress Catagloging-in-Publication Data

Svenbro, Jesper, 1944–
  [Phrasikleia. English]
  Phrasikleia : an anthropology of reading in ancient Greece / Jesper Svenbro :
translated by Janet Lloyd.
     p.   cm. — (Myth and poetics)
  Translation of: Phrasikleia : anthropologie de la lecture en Grèce ancienne.
  Includes bibliographical references and index.
  ISBN 0-8014-2519-0 (acid-free paper). — ISBN 0-8014-9752-3 (pbk. : acid-free
paper)
     1. Books and reading—Greece—History.   2. Language and culture—Greece.
3. Literacy—Greece—History.   4. Greece—Civilization.   I. Title.   II. Series.
Z1003.5.G8S9413   1992
028'.9'0938—dc20   92-52773